The Porter
of St. Bonaventure's

The Porter
of
Saint Bonaventure's

The Life of
Father Solanus Casey,
Capuchin

by James Patrick Derum

THE FIDELITY PRESS   DETROIT, MICHIGAN

Ninth printing, August, 1992

Jacket portrait of Father Solanus courtesy *The Detroit News*

The Fidelity Press
1780 Mt. Elliott, Detroit, Michigan 48207

Printed in the U.S.A.
Printed by Harlo Press, 50 Victor Avenue, Detroit, Michigan 48203

To the Divine Doorkeeper

—in Whose service
Father Solanus
opened material and spiritual doors
through forty years

Acknowledgments

Everything here related about Father Solanus comes out of interviews and correspondence with laymen, Capuchins, and his relatives; from material supplied by his brother, Monsignor Edward J. Casey, and from Father Solanus' correspondence and notes. Monsignor Casey, in interviews extending over an eight-day period in July, 1961, supplied facts about family history and background, and his brother's boyhood and young manhood.

Of the scores who have contributed information, many are named and quoted in the text. To credit in detail the assistance generously given by all who were interviewed, or who directed the author to sources of information, would require several pages. Specific acknowledgments are therefore confined to those without whose cooperation the writing of this biography would have presented perplexing difficulties. Foremost of these was Mrs. John P. Garrity, who supplied the notes made in her own interviews with many friends of Father Solanus. To this work, undertaken on behalf of the Father Solanus' Guild, she devoted countless hours, unflagging energy, pesistent enterprise, and notable sagacity.

Mrs. Garrity also read the manuscript, correcting, suggesting, and supplying valuable criticism.

—Miss Marion Smith, who researched Father Solanus' years at the diocesan seminary in Milwaukee.

—The Capuchin superiors, who made Father Solanus' correspondence and notebooks available.

—The Capuchin Fathers and Brothers who supplied data, anecdotes, and viewpoints.

—My wife, who read and re-read manuscript with her usual perception, and made most helpful criticisms and suggestions.

*   *   *

THE FIRST STEP TOWARD POSSIBLE CANONIZATION of Father Solanus was taken on October 4, 1966. This was the appointment by the Capuchin Generalate in Rome of a Vice-Postulator to investigate his life. The action was in response to evidences submitted and to a petition endorsed by thousands of the Capuchin's friends.

The never-hurried process leading to canonization is long and complicated; the majority are discontinued at some point along the way. To its progress in the instance of Father Solanus, the unusual powers so many have attributed to him will be of minor importance. The investigation will center, as does every such investigation, on whether the subject's holiness was of a degree constituting "heroic sanctity."

Whatever the examination's outcome, Father Solanus' apparent charisms, including his foreknowledge, will continue to mystify. The reader will judge for himself whether the humble priest-porter was one of those Daniel-Rops had in mind when he wrote, in *Jesus and His Times*: "In the accounts of all men of genius and sanctity, there is always something which evades our grasp and rebuffs our analysis. That something is, precisely, the genius and the sanctity."

HIS LIFE SHOWS US THE WAY TO PEACE

This is essentially the story of how one man's life touched and transformed the lives of tens of thousands.

Yet Father Solanus Casey was neither learned nor brilliant. Through most of his sixty Capuchin years he was a monastery doorkeeper.

But he was also a doorkeeper to souls.

He longed and prayed for man's wholehearted obedience to the two great commandments; this would, he was certain, change our misery-plagued world into a paradise.

Before his death he clearly saw that man must make his world a paradise, if he were not to turn it into a hell. For the humble priest beheld electric, chemical, nuclear and atomic power bringing men closer together, while they were becoming, spiritually, more alien, more hostile to one another than ever. And as man thus increasingly confronted man, his fingers were poised to press the buttons that could launch hydrogen bombs to obliterate himself and his world.

Father Solanus, who thought in elemental and essential terms, recognized the only solution. So he prayed ceaselessly as Christ had prayed, that all men might become one in God's love.

It was an ideal—but practical in that everyone can advance its realization by humbly freeing himself from prejudice and hatred.

Only his Creator could know how intensely the Capuchin porter lived the great commandment to love God with all his being; that was his inner life.

Necessarily, this account is largely limited to his exterior life; to his boundless charity in living the other great commandment—that love of neighbor which is the yardstick of one's love of God.

By that measurement Father Solanus was a giant.

—James Patrick Derum

The physical cures and other seemingly extraordinary favors attributed to Father Solanus Casey, O.F.M. Cap., are reported in this volume substantially as recounted by their recipients or by witnesses. The author reserves any decision concerning their supernatural character to the judgement of the Catholic Church, in obedience to the decree of Urban VIII and in conformity with the Apostolic Constitution of Pope Leo XIII.

Contents

The Porter
of Saint Bonaventure's

Chapter 1

The Porter of Saint Bonaventure's

I met him only once—in the early thirties—while visiting my mother in Detroit. I had driven her to Sunday afternoon services at St. Bonaventure's chapel on the city's near east side. Afterwards, she asked me to go with her to the monastery office next door; she wanted to talk briefly with a priest whose counsel she greatly valued.

When we entered the office, I saw a brown-robed friar sitting at a desk, conversing with a visitor—and I realized instantly why my mother had sought him out. For I had never beheld a masculine face so spiritually serene and kind.

We took our places among several men and women seated in chairs along the walls, and I studied him from across the room. He seemed quite ageless. Though his wiry, full beard was gray, and his head semi-bald, the rather penetrating light blue eyes were the eyes of youth. It was a strong face, with a well proportioned forehead rising above a sizeable humped nose and a wide, pleasant mouth.

When it came our turn to sit beside him at his desk, he talked with us as simply and leisurely as a friendly neighbor over a backyard fence. He was humble and without pretense.

You felt his goodness. It spoke to you with a force and eloquence utterly beyond the possibilities of words. He talked chiefly to my mother, but his presence spoke to me. Sitting there, I became aware of my own moral smallness, yet of an assurance that I could do better. Afterwards, only a sentence or two of his conversation remained with me, but I was never to forget the quiet, transparent spirituality of his face.

This was Father Solanus. At the time, I had heard nothing of the extraordinary powers attributed to him.

Sixteen years later, I was living in Detroit. One day, while talking with a business acquaintance—regarding, as I recall, some remote political possibility—he offhandedly observed that the "day of miracles has passed." Then he quickly added —"Perhaps I shouldn't have said that. After all, I was once cured through a miracle." He explained that when he was thirteen an hereditary disease—a disease that had proved fatal to relatives on both sides of his family—had fastened on him. Neighbors suggested to his mother that she take him to a remarkable priest "who cured people," and the next day she did so. The priest blessed him, and assured his mother— "Tommy will be all right." The next morning, all evidences of the disease had disappeared; that afternoon, the family physician could find no symptoms. It never recurred. My friend, pressed for the priest's name, searched his memory. He finally recalled that he had been a Capuchin friar, and that his name was Father Solanus.

Some months later, I was introduced in a downtown office to Father Quentin Heinrichs, then stationed at the Capuchin Monastery of St. Bonaventure. At the end of our business conference, I mentioned my friend's story of his cure. Father Quentin replied that any number of people claimed to have recovered from serious sicknesses through Father Solanus' intercession. He added that many also told of instances in which he seemed to have foreknowledge as to whether a cure or other development would, or would not, occur.

Asked whether Father Solanus was still living, Father Quentin said that he had died three years before, in 1957.

Father Quentin's words kindled my curiosity, and my interest grew as in following weeks I learned more about Father Solanus. In his long career he had become the most celebrated member of the Capuchin Order in the United States. Yet for most of that career he was officially a friary porter, or doorkeeper, a task usually assigned to a Brother. Thousands referred to him as a saint, and to him hundreds attributed cures of maladies that seemed beyond the power of medical science.

When Father Solanus died in 1957, he had been a Capuchin sixty years, a priest fifty-three years, a friary porter a total of about forty years.

Chapter 2

Why Thousands Mourned
the Humble Porter's Death

It was on a blizzardy Christmas eve in 1896 that the future Father Solanus rang the doorbell of St. Bonaventure's Capuchin Monastery in Detroit.

He came there as Barney Casey of Superior, Wisconsin. In his twenty-six years he had been a farm hand, a lumber jack, a brick maker, a prison guard, a motorman and a street car conductor. He was also a former seminarian.

He had come to the monastery door reluctantly, with dark doubts and forebodings of failure, because he felt himself required to obey what seemed to him a clear and unmistakable answer to prayer. Seventeen days before, while praying in his parish church to know God's will as to his calling in life, he had suddenly received a command—of this he never had the slightest doubt—from a supernatural source. It was a definite, three word message, directing him to join the Capuchin Order.

He acted at once, though necessary preliminaries delayed his departure until three days before Christmas. Then, as a great blizzard struck the middle west, he left father and mother, and nine brothers and four sisters, and entrained for Detroit and the Capuchin novitiate.

His coming to the Capuchins had been an act of faith requiring heroic humility. True, he was obeying what he believed to be a divine imperative. Nevertheless, his obedience must have been in painfully sharp conflict with his human judgement—judgement based on his previous seminary experience. In a human and formal sense, his future was to justify his presentiments. For more than sixty years in the Capuchin Order he would perform menial duties ordinarily considered below the dignity and office of a priest. Yet in his lowly position he would bring Christ's love and compassion to scores of thousands of the afflicted, of every faith and station—and these would never forget him. Though his last days were spent in Detroit, he had been absent from that city many years before his death. Yet the moment the news was broadcast, telephone calls began flooding into the monastery office. To the Capuchin superiors it quickly became evident that thousands remembered their dead brother, and would be deeply disappointed were they deprived of an opportunity to bid him a final farewell. Normal consideration for these old friends of the porter of St. Bonaventure's dictated that the body should lie in state until the funeral on Saturday. The monastery itself could provide no room sufficiently large, and the public chapel must be kept free for masses and devotions. It was, therefore, decided that on Thursday and part of Friday, the body should lie in state in a commodious funeral home, and should be transferred to the chapel on Friday afternoon, where it would lie till the funeral services on Saturday morning.

Wednesday evening, newscasters announced that the funeral home—on Detroit's far east side—would be open to the public at 10 o'clock Thursday morning. As early as 6:30 a.m., people began gathering on the sidewalk in front of the imposing building. The crowd continued to swell. To observers it seemed that every religion, occupation, and age was represented—priests, ministers, nuns, laborers, business men,

politicians, judges, doctors, lawyers, housewives, factory workers, adults, teen-agers, children.

Even after many had been standing for two or three hours
in the August day's increasing heat, the throng remained
orderly, quietly waiting. When at 10 o'clock the funeral
director and his assistants came out and asked the people to
form into two lines, they did so with every consideration for
one another. Then they moved forward at a deliberate pace
toward the funeral home's opened door.

Hour after hour, all through the day and up to 10:30
that evening, the long double queue continued to shuffle forward in perfect order. By the closing hour, more than five
thousand had passed before the brown-robed body lying within the rather incongruous tufted silk interior of the sleek
steel casket.

The long double line of viewers was endless; newcomers
joined it continuously through the day and evening. On the
street and in the funeral home the atmosphere was one of
awe and sorrow. All, including the many teen-agers, approached the coffin in deepest reverence. Many adults carried infants.

Some of the mourners, after kneeling a moment at the
coffin, would introduce themselves to the Capuchin Fathers
standing in the background. A man presented his son, saying:
"Fifteen years ago, Father, my son was dying of polio. Father
Solanus blessed him, and today he is in the best of health."
A woman introduced an elderly lady. "Father," she said, "this
is my mother. She was dying of cancer, and Father Solanus
blessed her and prayed for her, and here she is tonight."
Others were there, they said, in gratitude to the friar who
"had cured them" of some serious illness or other. One woman began to cry. Pointing toward the coffin, she said: "He
was the best friend I had in the world. Some years ago I was in
utter despair, and wanted only to die. He talked to me, and I
began to live again."

This went on all day and evening.

At 10:30 the funeral home doors were closed. Shortly thereafter, a couple rang and begged admittance; they had come a long distance. When the husband and wife were admitted, the woman explained that they owed their marriage to Father Solanus. She and her sister, as youngsters, had re-solved to become nuns. When eighteen years old, she had sought Father Solanus' counsel in the selection of a religious order. To her surprise, he told her she was not destined for a life in religion. This prediction shocked her, and he attempt-ed to overcome her arguments by becoming specific.

"You will," he told her, "marry a man now in military service. And you will have as many children as you can count on one hand, plus almost as many as you have fingers on the other."

She left his presence disappointed, chagrined, almost angered. For sometime thereafter she strove to realize a re-ligious life. Time, however, saw Father Solanus' prediction fulfilled. She eventually married a young man who had been in military service. They were now expecting their seventh child.

The funeral home doors were to remain closed to the public Friday morning, for at 10 o'clock the body was to be transferred to St. Bonaventure's chapel. But as early as 6:30, people began pressing the doorbell, and Arthur Van Ler-berghe, the funeral director, ordered the doors opened. At 10 o'clock the doors were again closed and the body was transported to the Capuchin chapel on Mt. Elliott Avenue. "By 3 p.m.," Mr. Van Lerberghe said, "six thousand persons had come through the chapel. That night, the flow of human-ity never stopped until the chapel was closed."

Shortly before 10 o'clock Saturday morning, the chapel was cleared in preparation for the Requiem Mass. From Thursday morning until that time, upwards of twenty thousand people had looked upon the ascetic face of the humble friar. Throughout the United States and Canada, two hundred thousand or more were said to have mourned his passing.

They thought of him as the holiest of priests, and few knew that his priestly powers had been crippled from the start. His Capuchin superiors had admitted him to the priesthood despite much doubt and after considerable debate, since he had been unable to meet the scholastic minimum normally required. They had permitted him to continue his seminary studies only after the seminary head, the Order's most learned member, had raised his powerful voice in his behalf.

He was ordained, but without the faculties for administering the sacrament of penance, or for formal preaching. In all his fifty-three years as a priest he never heard a confession, preached a mission, or conducted a retreat. Shortly after his ordination, more rigid requirements for ordination were established; the faculty-deprived priest became a survival from the past. Had these regulations been in effect during his clericate, they would have automatically excluded Father Solanus from the priesthood.

A simplex priest's field of usefulness was radically restricted. So for two years he served as a sacristan, then for forty years as a porter.

As a porter he became, in the eyes of the multitude—and of many other priests and religious—a saint.

Just what kind of a child, a boy, a young man, attains in his manhood to such holiness that thousands of his fellow Americans think and speak of him as a saint?

In the instance of the boy and man who became Father Solanus, we have firsthand accounts. The story of his childhood, boyhood, and young manhood, as well as of his priesthood, has been detailed to the author by relatives, friends, and confreres.

It is told in the following chapters.

Chapter 3

Young Barney Casey
Meets Bears and Books

Father Solanus' first remembered view of the world was of the shining Mississippi, and his mother, hanging out the washing beside their three-room log home on the Wisconsin bank. He had been born there on November 25, 1870.

He remembered his mother singing as she hung the clothes. Singing to Tommy, the current baby, lying in his crib just outside the cabin door. And waving and singing to Mrs. Cotter, their neighbor directly across the river, when she, too, came out to hang her wash.

The two women frequently bridged the river with song. For though comparatively narrow at the Casey homesite, the Mississippi was still too wide for easy conversation. In that wild pioneering country one grew lonely for the sound of neighborly voices, and song was a kind of companionship. Sometimes they would join their voices, singing together as they had sung twelve years before in the parish choir in Hastings which, like Prescott, was up the river a bit but on the Minnesota side. That had been during the first year of the war, which Lee's surrender had ended nine years before. It had been in the midst of the war, ten years before, that both had married. When there was important family news the women, hands cupped to mouth, shouted it over the water— and it was about this time that Mrs. Casey had highly important news for Mrs. Cotter. In a few days the Caseys would be moving. The autumn before, as Mrs. Cotter well knew, they had bought a partly cleared farm a little south and three or four miles inland, but closer to a school and a Catholic church. Three of the eight Casey children were now of school age.

The new acreage was partly cleared, and held a larger house, though it also was made of logs. Its first floor consisted of a large living room, and a combination dining room-kitchen, with a pantry. A stairway led to the upper floor with its two bedrooms. The Trimbelle River flowed nearby.

It was rolling, wooded country—a country Father Solanus always recalled as his boyhood paradise. The land was still primitive; deer roamed its heavily wooded hills and valleys. Once the boys came face to face with a bear, and it chased them. At least they thought it did—though in afteryears Father Solanus wondered whether they couldn't have made friends with it had they been less frightened. Blackbirds, prairie chickens and partridges abounded, and whippoorwills. Barney had a special liking for the whippoorwills—they frolicked and swept through the air and wheeled down close to earth as if daring him and his brothers to play tag with them.

This wilderness held dangers, as well as such joys as swimming in the Trimbelle's clear waters, or trying to snare its trout with a hook and a string attached to a sapling cut from a nearby copse. Here Barney lived enchanted years—from about four till a little after his twelfth year, when a boy's world is shining new, its colors brighter, its adventures more thrilling than ever they will be again. But still, there were hazards and perils, which generally struck when least expected. Once one of the boys, intending to burn off dead, dry grass, started a field fire. The wind suddenly veered, and the fire came within inches of destroying the family home, the barn and chicken house.

Disease threatened, too—particularly the dread childrens' diseases. It was in this second log home that black diphtheria, "the strangler," slowly choked the life out of twelve-year-old Mary Ann. Her mother, stunned, held three-year-old Martha to her breast, murmuring softly to herself—"Who will take the place of my Mary Ann?" and tiny Martha, squirming from her arms, toddled to the corner where the broom stood. Lifting it awkwardly she answered—"I will, mama. I will sweep the floor for you like Mary Ann." But upon Martha, too, the disease had fastened, and three days later she was dead.

Diphtheria also attacked several of the boys, including Barney. All recovered, but it was later said that Barney's weak, wispy voice resulted from this early sickness.

Basically, the Casey children were a healthy group, and certainly the family was one of the best nourished in the countryside. Barney Casey, Senior, was known as "a good provider." He was one of the few farmers in the township who fed milk-giving cows through the long winters, thus assuring fresh milk and butter the year 'round. This was profitable in another way, also, for he sold any surplus to eager neighbors. His vegetable and fruit garden was by far the largest and most varied in the township. Most of his neighbors fed their families chiefly on salt pork, beans and potatoes, particularly in the colder months when the Caseys were enjoying a diet of many vegetables and fruits.

It was a hearty, cheerful household. The Caseys were the kind of pioneers who transformed the frontier more than they were altered by it. To this new land they brought their Irish-Eastern States culture, enriching and brightening their primitive surroundings. Though both had left Ireland in their early years, they sang its folk songs and told its tales in the simple, direct Irish manner, sitting about the family table. Each child contributed his or her bit as a matter of course, informally and casually; it was the way their forefathers had entertained one another for generations. When deep snow shut the Caseys off from their neighbors for days at a time, the children amused one another, or father or mother would gather them about the dining room table for a literary evening. The senior Barney would read Tom Moore's poems, or Longfellow's or Whittier's—whose *Snowbound* translated into poetic metaphor the beauty of their snow-shrouded world. There was Grattan, too, and Lincoln, and Cooper with his *Deerslayer* stories. Dickens was a favorite and held the Caseys spellbound. Listening to their father or mother read these and other masters of the English language, or reading such authors themselves, the Casey children learned to use words well. In later years, this early acquaintanceship with good English served Barney in school, for no matter what grades he might achieve in other subjects, his marks in English were always excellent.

Young Barney liked to read, but he was, also, an explorer. He was spoken of as "the adventurer of the family," but he was a most practical adventurer. A quiet and thoughtful boy, he was forever working out ingenious ways to snare rabbits and prairie chickens—for game was important to the family larder. He was the one who discovered where wild berries were most plentiful. And when his mother wanted wild hops for yeast, she sent Barney on the search. He was a sociable lad, quick to join in family fun, and a willing entertainer, too. He learned, early, to play the mouth organ, and could produce a recognizable tune on an accordian. A fiddle also appeared one day in the Casey home; Barney Senior liked the sound of music about the house. Barney Junior tried his hand at the fiddle, and although his scraping was at times so unmusical his brothers advised him to practice in the barn, he kept at it. He was patient and determined, and if he pleased no one else he pleased his teacher—who was, for want of a competent one, his own untutored self.

Neighbors liked to visit at the Caseys; the Casey spirit was expansive, and the Casey home a gay and warming place. There was good talk, and singing, and a sympathetic political philosophy. Many of the neighbors were Irish, German or French-Canadian whom political and religious discrimination had driven to the United States. The Germans had fled the tyranny of Bismark's May Laws or still earlier political persecution; the French-Canadians the political and economic and social hostility of eastern Canada's Anglo-Saxon governments. The Caseys' French and German neighbors might have regretted that their pastor wasn't French, or German—but the main point was that he was a priest and could offer the Mass. It was that ancient sacrifice that drew them together and made them as one about the altar every Sunday, come fair weather or foul. All were grateful for their religious faith, and for living in a new land of hope where, free from oppression, they could build for themselves and their children a life of independent self-respect.

Among the most grateful—and with great good reason—was Ellen Elizabeth Casey. She was thankful above all for having escaped in her early childhood the enormous death-trap that Ireland became from 1845 to 1850, when famine killed a million of its sons and daughters. Ellen's father had died during the famine. Her mother, Brigid Shields Murphy, had sent her two older boys to relatives in Boston in 1848. The next year she landed in Boston with five-year-old Ellen, seven-year-old Mary Ann, and a three-year-old son, Maurice. From there they went to Portland, Maine, where Mrs. Murphy and her two older sons, Owen, twelve, and Patrick, ten, went to work twelve hours a day, six days a week, in the vast, gloomy textile mills. Care of the girls and little Maurice faced their mother with a problem, but she was lucky. A Portland lady offered to feed and shelter the girls for their help about the house, for even little Ellen could dust and wipe dishes. During the workdays, Maurice was cared for by a family friend. The combined wages of Mrs. Murphy and her sons meant survival, but little more.

The Barney Casey who was to marry Ellen Murphy, and whose son and namesake was to become Father Solanus, left County Monoghan with a sister in 1857. He was seventeen years old. They joined an elder brother and two sisters who had settled near Boston, and Barney immediately began to learn shoemaking. When the War Between the States broke out, he contracted to make shoes for the Union armies.

Two years after landing in Boston, Barney met Ellen Murphy at a Fourth of July picnic, through a cousin to whom both were related. He instantly lost his heart to the sweet, serious sixteen-year-old—but soon lost Ellen herself. For when Ellen wrote her mother in Minnesota—where she had gone a few months before—that Barney had proposed, Mrs. Murphy's answer was an abrupt command. She ordered Ellen to leave Boston and join her immediately. Mrs. Murphy was living with her daughter Mary Ann, in the vicinity of Hastings, Minnesota; she had gone to her when Mary Ann, who had married at sixteen, wrote her that she was soon to be a mother.

When Ellen arrived in Hastings, her mother gave her a talking to. "You're still but a girl," she told her. "You should enjoy the years of your girlhood; then you can take on family responsibilities." Her elder daughter was an instance that such responsibilities can develop quickly; Mary Ann had borne twin boys.

Though Ellen had obediently joined her mother in far away Minnesota, her heart was still with Barney in Boston. It wasn't long after her arrival in the west that she had met a most influential friend who aided the romance. This was Mrs. Ignatius Donnelly, whose husband was a celebrated writer, lecturer, apostle of midwest development, political reformer, and a leader of the Bacon-wrote-Shakespeare cult. He was to become the youngest member of the House of Representatives and later a United States senator from Minnesota.

Mrs. Donnelly and Mrs. Murphy were parishoners of Guardian Angels Church in Hastings. In a day of "national" churches, this was the "Irish Church," as St. Boniface Church, less than a block away, was the "German Church." In Guardian Angels parish the people were almost as close as members of the same family. Mrs. Donnelly and Mrs. Murphy sang in the choir, and became intimate friends. When Ellen arrived from Boston she took her place beside them in the choir to lift her clear young voice in the operatic church music of the times.

Mrs. Donnelly, lonely during her husband's extended lecture tours, begged Mrs. Murphy to let Ellen live with her, and the mother agreed. To the older woman she became as a daughter, and Mrs. Donnelly finally persuaded Mrs. Murphy to approve Ellen's formal engagement to Barney Casey. Three years later, she invited Ellen to accompany her and her husband on a trip to Boston, where Ellen and Barney would wed. So on October 6, 1863, they were married in Danvers, a Boston suburb. Theirs was a half-day honeymoon; the young husband was too busy turning out shoes for soldiers to afford more time.

When the war ended, he set up as a shoe merchant in Germantown, near Philadelphia, and sent for his brother Terrence to assist him in the business. Terrence, who had immigrated to England, joined Barney in time to help him open a new store in New Castle, Pennsylvania, then a booming mining town. But a period of bad times and the brothers' inability to refuse credit to the parents of shoeless children, reduced profits, and Barney decided to take his wife's advice and move west. Ellen's brothers Owen and Pat were now prosperous Wisconsin farmers and had been urging Barney to come out to the golden land of opportunity. Good land was available on the Mississippi, just below Prescott, on the Wisconsin side, and they advised their brother-in-law to file a claim there. If Barney came west, his family—the Caseys now had two babies—could stay with them while a house was built and land was cleared. If all went well, he would be sending crops to market within two years. Terrence, after advising him to make the move, went to Boston. There he would study law, become a prominent counselor, and win appointment to the judicial bench.

In the fall of 1865, the young Caseys and little Ellen and James, entrained for western Wisconsin. There Owen and Pat Murphy assisted Barney in constructing a stout log house beside the Mississippi, helped clear some of his 80-acre claim, and with a huge breaking plow pulled by three span of oxen, aided him break the "wild" soil. Barney had learned farming as a young man in Ireland, but this was new. He saw in amazement the razor sharp plough cut through roots as thick as a man's arm and said to be a hundred years old or more. The log house had three rooms, and there was a lean-to shelter for the stock—a span of oxen and a cow.

They had been seven years in their "temporary" home when the Caseys acquired the Trimbelle property.

It was well that the Caseys had moved to Trimbelle, with its larger house and its closer school and church. For here, within eight years and three or four months, seven more children were born to them. In 1882, despite the loss of two girls, the family totaled twelve. Ellen, their first born, now eighteen, was completing a normal school course, and would soon be teaching. Steady, stalwart Jim, the oldest son, was seventeen, and already his father's strong right hand. The log house had been roomy enough in 1873 but seemed much smaller now, and Barney Senior wanted more acreage, and a shorter haul to a freight depot. He and Ellen began planning a new home, to be built on land he was acquiring fifteen miles to the north, in St. Croix County.

When the harvest of 1882 was gathered, they moved again.

Chapter 4

At Fifteen, a Lumberjack

Moving was an enormous job. Farm equipment, household furniture, the winter fruits and vegetables, the fodder for horses, cattle, pigs and sheep, all must be transported—excepting, of course, the horses, which transported themselves and everything else.

All the Caseys of school age, including twelve-year-old Barney, pitched in, and the word was "speed." For the move was started late in October, and Mr. Casey and his son Jim were fearful that an early snowstorm might delay the operation.

The new home on the Casey's new, 345-acre farm was of clapboard construction, with a large living room, a large kitchen and a bedroom on the first floor, and three bedrooms upstairs. There were two barns, a substantial ice house—a luxury few farms boasted—and a deep root house. Barney Senior, aided by Jim and Maurice, painted the buildings white and trimmed them in green. On either side of the house they had planted fruit trees that every spring embowered it in flowers, and two giant maples stood sentinel-like in front. Nearby flowed the Willow River, and within easy walking distance was a small lake. A railroad line, running through the farm, brought the Caseys within less than an hour's ride of St. Paul, only thirty miles to the west. Two miles away was the town of Burkhardt with its freight and passenger depot and its district school. About nine miles away, toward the Mississippi, was the little town of Hudson with its Catholic church.

The Caseys' relative prosperity had made the new house and farm possible. It was prosperity won despite blizzards, floods, droughts, blights, grass fires, and grasshopper and cinch bug invasions. Horses had superseded oxen; with them, one could travel to town in reasonable time.

The move promised increased farm profits, and Mr. Casey, an enterprising man, developed ways of adding to income between harvest and spring planting. He established connections with manufacturers of religious goods, with magazine and book publishers, and sold their products. He became agent for the *Irish Standard* and for *Extension Magazine,* and made business still further serve his Catholicity by promoting Catholic books. Ingeniously, he made his book business do double duty by encouraging his children to read those books he thought might interest them, with due cautions not to soil them and thus render them unfit for sale.

He always went to St. Paul to buy books, selecting them with care. Transporting the books was an operation in logistics. As his train approached the Casey farm, he would lug the heavy canvas sack of books to the rear platform, and heave it into a snowbank. His sons would be waiting to pick it up, and he himself would walk back from the Burghart station unimpeded. This was repeated three or four times during the season.

Getting to Mass on Sunday was more of a problem. There was only one wagon, and always a baby too young to make the journey. So one parent and about half the children traveled to church on alternate Sundays. In the narrow, springless wagon it was a slow, jolting ride that in rain, snow or cold,

could become a hardship. Two hours before the ten o'clock
Mass, the Caseys would set out. Those who were to receive
Holy Communion would be fasting from midnight. When St.
Patrick's first bell rang out over the hills and valleys, they
must be half way to Hudson, or they were certain to be late.
And that, with the Caseys, was unthinkable.

For those at home there were Sunday devotions, also. At
ten o'clock, just as the holy sacrifice was starting at St. Patrick's, the home-staying parent would call the children together and read the Mass liturgy of the day. The older children would make the responses. When Mr. Casey led the
services, he would talk on the text of the day's Epistle or
Gospel; he was somewhat addicted to sermonizing.

In exercising discipline, however, he sometimes went beyond mere words. Of this young Barney became aware when
six years old. He had thrown a fork at one of his sisters.

"This is the first time you have ever done anything like
this," his father told him. "So your punishment will be only
three lashes. But if you do any such thing again, you'll receive six lashes. And if it should happen a third time, you'll
get nine lashes."

Seventy years later, Father Solanus referred to this instance of paternal sternness with high approval, pointing
out that it was a discipline rooted in enlightened and responsible love. The children experienced that love in their
parent's daily care, and could read it, particularly, in their
mother's countenance. "Her face beamed kindness," were the
words in which a neighbor described her. She was small and
graceful, with earnest, innocent blue eyes. All thought her
younger than her age; perhaps it was her outgoing love, her
forgetfulness of self, that kept her youthful. An excellent
organizer, Ellen Casey assigned each of the children household duties and saw to it that they fulfilled them. As a result
her family and her house were kept in order. Her friends

declared that in the Casey home, "one could eat off the floor"
—woman's highest tribute to an efficient housekeeper. And
organization and good housekeeping were almost a necessity,
for the large family was still increasing, and two children
were to be born in the Willow River home.

Discipline also applied to learning, and the children were
required to do their school homework as well as their various
chores. Learning the catechism was a never ending task that
started when the children reached their seventh year and
continued until they had made their first Communion. Week
after week a certain number of questions from the penny
catechism had to be learned, word for word, in preparation for
the catechism classes which would follow the Mass the next
Sunday. In these classes, women taught the smaller children,
while Father Thomas A. Kelly, the pastor, instructed the older girls and boys. He also taught the First Communion class
—whose members, according to custom, must have reached
their twelfth birthday by the scheduled first Communion date.
Many didn't receive first Communion until they were a year
or two older, particularly when they couldn't get to the
catechism class every Sunday. Barney was one of these; he
did not make his first Communion until thirteen years old.

Two weeks before the great day, he and other farm children of the first Communion class came to Hudson for a two
weeks' stay in the houses of city parishioners. Morning and
afternoon, sitting in the church pews, they listened to Father
Kelly expound Catholicity's chief doctrines. In the spring of
1883, with other boys and girls of twelve and thirteen, and a
few fourteen years old, Barney knelt at the altar in St. Patrick's church and for the first time received his Eucharistic
Lord in Holy Communion.

It was about this time that Maurice, Barney's elder by
three years, entered the Milwaukee seminary, known as St.

Francis de Sales Seminary but more commonly referred to as
"the German seminary." This was because most of the students were German and because German was the common
language. After eight years of study Maurice would be ordained a priest, if all went well. His parents and particularly his
father never permitted themselves to doubt that all would go
well. They must have realized that Maurice would be in an
alien environment, an enclave in which the language and
racial characteristics of most of the students would be strange
to him. But a seminary was a seminary, and they were sure
that Maurice possessed all the qualities needed for a priestly
calling. He was talented, thoughtful, retiring, modest. With
him, memorizing prayers and the catechism was not a task
but almost a hobby—he studied prayerbook or catechism
even while herding the cattle or waiting for a fish to take the
hook.

Barney noted his parents' happiness that Maurice was
destined to be "the priest of the family," but at this time his
own interest was centered on a less spiritual activity. His oldest brother Jim had been given a new rifle, and it drew the
boy like a magnet. Whenever the senior brother found time
for hunting, Barney tagged along, and occasionally Jim
would let him try a shot at a squirrel or a rabbit. Jim hunted
for food, not pleasure. Fresh meat was scarce, and rabbit
stew was looked upon as a standby. As his older brothers became more burdened with farm work and Barney's markman-
ship improved, he gradually took over the rifle. With Chris
Adam, a boy living on a neighboring farm, Barney wandered
through fields and woodlands. Besides the nearly always
plentiful rabbits, he brought home quail, wild ducks, geese,
and prairie chickens—and, as he grew older, an occasional
deer.

The woodlands that covered much of the Casey farm
supplied fuel and fencing. As Barney grew older, he helped

fell trees for fence rails and posts, and cut endless cords of wood for the insatiable heating and cooking stoves. Wood cutting was mostly an autumn job, when sugar maples, locust, oak and a dozen other kinds of trees defied on-coming winter with the flaunting of their crimson and yellow banners. But until he was fourteen Barney's labors were lighter. With his younger brothers he drove cows to and from pasture, helped feed cattle and horses, swilled the pigs, hunted hens' eggs, brought in firewood, and endlessly weeded the huge family vegetable gardens. The boys fished, too, particularly on Fridays, and generally brought home ample strings of perch or bass or pickerel for the family table.

With his sons' help, Mr. Casey operated one of the best kept and cultivated farms in the township. Black-bearded, patriarchial, friendly, he was esteemed and liked throughout the countryside. His neighbors elected and re-elected him township treasurer, regarded as a position of trust. This responsibility he administered from an office in Hudson. He also served year after year as a school trustee.

Though he managed efficiently, he refused to allow farming to enslave his family. Too many farmers, he thought, made financial success their driving motive. They were harsh taskmasters to themselves, their children, their wives. They led grim, joyless lives; overworked their sons; tolerated their daughters. Mr. Casey preferred to make farming a more socially enjoyable way of life.

At the Casey farm everyone worked hard, but there was always awaiting them the reward of fun and relaxation. Most of this centered about Dry Dam Lake, a spring fed, oval pond bordering the farm. It was about three-quarters of a mile long and a little less wide, in the midst of an oak and maple woodland. Summer and winter, spring and fall, Dry Dam Lake and its surrounding area was the Casey boys private

playground. There they swam, speared frogs, and fished. On
its mirror-smooth ice they skated in winter.

A small flatboat was used for fishing, the lake yielding,
almost unfailingly, pan fish and small mouth black bass.

Two or three hundred feet from the lake, in a little
meadow amidst the trees, was the field-games arena. This was
known simply as "the green place." It was a 50-foot diameter
hollow, thought to have been formed by a meteor in ages
past. When in late summer the grass all about was burnt
brown, the hollow remained invitingly green. Sloping gently
to a five foot depth, it provided just the right angle for foot
racing. Around the slope of this natural running track the
Casey brothers and their neighborhood friends, grimly com-
petitive, raced one another. In other games, too, they strove
for victory—going in for broad jumping, high jumping, pole
vaulting, and shot putting. The vaulting pole was a hickory
sapling, and the shot a round stone, but the do-or-die spirit
would have done credit to college athletes. The boys also
played horseshoes in the yard near the house, and baseball in
a nearby field. In the backyard, or in the barn, they boxed.
Their father enjoyed all this; he had an Irishman's love of
sports.

Young Barney played hard, but always with an air of
playing largely for the fun of the game. Winning or losing,
he remained good natured. He was never known to find fault
with another player; never argued a point as if the world
depended on it; never, as one of his brothers put it, got
"huffy." He had no enemies.

He was spoken of as a good ball player. His throwing arm
was quick and strong, and he hit well. Generally, he was the
catcher.

He went in for all sports except boxing—despite the fact
that his brothers avidly followed the fortunes of the mighty

John L. Sullivan and of the unbeatable Jack McAuliffe. They pooled their savings, purchased a set of eight-ounce gloves, and ardently practiced the manly art. That is, all but Barney. He gave no reason—he was adept at turning aside with a whimsical quip any question he didn't care to answer. It was thought that he just didn't want to hurt anyone. Perhaps, too, he had matured spiritually to a degree which enabled him to realize boxing's inherent cruelty. For a boxer, unless phenominally clever, must punish his opponent to win. That evidently was not Barney's idea of sport.

His clear-headed courage was, however, widely recognized—largely because of the way he had killed a wildcat. It happened one afternoon late in spring when fifteen-year-old Barney and three younger brothers were returning home after weeding an onion field over toward Dry Dam Lake. Pat, a year younger than Barney, had gone ahead with Rover to round up the cows. Suddenly he reappeared, racing toward his brothers and yelling—"Rover's tangled with a wildcat! He's chasing it towards the river! He's all red!"

The boys sped toward the Willow River. They were intent on saving Rover. He was one of the family, and a big wildcat might slash a brave dog to ribbons. Frantic barking led them to a big maple overlooking the ravine through which flowed the river. Rover, madly barking his sheepdog's heart out, and with a great red smear across his shoulders, was bounding up against the tree trunk. A seemingly indifferent wildcat lay relaxed on the tree's lowest limb.

As they drew nearer, the cat advanced cautiously down the tree trunk, stopped just beyond Rover's reach, then jumped, slashing sideways. The dog whirled aside and as the big cat landed, leaped for its throat and hurled it down the ravine.

The animal struck a clump of alders near the river's edge, and Rover instantly attacked. Dashing in and out he avoided the knife-like claws but kept the cat too busy for it to turn and run for the trees. Pat, recklessly brave, came up with a stout stick and began to strike at the cat, and Barney shouted to him, "Play it safe." He ordered little Leo and Ed to stay on the upper bank, then plunged down the ravine toward a heap of stones near a bend in the river. Circling, he reappeared through the alders back of the wildcat. Arms extended before him, his hands held a heavy stone.

Slowly, silently he edged forward. The slightest sound, and the snarling fury would turn and slash him—for he would have had to be incredibly lucky to hit a charging wildcat with the weighty stone.

He drew within two feet, poised the stone, and cast it. It struck the wildcat's skull with a dull thud, and the beast collapsed. The boys poked it with long sticks, but it was literally stone-dead. Then they tied it with wild grape runners to a carrying limb, and started home in triumph.

As they neared the house, Barney suggested that they set the wildcat on the side lawn in a crouching position. This done, Leo rushed into the kitchen, shouting—"There's a wildcat outside!"

Wide-eyed, father, and mother with four-month old Gracie in her arms, together with Jim and John, Tom, Gus, and Ellen with three-year-old Margaret by the hand, hurried out. Before they realized that the crouching cat was dead, its conquerors rushed from behind concealing trees to tell the great adventure.

A wildcat bounty was ten dollars—a small fortune. Barney and Pat insisted their father keep it. They knew he was worried about the threatened wheat crop, usually depended on for the larger portion of the year's income. Driving about the farm only a week before, Barney and his father had come to the wheat fields, and saw a mist hanging over them. His father groaned; it was the dreaded blight. Barney said— "Don't worry, Pa. We'll all pray for good crops, and we'll have a good year without the wheat." That night, and for many nights thereafter, Mr. Casey added to the usual fifteen minutes of family prayer a petition that the harvest not totally fail. Barney, now of an age when a farm boy ordinarily took his place beside adults in the fields, was deeply concerned. He had formed the habit of prayer. He recited the rosary each night, kneeling at his bedside. Now he began to pray for a harvest that would prove profitable despite the lost wheat crop.

He had resolved to say the rosary every day, but it was sometimes a resolve hard to keep. Harvesting and chores made the workday extend from early morning to late at night. One evening almost unbearable weariness tempted him to skip the rosary just that once. Fighting against a desperate desire to throw himself into bed, he knelt, determined to recite at least one of the five decades. He knelt upright, without support, a habit he had formed as a child, from observing his mother and his sister Ellen, and one that he never relinquished. To his surprise, he remained fully awake until the last decade was completed. Sleep came almost instantly.

During the night he dreamed that he was suspended over a great pit of fire, and in danger of falling into it. He looked up, and saw a huge rosary hanging just above him. He grasped it; it supported him securely.

It was a dream he never forgot. He was to tell of it years later when preaching at his parents' golden wedding anniversary.

Young Barney was searching his mind for some way in which he himself might increase the family income. For this purpose, he now felt free to leave the farm if he could obtain his parents' consent. For Maurice, after three years' study, had recently dropped out of the seminary. His trouble probably was neurasthenia, a serious but generally temporary condition. Nevertheless, he had returned home to stay, and had taken his place in the fields beside his brothers. For a time he felt frustrated and futile, and accused himself of being "a misfit" wherever he turned.

His parents were sympathic, though his father was unable to conceal his disappointment. Now and then he could be heard muttering into his beard—"If I were to start life over, I'd be a priest."

Whatever Mrs. Casey might have thought of so ungallant a sentiment, its unguarded expression must have made Maurice all the more painfully conscious of his "failure." But eventually, aided by the tonic of hard physical work, he pulled himself out of his depression. If he could not be a priest himself, he resolved to pray and work that others might be, and to contribute what he could to the upkeep of missionaries.

Barney's ideas were closer to home, and he finally decided on a way of earning money to help offset the wheat crop failure. In Stillwater, Minnesota, only twenty miles away, logs were choking the St. Croix river; the sawmills were desperate for more hands. Men were making good wages on the log booms. He realized that he was a pretty slim youngster to be putting himself forward to do a man's work. But he determined to try. The fact that his uncle, Father Maurice Murphy, was the Catholic pastor in Stillwater, would help to win his parents' consent. For Father Murphy, his mother's youngest brother, was a potent influence in the Casey family.

Ellen had always been close in spirit to her brother, and even, at times, in his work. When he was planning to erect St. Michael's Church—in the last century a noteworthy edifice—she had helped raise money for its building. Rowing herself up and down the St. Croix River, she had stopped at every Catholic household along the Minnesota bank to gather pledges.

So, approval won, Barney went to Stillwater. The log boom boss might have looked doubtfully at his stringy figure, but he hired him to work on the catwalks built over the lake of "still water" that gave the city its name. Armed with a peavey, Barney labored through the long days, feeding logs into the Stillwater mills, then turning out over a hundred million feet of lumber a year. The work demanded endurance and skill, and Barney was proud to measure up to it.

To him the Stillwater of the mid 1880's presented marvels. The town was at the height of prosperity, and displayed the fact. Its fire engine, purchased for an enormous $7,000, could shoot a stream of water through 1500 feet of hose, and over the courthouse dome! Its opera house was one of the largest and most beautiful west of Pittsburgh.

Stillwater citizens were even talking of building one of those new electric trolley railways for faster transportation about the city streets. One had just started operation in Baltimore; it was exciting the whole nation.

When winter approached, Barney returned home to take up school where he had left off the previous spring, and to work on the farm. A few days later, his father showed him his accounts. They revealed that though the wheat had failed, other crops had yielded heavily, and had brought excellent prices.

With Barney's contributions from his logger's pay, all debts had been discharged, and there was a surplus.

Chapter 5

Barney Knocks
at His Pastor's Door

His eagerness to help his parents had introduced Barney
to a wider world; that continuing desire was to keep him
there. True, when winter's approach brought a decrease in
the volume of logs being floated down to Stillwater, he returned to the farm. But he had come to realize what a comforting assurance the money he could send home was to a
family that might any year face a disastrous crop failure. So,
even as he studied at the district school to complete its course,
his mind was on Stillwater and its opportunities.

Between farm chores and school he took part in other
activities, which included debating. It was near Barney's
sixteenth birthday, on November 25, that Mr. Hughes, the
district schoolmaster, began training him in the art of formal
disputation. Sometime later, he joined with Mr. Hughes in
meeting his father and his older brother John in a debate to
which the public was invited. The subject was a popular one
in those times: "Resolved, that the intemperate consumption
of alcohol has been a greater evil than war." And the debaters
were even more popular than the subject. Mr. Casey was
township treasurer and a school trustee, and as everyone well
knew, most of the Caseys had a ready way with words. People
from all over the countryside crowded into the hall, and if
the debate's title was stilted, the debaters weren't. They start-

ed out as if determined to uphold decorum and dignity. But as the argument and the room grew warmer, each team began slam-banging the other with robust abandon.

If the debate failed to settle the issue, it probably increased Rebecca Tobin's admiration for Barney Casey. For Rebecca, who lived on a neighboring farm, liked Barney, and to Barney she was undoubtedly the ideal girl. Black eyed, black haired, sweet and pleasant, she was at fifteen years the kind of a young lady even other girls admire.

Generally, adolescent romances are not too serious or permanent, and it is not known whether, despite their youth, the mutual regard of the sixteen-year-old Barney and the fifteen-year-old Rebecca attained any degree of mature development. They did not "keep company," but Barney, at least, felt more than brotherly affection for Rebecca. He liked her far more than he disliked her brother Andy, and Andy was the only neighbor boy against whom Barney was ever known to have shown anger. Andy had been accused, on circumstantial evidence, of poisoning Rover, the Casey dog that had helped kill the wildcat. When Barney first saw the dog's stiffened body, he paled with anger. Andy, he threatened, would pay for the crime. Grief stricken, he went to his room. When he came down again, he was calm. He never uttered another word about punishing Andy.

Sometime after the debate, Barney completed his district school studies to the satisfaction of Mr. Hughes, and returned to Stillwater. He had obtained a job at the state prison as a handy man and relief guard.

This experience must have accelerated his discovery of the adult world, its evils and its sorrows and tragedies. It was, fortunately for him, a world into which he entered spiritually well-armed. His love for God and his faith were strong. So was his love of family, whose affection and care he had probably, as do most young people, taken for granted. Now, guarding largely friendless prisoners in the Stillwater penitentiary, he must have learned in larger measure what loving, devoted and well-balanced parents, and a morally sound family, can mean to a man.

Among the state prison's inmates were several notorious outlaws. Barney, intensely interested in people, came to know some of them well. These included Jim and Cole Younger, whose sensational exploits were familiar stories throughout the nation.

He had other exciting interests. By summer, Stillwater's talk of an electric street railway had become reality, and Barney, working as a part-time motorman, had learned to drive the new street cars. He was thus one of the first motormen, and quite possibly the youngest, in the United States.

In the 1880's the trolly car was as great a sensation as the motor car was to be thirty years later. All America was singing—

> "We'll have a house in Baltimore,
>   Streetcars running by our door. . ."

—Baltimore having been the first city to boast an electric railway. A mighty thrill it must have been to the farmer boy, he who had never driven anything faster than a team of plow horses, to speed over iron rails, driving a car powered by silent, mysterious current.

During this period he seemed to have had some correspondence with Rebecca. At least, she wrote him one letter which was read, quite improperly, by three of his younger brothers.

One day, while Barney was visiting home, Gus, with his younger brothers Leo and Ed, came upon Barney's half-open valise in a bedroom. Possibly seeking gifts—for Barney was generous—they probed thoroughly. In a side-pocket of the bag, sharp-eyed Gus discovered Rebecca's letter to Barney.

With conspiratorial eagerness, the nine-year-old boy gleefully read it to Leo and Ed. Even to the youngest of the three, its contents were sensational. In it, Rebecca informed Barney that she had told her mother he wanted her to become engaged to him, and that her mother had refused approval.

His brief experience driving a car in Stillwater moved Barney to try for a full time motorman's job. He applied by letter to a new street car company in Appleton, Wisconsin, about 230 miles to the southwest of his home. While hoping and waiting for a favorable answer, he started a small business of his own. Clever at picking up skills, he had learned how to color photographs—an art then much patronized. Several Casey relatives were living near the old Casey home in Trimbelle, and Barney stayed with his Aunt Mary Moran in her pleasant white house, while practicing his new trade. As he wrote in later years, he "learned to take an interest in the attractive young people of that neighborhood—among them a modest school friend of cousin Tess." This was Nellie O'Brien, later his brother John's wife.

His interest in "the attractive young people," following so shortly upon his rejection by Rebecca, may indicate that he had not been too cast down by his failure to become engaged to her.

About this time, Rebecca completed her studies in the district school, and her parents sent her to a boarding school in St. Paul. Barney was never to see her again, though he asked about her whenever he returned home.

Barney had many a gay time in the Trimbelle countryside. Genial, humorous and unassuming, he enjoyed people himself and had a knack of promoting their enjoyment. He had continued his attempts to master the violin, and he could now play the latest dance tunes. Naturally he was in demand at small gatherings of young people. His music was only passable, but they could afford it, for it was free.

While in Trimbelle, Barney received word that a motorman's job was at last open in Appleton. His move there marked his permanent separation from his family. After that, he would return only on visits until some years later, when for a brief time the entire family would be reunited in Superior.

In Appleton, he kept closely informed of home developments, which began to spell cumulative disaster. In 1887 and 1888, drought and cinch bugs caused successive crop failures, and the money he was sending home became highly important.

Toward the latter part of 1889, Barney learned that a trolley system was being built in Superior, Wisconsin. This booming port city at the northwestern tip of the state, was only a hundred miles from his home. Late in the spring of 1890, he took a job as motorman in Superior, a move that was to influence the fortunes of each member of his family.

Barney saw in booming Superior the solutions to all his family's needs and aspirations, at a moment when the needs had become acute, and the aspirations were demanding realization. The Casey clan was ambitious and farseeing, and eager for higher education and the progress it seemed to promise. But crop failures in 1887, 1888 and 1889, had dealt their hopes devastating blows. The older sons met the crisis by finding jobs wherever in surrounding towns jobs could be found. But all this was hit and miss and temporary.

Barney wrote the family about the demand for able men in Superior, and the educational opportunities the city offered for all the children, large and small. As a result, the three older brothers soon joined him. Jim and John, while working at various jobs, studied for post office examinations and were soon helping the mail go through on time. Maurice took up the plumbing trade. The four brothers rented a house at 1605 Belknap Street, and Nell gave up schoolteaching to keep house for them. Now they joined in influencing their father to sell the farm and come to Superior. Why not bring the dairy cows, and the horses, they urged, and start a dairy business? When he asked them how he could find a buyer for the farm in such times, Barney answered by having a real estate company take it over in return for ten city lots. In the fall of 1890 Mrs. Casey and her three younger daughters came to Superior, while Nell returned to schoolteaching. Pat—who was an excellent cook—remained on the farm with his father and younger brothers, who were attending the district school. The next March, the day after the school dismissed for the season, Mr. Casey and his sons loaded household furniture, farm implements, fodder, cows and horses into two box cars standing on a railroad siding at Burkhardt, and were off to Superior.

To house the dairy venture, Barney and his brothers had rented a huge barn and forty acres of the Perkins farm on the city's outskirts. More stock was purchased, and the dairy flourished. To the forty acres were added one hundred and sixty more. The enlarged farm supplied oats and hay for the livestock, and vegetables and fruits for the family.

The move brought stabilized prosperity. A few months after coming to Superior, the Caseys built a new ten room house on Spruce Street. The younger children attended the Sacred Heart parochial school; the adolescents entered high school. It wasn't long before John was studying law after work hours. To all the children the move opened new vistas of opportunity.

Through the long months of persuasion and planning which finally saw his family established in Superior, Barney Junior drove his lurching little street car over strap-metal tracks laid on an uneven, poorly drained clay roadbed. All his skill couldn't prevent the car—it was only sixteen feet long—from bounding off the tracks now and then. At this, the male passengers would dismount, and heave and push— and soon the little car would be on its way once more.

Generally he had a trainee at his side; the management had told him that as soon as he had schooled a few new motormen he would be promoted to conductor. He was instructing candidates years older than himself.

When he became conductor, he was lead man in a three man crew, the others being a motorman and a "trolley guider." The latter strove constantly to keep the trolley pole's double wheels in contact with the two overhead wires that carried the current.

Outwardly, Barney seemed content with endless riding around the trolley system's tracks, seven days a week. He worked long hours. He attended Sunday Mass in his conductor's uniform, his coin changer hooked to his belt, for he had to hurry from church to car barn to be on schedule. Such a job would seem to have left him little time for thinking, but his mind was busy about his future, and unsettled. He was endlessly questioning himself as to his personal responsibility to his Creator, and to his fellow men in a world in which so many people loved God so little. For all his easy casual manner he was intensely serious, and he had begun to ask himself how he could be of greatest service in the world. Such soul searching in a young man of twenty-one requires an answer, and the answer may demand a decision. Somewhat vaguely, Barney had begun to realize that the decision might lead him toward 'God's holy mountain, and His dwelling place.'

Possibly, if he had felt less responsible about helping his family, he might have been more immediately responsive when he experienced the first faint impulse toward a life in religion. His faith, even in youth, seems to have been deep.

Incidents such as his assurance to his father that prayer would save the crops, are indicative of this.

At fourteen or fifteen Barney seems to have developed a religious life of his own. At that age he became devoted to the recital of the rosary. He prayed it daily. In doing so he necessarily contemplated repeatedly a number of Christianity's chief truths. This suggests that he early formed in some degree the habit of mental prayer—basic to appreciation of the supernatural.

He was, by nature, a most friendly person. He made friends easily. His easy manner, his unpretentiousness, his quiet humor made him a favorite in any gathering. As catcher on the celebrated "all-brothers" Casey baseball team, he enjoyed a certain distinction among the sports-minded. The Casey All-Brothers Nine held its own with good baseball teams in and about Superior, and Barney, as catcher, was one of the chief reasons for its success. He thought well of nearly everyone, and he hobnobbed with people in all walks of life, but he had principles and he never violated them. At his first Communion he had taken a pledge—as was then the custom —not to drink alcoholic beverages until he was twenty-one. This he observed, and it was probably a good thing he did, for the Superior of that day, a port town, supported a saloon to every eighty-six inhabitants.

It was a booming, exciting town, offering money-making opportunities on all sides, but Barney was becoming less and less interested in such things. Gradually the conviction grew that he should take some step toward the priesthood.

That first step, he knew, would be a talk with the pastor of Sacred Heart parish, Father Sturm—but he delayed acting. Perhaps he feared that the pastor might advise that he was too old to begin seminary studies. He was close to voting age, but his education was only that of most town boys of fourteen or fifteen years. If a seminary should admit him, he would be classed with students six or seven years younger. Possibly, too, he felt that the family still needed his help. Whatever the reason for his reluctance, he made no move.

Sometimes when a person remains thus indecisive, a force outside himself, some unexpected, perhaps shocking incident, may give the needed push toward a final resolve. In Barney Casey's life such an event happened on a cold, drizzly afternoon in late fall as his car rounded a corner in Superior's toughest district. The streetcar stopped with a jolt; a crowd was surrounding some object in the middle of the street. Barney and his two crewmen, running to the scene, saw a drunken sailor, a dagger in his hand, standing over a young woman lying across the tracks, blood trickling through rents the knife had made in her coat. No one had dared step forward against the threatening knife, and as Barney reached the crowd the drunk was shouting foul accusations against the woman. At this moment, two policemen came rushing up and disarmed the man at gunpoint. The policemen secured him and moved the woman to the side of the road. Barney and his crew drove off.

But the scene remained with him. To him, the brutal stabbing and the sailor's hysterical cursing symbolized the world's sin and hate and man-made misery. He began to pray for the woman and her assailant, and realized while praying that he must pray for the entire world. He saw as in a white light that the only cure for mankind's crime and wretchedness was the love that can be learned only from and through Him who died to show men what love is. He felt an intense desire to join himself to his Savior in making reparation for himself and for his fellowmen.

A few days later he made his way to the Sacred Heart parish rectory. Father Sturm welcomed him to his study, and Barney was soon telling him of his desire to serve God in the priesthood. The pastor knew the Caseys as a devout family, and Barney as a steady, self-respecting young man. If Barney was willing to enter a seminary with younger students, his pastor saw no reason why he shouldn't propose him. The chief requirements were an unselfish love of God, and a desire to give oneself to His service.

Certain preliminaries, Father Sturm explained, were necessary. A baptismal certificate must be presented, and the diocesan bishop's approval obtained. There was also the matter of seminary tuition. Once these matters were arranged, Barney could enter the seminary the following January.

When the German pastor spoke of "the seminary" he meant the same German seminary of St. Francis de Sales in Milwaukee which Maurice Casey had attended. There the classes and campus conversation were for the most part in German. A minority of non-German students were included in the student body and some non-German instructors were on the faculty. On the whole, however, a student from Germany would have found it not too different from a seminary in his native land.

There is nothing to indicate that Barney was troubled by the prospect of attending the same institution from which, six years before, an unhappy Maurice had returned home with a nagging sense of futility and failure. Possibly his joy at the opportunity of beginning studies that could lead to the priesthood drove all other considerations from his mind. As for his family, all were elated. His brother Gus asked how advanced his classes would be, and Barney explained that the first four seminary years were a kind of high school.

"Then I'll be one semester ahead of you!" exclaimed Gus, a sharp lad who had started high school the previous September.

He was seven years Barney's junior.

Chapter 6

Progress towards Frustration

The "German seminary" combined aspects of monastery, college, and army barracks. Its students prayed at scheduled times. They studied prescribed subjects at scheduled times. They were subject to semi-military discipline.

The school's five-story, domed central structure overlooked lesser buildings and Lake Michigan's sparkling waters on Milwaukee's south side. Its name honored St. Francis de Sales, and it was frequently referred to as The Salesianum.

The common language was German, though the non-German minority—largely Irish and Polish—attended classes that at least during the first four years were probably taught in English. German, however, was a required subject, though the touchstone subject was Latin. Should a student fail in Latin, the faculty would be forced to consider whether he should be advanced to the philosophy and theology courses. In these, the textbooks were in Latin.

In studying, the student benefited from the seminary's order and discipline, strictly enforced to the sound of bells. Bells governed virtually all major activities. At the sound of a bell—even the five-thirty rising bell—one moved instantly. Response to bells became semi-automatic. To Barney, this was to prove of enduring advantage. Little as he could then have anticipated, through his next sixty-five years he would arise, pray, eat, recreate and sleep to the uncompromising metallic signals that help a religious house maintain promptness and order.

The bells summoned to morning prayers, which were followed by an hour's meditation. In this a priest assisted the lower classes, reading from a devotional work and commenting on the text. Beginning at six-forty-five, Mass was sung. Breakfast was at seven-thirty; the first class started at eight o'clock.

So went the bell-timed day, with few minutes unaccounted for. The dinner bell rang at twelve; a class bell at two; a recess bell at four; a rosary bell at five; a supper bell sometime thereafter; a study bell at seven-thirty; the night prayers bell at nine; the retiring bell at nine-thirty.

The most welcome bells were those that called to meals. Thanks to the devoted Franciscan Sisters who labored in the kitchen, the food was wholesome and well prepared. They also kept the rooms and corridors spick-and-span, laundered clothes, and nursed the students when they fell sick. Without their good German cooking, their washing, cleaning and nursing, the seminary could hardly have operated.

Among students the Sisters nursed was Barney himself. Time after time, during his four-and-a-half years at St. Francis, quinsy sore throat—the layman's name for peritonsillar abcess—made his life miserable. The disease caused throat swelling, penetrating pain, sickening fever; each word became a straining gasp. This recurrent sickness must have interfered with his study. He was further handicapped by an extra-curricular activity; to earn his tuition he had become the seminary barber. This was another skill that he had picked up somewhere along the way of his adventurous career, but the work must have limited his time for study.

Nevertheless, in his first semester his grades were excellent. Strangely, his lowest mark was in "vocal music";

possibly this was due to quinsy. His other subjects were Latin, German, English, arithmetic, Christian doctrine, and geography, and he passed all tests in these with high marks.

He was an earnest student. His mark in Application, all through his nine semesters at St. Francis, was "1." This was his rating, also, for Conduct.

During the fall and winter of 1892-93, his averages showed a slight falling off, but his marks were still in the 80's and 90's. He had no serious reason to fear ultimate failure.

On his return home for the summer vacation of 1893, he organized a small literary society among his brothers and friends. He also helped his father farm.

In the second half of 1893, Barney's grades slipped a notch or two, but were still satisfactory. Despite his studies and his barbering activities, he permitted himself a little time for needed outdoor recreation. In winter he skated on the big rink the students had made; in spring, he played baseball occasionally when his class team demanded his help against one of the tougher school nines. Because he could give so little time to the game, he was officially designated the relief catcher, and his first appearance in that role astounded his classmates—for he refused to wear a catcher's mask. Despite urgent warnings predicting a smashed face from bat or ball, he waved the mask aside, made a huge sign of the cross, and crouched as close to the batter as if he were wearing full protection. He was never injured.

The boys, noticing that the middle finger of his throwing hand was bent at a rather sharp angle, assumed he had injured it catching. But he explained that he had broken it when a Casey horse he was exercising threw him—and his small sister, Gracie, to whom he was giving a ride. His hands protected the child, but the finger was broken, and he hadn't bothered having it properly set. He carried the disfiguration throughout his life.

The students looked upon him as an older brother. When their skylarking flared into sudden combat, he—who, generally, strictly minded his own business—would come between the combatants. His—"Now, boys, take it easy!"—would bring calm, and in another moment the belligerents were friends.

Now in his twenty-fourth year, he returned to Superior for the long vacation of 1894. That summer, as usual, he aided in the farm work and helped operate the dairy business. Jim was now a mail carrier, and Maurice had learned the plumbing trade and was indulging a desire to see the world while practicing it. He wrote regularly from whatever city he was in, from middle west to far west. John was managing the dairy business while reading law in the office of Judge Smith, a family friend. Edward was attending the Sacred Heart High School and already thinking of the seminary. The younger children were in grade school or high school.

During the seminary year of 1894-95, Barney brought up his marks a little—they had declined in the previous year—and in the fall of 1895 entered Class Five, equivalent to the first year of college. As usual he received top grades in Application and Conduct, and very good grades in Christian Doctrine, and English. But in the second semester of Class Five he was in the 70 to 77 range in Latin, algebra, geometry, and history, and in the 77 to 85 range in German. He was in the 85 to 93 range in vocal music, United States history, and natural philosophy.

At this point the seminary superiors informed Barney—this he was to tell some of his Capuchin brethren many years later—that he would not be able to manage his studies if he continued in the diocesan seminary. How this judgment was arrived at must remain conjectural; the grades for his last two semesters, while low in what were considered the more difficult subjects, were not failing marks. The seminary au-

thorities today can throw no light. If some of his classes were
taught in German, this would go far to explain his low
grades; he had not succeeded in mastering that language.
That, with his still lower marks in Latin, might have been
decisive.

The authorities did not, however, advise him to seek his
vocation in the world. Their suggestion was quite the opposite; they urged him to ask admittance to a religious order.
It is possible that they might have had in mind an English-
speaking religious order, in whose seminary language difficulties might be to some degree eliminated. Also, his intense
spirituality might have suggested to them that he should join
a religious order where he could lead a more contemplative
life.

Whatever the motivation of the seminary superiors, it is
evident that Barney, humble and conscientiously concerned
with serving God in any way God desired, took their advice
most seriously. Acting on it, he visited the Capuchin major
seminary, or clericate, at that time in downtown Milwaukee.
Apparently, the visit did little to implant in his mind any idea
that his future lay with the Capuchins.

He returned home for the long vacation of 1896 uncertain and unsettled. He had become unsure of his calling, not
only to the diocesan priesthood, but to a life in religion.

Chapter 7

At a Word from a Lady

Through the summer and fall of 1896, the ex-seminarian prayed to know God's will. Part of this period he was sick; the quinsy sore throat had become chronic.

He opened his heart to his mother and to his newly married sister, Ellen, who though married that summer was often at the family home. His chief question was, "Does God want me to be a priest?" They could do little to help him find an answer.

Finally, the counsel he needed came to him when he sought out Father Eustace Vollmer, a Franciscan to whom he had gone in the past for spiritual advice. Father Eustace was celebrated; people of all faiths went to him for counsel.

In the most positive manner, Father Eustace brushed aside Barney's doubts and fears. The seminary counselors, he insisted, had been right; Barney most certainly did have a vocation to the priesthood in some religious order. He encouraged him to apply to his own Franciscan Order and to others, including the Capuchin.

Barney received the Franciscan's mention of the Capuchins without enthusiasm. Perhaps his chief objection to the Capuchins was the fact that theirs was, in the United States at that time, a German-speaking Order. So was their seminary —and Barney must have considered that it was in another German seminary that he had found the going hard. There is

no record that he raised this fact as an objection, but he did
mention to Father Eustace one circumstance he considered a
drawback. He must have done so in a semi-humorous vein,
for his disapproval was merely a matter of personal taste: he
disliked the enormous beards Capuchins then wore. Many of
them, in imitation of St. Francis, never trimmed their beards,
and Barney told Father Eustace that he shrank from going
through life with such a cumbersome adornment.

"You above all, Barney, should value the Capuchin beard!"
answered the Franciscan. "Those big beards protect the
throat and chest. With that troublesome quinsy of yours, a
heavy beard is precisely what you need."

So Barney sought to quiet whatever doubts he may have
had about the Capuchins, and to rid himself of his prejudice
against their beards, and he sent off a letter of application to
the Capuchin Provincial in Detroit.

In the Capuchin friary on Mt. Elliott Avenue in Detroit,
Father Bonaventure Frey read Barney's letter and stroked his
own full and flowing beard. Then his large brown eyes re-
read other letters relating to Barney Casey.

In one letter, particularly, the Capuchin Provincial—who
was also Co-Founder of the Order in the United States—
found a most convincing evaluation. It was from the eminent
Monsignor Joseph Rainer, incoming rector of St. Francis
Seminary in Milwaukee. The Monsignor stated that he was
quite certain that Barney Casey possessed a true vocation to
the monastic life—the rector using that term roughly as
inclusive of friars as well as monks.

Summing up the evidence before him, Father Bonaventure concluded that Barney Casey was devout and humble,
and therefore in the Franciscan spirit. If any question of
Barney's scholarship entered his mind, he evidently decided

to leave its answer to the future judgment of the Capuchin seminary's instructors. Yes, and to the good Lord, whose judgments and ways were so often so surprising to men. He had seen that proved more than once since Father Francis Haas and he left Europe for the United States many years before.

He and Father Francis had set out from Switzerland in the summer of 1856. They proposed to establish in the largely Protestant United States a branch of the Capuchin Order. Though not Capuchins, they had bound themselves to observe the Capuchin rule, and were sanctioned by the Swiss Capuchin Provincial. When they landed in New York from their vermin-ridden windjammer—they hadn't been able to afford a steamer—their capital added up to two dollars and fifty cents.

In Wisconsin, despite misunderstandings, rebuffs, misfortunes and threatened disasters, they had built their community's foundation. Now, after forty years, it was flourishing—with a great mother house in Mt. Calvary, Wisconsin, and establishments in Milwaukee, New York City, and Detroit. It was supplying priests who served in the spirit of St. Francis; like him, they considered love of God even more important than love of learning. Perhaps this former student so strongly recommended by the rector of Milwaukee's diocesan seminary was a man after the Poverello's heart. Father Bonaventure drew a sheet of letter paper toward him and wrote:

Dear Mr. Casey:
I will make no objection now to your application to join the novitiate, as the Reverend Rector of the Salesianum [St. Francis Seminary] thinks you have a vocation for monastic life. You may therefore come to Detroit as soon as circumstances will allow you.

At the Casey home in Superior, Barney read the Provincial's letter without enthusiasm. He still preferred any other religious community to the Capuchins.

He did not act immediately. He continued to pray. It occurred to him that the great feast of the Immaculate Conception of the Blessed Virgin was soon to be celebrated—on December eighth. He decided to make a novena for guidance to the Mother of God, to end on her feastday. He asked his mother and sister Ellie to join him in the nine days of prayer.

Just before the close of the novena, as he recorded in a memo book twelve years later, he made a vow of perpetual chastity.

It is probable that Father Eustace knew about and approved this solemn promise. It was a weighty matter, for it bound Barney to devote himself directly to God's service totally, whether or not he entered a religious order. He made the vow, evidently, on the eve of the feastday. The note which he jotted down in his notebook on December 8, 1908, reads —"Dec. 8th, 1895—Vow of Chastity—and—at once—Decision in vocation to Detroit. Deo Gratias." He wrote "1895" for "1896." It was an error such as one can easily make years after an event.

During the feastday Mass, he became intensely aware of the presence of the Mother of God. At the same time, he was distinctly conscious of the command, as coming from her: "Go to Detroit." There was no visualization.

The simple directive could have only one meaning. The Capuchin Order at that time was the only religious order for men with a novitiate in Detroit. The command meant, therefore, "Join the Capuchins."

He never questioned the command for an instant, and he got to Detroit as quickly as he could manage.

Clearances had to be obtained from the Chancery, for he had been a seminarian. This required ten days. By Sunday,

December 20, he was ready. He informed his parents that he would be starting for Detroit the next day.

The family remonstrated. Why could he not go to the Capuchins after Christmas? Moreover, heavy snowfall was predicted; the first flakes were already coming down. His brothers warned him that this could slow trains to a snail's pace; insisted that he was foolhardy to set out in the face of such weather. Their words were wasted, and they could not understand his inflexibility.

On the night of December twenty-first, he was on the 11 p.m. train for St. Paul when it pulled out of the Superior depot.

The snow proved to be as heavy, the train as slow as his brothers had predicted. All the way from St. Paul, across Wisconsin to Milwaukee, the locomotive battled the drifts. The crowded cars, when not stifling hot, were miserably cold, their air dried out and stale. In Milwaukee, there was a lay-over. Early Wednesday morning, he left Chicago on another train, pulled by two locomotives, for Detroit. At times, the train slowed to twelve miles an hour through ever-deepening snow. Long before it pulled into the Detroit station, darkness had fallen. It was Christmas eve.

Lugging his valise, an exhausted Barney found his way to a streetcar, arrived downtown and made the necessary transfer. When finally the conductor called his stop, he found himself but a few steps from the Capuchin friary and its adjoining church.

A bearded Brother, answering the doorbell, informed him that he was expected. He waved the weary traveler to a chair and vanished, soon reappearing with two friars. The more elderly was the Guardian, Father Casimir; the other was Father Gabriel, the novice master. They offered him food; Barney replied that he wanted only sleep. At the head of the stairs, they showed him his "cell." It was a small room on the building's east side, overlooking the grounds at the rear of the friary.

As he closed his room door, Barney's earlier prejudices against joining the Capuchins swept over him again, full force. Perhaps fatigue contributed to the feeling; he was physically drained. He asked himself—"Why did our Blessed Lady send me here?"

He removed his outer clothes, and stretching himself on the narrow iron bed, pulled a blanket around him against the cold.

In seconds, he was sound asleep.

Out of a fathomless oblivion he felt himself climbing back to consciousness, vaguely aware that something unusual had awakened him. Listening, he detected in the near distance the jingling of bells, and many voices shouting out a joyful song. There came a brief silence, and then, closer this time, the singing and the bells burst forth again. Now the jubilant invitation fell clearly on his ears—

> Adeste fideles,
> Laeti triumphantes,
> Venite, venite in Bethlehem!

Swinging out of bed, he opened the door and peered down the corridor. A brown-robed procession was approaching. It stopped before a door as the friars continued to sing out their appeal to all the faithful to join them on the road to Bethlehem. From a friar's hands, a censer swung rhythmically, white smoke puffs rising at the top of every arc. As he watched, a friar emerged from the cell and joined the group, which again moved toward him.

He hurried into his shoes, and glanced at his watch; he had been asleep only an hour. Yet he felt fresh and thoroughly rested.

The friars were now before his half-opened door. The

little white clouds from the swinging censer, drifting into his cell, filled it with their purifying fragrance, man's ancient symbol of clean hearts on fire with love of God. Again the voices rang out—

> Natum videte
> Regem Angelorum!
> Venite adoremus,
> Venite adoremus,
> Venite adoremus
> Dominum!

Barney, responding to welcoming smiles and gestures, shrugged himself into his suit coat and moved in among friars going forward to adore the Lord. The gloomy fog that had enveloped his mind only an hour before had dissipated. Exhilarated and exalted, he fell into step with these bearded religious with whom he was to walk and sing praise to his Creator through the next sixty years.

Led by Father Bonaventure, the friars continued their tour of the corridors, their number increasing until all the cells had been visited. Then they moved toward the choir chapel.

Years later, he often told of that Christmas night, and of the deep serene happiness that flooded his heart as he joined in the responses at Midnight Mass. He felt himself one with these earnest, humble men crying out in the "Kyrie" to the Lord to have mercy on themselves and on all sinners; jubiliantly praising the Holy Trinity in the Gloria, and imploring heaven's peace on earth to men of good will. He was experiencing a new fervor, a deeper love of God. Never again would he doubt that—if he was to serve God as a religious—it must be as a Capuchin.

All through that Holy Mass, his spirit rejoiced. He realized that He Who had been homeless on this Christmas night, had brought him home at last.

Barney felt truly at home, but his suroundings were still somewhat strange the next day as he entered the large, plain, rectangular refectory and took his seat at one of the long oak tables running along each of its four walls. The friars sat on benches with their backs toward the wall. He could see every face, and every face wore a beard. As Father Guardian introduced him, beardless Barney in his layman's clothes felt as conspicuous as a white crow. But he was soon taken up in the affable conversation, for the spirit was one of festival. During the year the friars ate plain food, but such days as Christmas and Easter they honored by feasting and singing, and relaxing from their labors.

Today, every table held bowls of oranges, apples, bananas and nuts, and the serving Brothers were carrying in great platters of turkey, and bowls of mashed potatoes, sausage dressing and vegetables. Beside every plate, too, there stood a wineglass. Into this, if an abstemious diner had not turned it down, Brother Server poured good Rhine wine. It would be sipped and savored slowly, appreciatively, for no second glass would follow.

Among those who most knowledgeably relished the wine was the Father Provincial. In his youth Father Bonaventure, as John Frey of the Swiss canton of Thurgau, had been a dashing member of the University of Bonn's famed Bavarian Student's Corps. He had worn the smart Corps regalia with cap of blue and white, and a sword dangling from his hip. Upon those student days he looked back with pleasure, and with special affection remembered his beloved Bavarian Corps. Indeed, quite recently, when a friend had given him money "to do with as he would," he had sent the Corps a hundred Marks as a token of his esteem.

In the recreation room after dinner a friar played the piano softly while priests and brothers relaxed. Cigars were freely passed—benefactors had been generous that season.

Even some friars who smoked but seldom, lighted up, albeit somewhat awkwardly, and the room was soon fragrant with the scent of good Havana.

When singing started, Barney joined in, happy that his years in the "German seminary" had made him familiar with the Deutsch. With these German-singing friars he lustily praised the *Tannenbaum,* tenderly paid homage to *Heilige Nacht,* and sang many other songs of Christmastide. As these men, strong in mind and strong in faith, sang their love for the Babe of Bethlehem, Barney felt his Irish heart warmed to its very core. He sang well, for the quinsy sore throat that had afflicted him till recently had gone. Nor would it ever return through all his Capuchin days.

At St. Bonaventure's, Christmas observance was liturgical. It began Christmas eve, and extended to Epiphany. During this time a deep, a special joy pervaded the friary—joy that overflowed Barney's heart and made him feel truly a member of this spiritual family.

He was eagerly looking forward to the day when he, too, would wear the brown robe. That day would come three weeks after Christmas, when he would be formally invested with the Capuchin habit.

Chapter 8

A New Garb,
and a New Life

Sometime between Barney's first, heart-warming Christmas day at St. Bonaventure's and his investiture three weeks later, darkness descended upon his mind and soul.

During this darkness he was powerfully tempted to leave the monastery. He resisted, praying for light. He always considered this experience the most trying of his life. The temptation was not rooted in any dissatisfaction with the Capuchin Order; all his doubts about joining that branch of the Franciscans had faded away on Christmas eve. It seems to have been, rather, an overpowering fear of entrance into any religious community.

He prayed for strength to repel this terrorizing attack. He won the battle—and this victory he always considered one of the memorable dates in his Capuchin career. He includes it among thirteen events which he noted on one of the pages of a small book entitled "Rule of St. Francis." Every Capuchin receives one of these when entering the order. The note referring to the temptation reads cryptically—"January 13, 1897. Dark indeed." This was the day before his investiture. Years later, in a letter to one of his brothers, he feelingly mentions this spiritual struggle.

The temptation to leave St. Bonaventure's seems to have

persisted up to the moment he entered the choir chapel on Thursday, January 14, 1897, for the investiture ceremony. There it ceased.

Dressed in his layman's clothes, he walked alone; he was the only one invested at this time. The entire community was gathered, each friar in his stall, and the Provincial, who officiated, waiting for him at the foot of the altar. To the altar's left, draped over a prie-dieu, was a Capuchin's habit— dark brown robe, cowl, and white waist cord or cincture. Turning and facing the tabernacle, Father Bonaventure recited in a loud voice—"The Lord be with you," to which the choir made the age-old response, "And with your spirit."

Then Father Bonaventure prayed aloud, asking God to "enlarge the heart of Your servant with all heavenly gifts . . . infuse into him Your holy grace by which he will be able to persevere in that which he has begun . . ."

Next, accompanied by two Brothers as acolytes, the Provincial moved to the Epistle or left side of the altar, and blessed the habit, the cowl, and the cincture. Assisted by the acolytes, Barney now put on these articles of the simple Franciscan habit—a habit he was to wear for the next sixty years. As he clothed himself, Father Bonaventure prayed: "May the Lord clothe you with the 'new man,' who according to God is created in justice, and in the holiness of truth . . . . O Lord Jesus Christ, Who has said, 'My yoke is sweet and My burden light,' we beseech You, that this Your servant may wear this habit in such manner that he may obtain Your grace in this present life and the glory of the life to come."

As the candidate put on the cowl, Father Bonaventure continued to pray: "O Lord, deign to place this helmet of salvation upon his head, so that he may withstand the attacks of the infernal enemy." Barney drew the cincture about him, as the priest asked the Lord to "gird him with the cincture of purity." The investiture completed, Barney was placed under the special patronage of St. Francis Solanus, by whose name he would henceforth be known.*

The new Frater Solanus resembled his patron in language difficulties, in devotion to—though not in mastery of—the violin, and in ardent willingness to sacrifice himself for God and souls. Here the similarities ended. For Saint Francis Solanus had been a Spanish nobleman, an intellectual, a more than capable violinist, a phenominally successful missionary, a brilliant preacher. Through twenty years he hazarded his life, evangelizing savage tribes in vast regions of seventeenth century South America. His twentieth century namesake was to spend his life behind a desk; would never see a mission country; would never preach a doctrinal sermon.

In the novitiate Frater Solanus was introduced to two other novices. They had been invested six months before. But Fraters Leo Steinberg and Salesius Schneweis would be departing for the Capuchin seminary in Milwaukee the following July. He, having entered at an irregular time, would remain a novice until the following July—six months longer than the twelve months minimum.

The novitiate was not the regular Capuchin life, but an introduction to it; a time of test and trial, of self-measurement and self-examination. Like the West Pointer during pleb year, the novice would possibly never again find life so difficult.

Even as an engagement which, it is anticipated, will lead to marriage, so with the novitiate. It is a period of getting acquainted with new demands on one's generosity and self-

---

* This was once the custom with the Capuchins and most other religious orders. Today—stressing one's baptismal consecration to Christ—the candidate in many orders, including the Capuchin, is not given a "name in religion." He continues to be known by his baptismal name, to which, in the Capuchin Order, "Frater" or "Brother" is prefixed.

discipline, and of getting to know oneself in the light of those demands. The novice has been moved by love of God to want to live closer to Him. He may eventually learn that he and the religious life are incompatible. And so he may finally reject the idea of becoming a religious, or the order's superiors may find, for various reasons, that his life's service lies elsewhere.

His Capuchin brethren would be studying whether he possessed the spiritual maturity to love poverty—not merely material poverty, but that inner poverty which is a denial of egoism and egocentricity. They would want to know whether he could be sufficiently a man to find in obedience to recognized authority, not repression, but spiritual liberty and fulfillment. He must face up, also, to the question of whether he possessed the spiritual strength to lead a celibate life.

Though Frater Solanus, obviously, was more certain of his vocation than younger novices could be, he must meet the Capuchin novitiate test as fully and be scrutinized as carefully.

During his novitiate, therefore, Barney was called upon to settle, for all his future life, the questions every novice must answer: "Is this life for me? Have I really met the risen Christ, and fully accepted Him? Has He called me to be His disciple? Do I really see the value, for me, of giving up all things to follow Him?"

To help him formulate these questions fully and clearly, and answer them honestly, called for expert counsel and guidance. This supremely important responsibility was the burden of the Novice Master—in this instance Father Gabriel Messmer, a priest of unusual background and ability. In Switzerland he had been Joseph Messmer—cavalry lieutenant in the Swiss army; director of extensive land holdings on celebrated Lake Constance; proprietor of a large hostelry; a professional in agriculture and hotel management. These activities he turned away from, hoping to become a Brother in the Capuchin Order. But when he arrived in the United States to join the American Capuchins, his spiritual adviser induced him to study for the priesthood. It is thought that this counsel was reinforced by Joseph's brother, Dr. Sebastian Messmer, then priest-professor of Canon Law at Seton Hall College (now University) in New Jersey. He was later to become Archbishop of Milwaukee.

Appointed a professor in the Order's clericate, Father Gabriel begged to be transferred to pastoral work. He served several years in Capuchin parishes, then was made novice master in Detroit. In that office, he worked wonders with the novices through fatherly kindness, endless patience, serenity, sensible discipline, and deep interest in their welfare.

Under him, Frater Solanus studied the Franciscan rule and the Capuchin Constitutions, or outline of life. So careful were the superiors that novices be wholly uninfluenced while weighing their final decision, that conversation between them and professed friars was not permitted during the novitiate year.

Despite this restriction, Frater Solanus, in the friary's peaceful atmosphere, felt very much a brother to the quiet-faced Capuchins. Even his loose brown robe, so comfortable and convenient, must have added to his ease. It eliminated the layman's dress shirt, necktie, and the starched collar and cuffs then in style. And it saved time—of which Capuchins, for all that they seldom seemed to hurry, were in fact quite miserly. One could slip into habit and sandals in a moment.

This was doubly appreciated when, at four-forty-five each morning, a loud, hollow clapping resounded up and down the corridors. It was the community's Archangel Gabriel, awakening the dead-to-the-world. To the youngest Brother was assigned this thankless task. With uncommendable zeal, he slammed together two-by-four sections as he moved through the echoing corridor. Possibly, as some hinted, his enthusiasm was inspired by unconscious resentment at being required to arise even earlier than his fellows. Whatever the reason, the hideous clamor seemed to the more sleep-prone indicative of a spirit alien to true brotherhood.

In the fifteen minutes following Brother Bedlam's racket, friars and novices dressed, washed—the icy cold water of mid-winter was particularly stimulating—and took their places in choir.

At ten minutes after five, there commenced the chanting of Lauds, the morning prayer of the Church, followed by the Litany of the Saints. Then came a period of twenty minutes or so for silent meditation. Just before six o'clock, the friars recited the Angelus, that age-old commemoration of Christianity's central mystery, the Incarnation. At six o'clock there began the celebration of the community Mass.

For fifteen or twenty minutes after Mass, the novices and most of the friars remained in chapel, praying, offering their thanksgivings. A little before seven, the breakfast bell called all to the refectory and a fifteen minute meal of coffee and bread or cereal, eaten in silence. After breakfast, those who had no immediate duties, such as hearing confessions in the public chapel, retired to their cells for twenty or thirty minutes of spiritual reading. Or they meditated, walking about the friary garden. By 8 o'clock all had begun their daily duties.

Generally, several of the Fathers were absent, preaching missions in parishes throughout the midwest.

Almost every morning priests were called upon to officiate at burials in the cemetery across the street from the friary. The Fathers also assisted at various parishes in the surrounding community, particularly on weekends.

The Brothers bought the food and prepared it; cleaned and maintained the buildings, ran the printing press; tailored

new habits and repaired old ones, and performed various
office duties, including that of porter or doorkeeper.

Novices who were to become Brothers attended two lec-
tures a day. Those aiming for the priesthood heard a third
lecture. The latter also read assigned books and articles;
learned to recite the divine office; took part in chanting the
canonical hours in choir, and assisted in the various liturgical
functions throughout the year. They also helped the Brothers
with various jobs about the friary. Every minute was filled;
time-wasting was held a serious fault.

After the noonday meal, the novices relaxed in their
quarters, while the friars were enjoying their own thirty
minutes of leisure in the recreation room. Thursday afternoon
was a free period. On Sundays, the novices attended only one
lecture. On that day, too, as well as on feastdays, the usual
reading at dinner and supper was dispensed with, and the
usual mealtime silence was not observed.

On ordinary days, the reading aloud at dinner and supper
started with a passage from one of the four gospels. This was
followed by reading from the biography of a saint, or from
some devotional work, or from one of the Papal Encyclicals.
A Father would read about five minutes, then pass the book
to a priest at his right. In this way, all the Fathers would
contribute to the reading, which ended only with the end of
the meal. It was another way of making every minute count;
of keeping the community's collective mind centered on the
supernatural.

Throughout the friary, living was reduced to essentials.
Frater Solanus' cell was a room about nine by twelve feet,
with a single window. Its furnishings were a narrow iron bed,
a small table, a straight, armless chair. Two clothes hooks on
a wall substituted for a clothes closet; they were ample for all
the clothes a friar possessed.

In its government, the friary was equally simple. The

Father Guardian was its spiritual and temporal head. Obedience was due him in everything that was "honorable and just and in accordance with the rule of the religious life." Everything out of the routine was done with his specific permission. Despite this, basic democracy prevailed. The next year, or the next week, the Father Guardian himself might be under obedience to another Guardian.

Through daily reading, contemplation, instruction and action, Frater Solanus and his fellow novices grew in spiritual maturity. One of the most significant lessons taught them the deeper meaning of the term "Friars Minor," which St. Francis of Assisi had applied to himself and his followers. To every Franciscan it meant what the Assisian took it to mean—that Franciscans must consider themselves the lesser, the least consequential, not only of religious, but of men. At the same time, the term expressed the fact that they were brothers—brothers not only to one another, but to all men. Not Big Brothers, but minor brothers—little brothers, poor, humble, willing and ready to serve as smaller brothers do.

The novice tried to see himself as all men actually are—as weak, fault-ridden; to recognize God as sole origin of any good that was in himself; to appreciate the truth of St. Francis' aphorism, that "what a man is in the sight of God, so much he is, and no more."

Throughout his novitiate year he is conscious that within the twelve months he must arrive at a major decision, a decision that will radically change his life. He must make that decision with full knowledge of all its implications; he must therefore make it honestly and after long self-study and self-questioning. He must be free from any influence other than that of the novice master, who must act as his objective and impartial guide and counselor.

When he enters the novitiate, the candidate is probably

more mature, spiritually, than the average young man. Otherwise, he would hardly have been sufficiently interested in the
religious life to have thought seriously about embracing it.

By the end of the novitiate year, the would-be Capuchin
has learned the necessity of continuous spiritual growth. He
is resolved, with God's help, to improve, and never to allow
spiritual fatigue or discouragement to stop his progress.

By July, 1898, Barney had passed his long novitiate test,
along with four candidates who had entered the previous
July. With these, he made his solemn Capuchin promises in
the presence of the entire community.

The rite was comparatively brief. Father Bonaventure, as
Provincial, received his vow to "observe throughout my life
the Rule of the Friars Minor . . . living in obedience, without
property, and in chastity." Again, the Fathers and Brothers
gave Frater Solanus and his novice companions the cere-
monial kiss of peace, as the choir chanted Psalm 132, beginning—

> Behold how good and pleasant it is
> For brothers to live together in unity . . .

Thus the novices became Capuchins. But before they
could become priests, years of hard study were ahead. To begin these studies, they entrained for Milwaukee and the Order's major seminary on a July day in 1898.

Chapter 9

"He Will be Something Like the Cure of Ars"

To Frater Solanus the most impressive feature of the Capuchin Seminary was its stern director, Father Anthony. Ten years before, he had been the Order's Provincial. Now in his sixty-eighth year, he had mellowed somewhat, but he was still considered heavy-tempered and unyielding.

Austere, exacting, he demanded high scholastic achievement. To this end, students were not permitted to receive relations and friends. The "no visitors" rule had some exceptions, and at least one of them was made in Frater Solanus' favor. His brother John had married Nellie O'Brien, one of the lively teen-age group with whom Barney had had many a good time in and around Trimbelle. When the newlyweds came to Milwaukee, Father Anthony gave him permission to visit with them.

To the students, the director was an awesome figure, and not only because of his impressive scholarship. Stockily built, he was as grim and resolute as a battleship. A high, square forehead and a grizzled gray beard cascading down his broad chest accentuated his granite facial features. His lively and observant gray eyes, the seminarians told one another, "looked right through you."

Father Anthony—who was to make the great key decision in Frater Solanus' life—had joined the Order in 1867.

To the struggling Capuchins, his request for admission seemed literally a Godsend. The Fathers who then constituted the young "Custody"—the designation of the foundation before it became a Province—had been kept too busy to concentrate on graduate and post-graduate studies in philosophy and theology. The clericate was in crying need of a first-rate scholar to direct its studies, and Father Anthony filled the need.

He had made brilliant records as a student in Germany. A driving desire to dedicate himself to missionary work had brought him to the United States, a mission country. When he joined the Capuchins he was thirty-six years old. Even in his Capuchin novitiate he was called upon to teach Greek and Church history. When the Founder, Father Francis, was thought to be dying, he sent for Father Anthony. As the latter leaned over his bedside, he earnestly asked him—"Do you intend persevering in your Capuchin vocation?" Upon receiving Father Anthony's warm assurance, he said—"Then I am ready and willing to die."

He recovered, but thereafter he and Co-Founder Father Bonaventure relied heavily on Father Anthony's counsel, particularly in regard to the fitness of clerics for ordination to the priesthood.

During his first three semesters in the seminary Frater Solanus' scholastic rating was a little less than average. In philosophy he was below average all the way, with one "3," the passing grade—and two "2-3's," which indicated somewhat less than average, but better than merely "passing."

He was not the least of the six students in his class. Frater Damasus, a patient, cheerful cleric, was a rung or two below him. His, too, was a delayed vocation; he had been thirty-two years old when he entered the novitiate. German, the classroom language, presented no difficulties to him, since he

came from a German-speaking home—as did Fraters Maurus
Ascherl, Pius Stutzer, and Fabian Fetha. Fraters John O'Dono-
van and Solanus Casey must have envied these students their
easy command of the German tongue.

Perhaps Frater Solanus' somewhat limited grasp of German* accounted for Father Anthony's extraordinary consideration when finally, at the beginning of the fourth semester, he began to instruct him. The director of the clericate
would at times so formulate his questions to Frater Solanus as
virtually to put the answer on his lips! This practice, which
would have scandalized students and faculty in a university,
received no criticism. On the contrary, the students favored it.
It was not only that in the little seminary the students were all
charitable and truly brothers in spirit; they admired and loved
Frater Solanus in a special way. Like Father Anthony and the
rest of the faculty, they observed Frater Solanus with admiring
interest. All recognized in him a high spirituality, a burning
love for God, and deep humility. They noted how meticulous
he was in observance of the Franciscan Rule, and in performance of every duty. When acting as sacristan, for example, he
would go about decorating the altar so painstakingly that
the task would take him three or four times as long as most

---

* It is certain that Father Solanus himself believed that his im-
perfect grasp of German handicapped him in the seminary. A
scholarly nephew has quoted him as telling him that "the reason
he never received faculties to hear confessions was that the classes
in the seminary were taught completely in German." Father Boniface, who although ordained a year later attended some classes
with Father Solanus, says: "As far as study was concerned, all
clerics were on equal scholastic grounds, because all textbooks,
except Church History, were in Latin. . . . In the examination the
teachers limited themselves to the contents of the textbooks, which
gave every cleric a chance to pass the examinations." It seems
obvious, however, that a student who lacked a ready and perfect
understanding of German might have failed to grasp many of the
instructor's explanations and clarifications that would have enabled him to thoroughly comprehend the text.

would have devoted to it. They loved him, too, because of his unassuming manner, his open heartedness, his unfailing good humor and easy give-and-take during recreation, and his utter lack of self-centeredness.

They realized that he was no perfectionist, even if he did consume fifteen minutes or so merely adjusting candles and flowers on the altar. Had he been a perfectionist, he probably would have found some excuse when Father Anthony, during recreation, asked him for a violin solo—for his technical deficiencies were considerable. Yet he would respond to Father Anthony's request with such a generous desire to please, and in a manner so eloquently reflecting his candor and simplicity, that his performance won all hearts. Unfailingly, when he had concluded his little concert, Father Anthony would show his satisfaction by leading the applause.

His grades fell off in the fall term of 1899, coincident with the beginning of the study of dogma, moral theology, canon law, sacred scripture and liturgy. In these subjects, from January, 1900 to June, 1902, he received three "3's" and a "2-3" in dogma; three "2-3's" and a "2" in morals, and like grades in canon law; three "3's" and a "2-3" in scripture, and all "2's" in liturgy. It may have been that Latin, as well as German, held him back. He had received low Latin grades in the diocesan seminary, and in the Capuchin seminary all textbooks, except one, were in Latin.

The faculty did not, of course, base its judgment of a candidate for the priesthood entirely on scholastic grades; other considerations could be far more important. A student's degree of scholastic ability, however, indicated his knowledge of essential subjects and aided the faculty in determining whether they should continue to advance him on the road to the priesthood.

Whatever the reasons for his mediocre scholarship, Frater Solanus continued in the seminary, and with his classmates received tonsure. This marked his official entrance into the clerical state, and preceded the reception of minor orders.

In due course, and if their superiors approved, Frater Solanus and his five classmates would receive major orders, the first of which was the subdiaconate. Before they could be recommended for the subdiaconate, however, their superiors would meet, discuss each one and his qualifications, and decide whether he should be admitted to this first of the major orders. This decision was of the gravest importance. Up to ordination as subdeacon, a cleric had formed no permanent bond to the clerical life. But this step would obligate him to clerical celibacy and daily recitation of the divine office the rest of his earthly days.

No written record has been found of the meeting at which the Capuchin superiors decided which members of the ordination class of 1904 were to be ordained subdeacons; known records of such meetings go back only to 1912. According to Father Boniface, there was some opposition to the ordination of Frater Solanus as subdeacon, and it was Father Anthony's powerful support that overrode whatever objections were voiced. Perhaps alluding to Frater Solanus' extraordinary spirituality, and to practical abilities he may have recognized in him, the old director of the seminary said— "We shall ordain Frater Solanus, and as a priest, he will be to the people something like the Curé of Ars." [Since his canonization in 1925, St. John Vianney.]

The Curé of Ars had been an even less able student than Frater Solanus. At his ordination, faculties had been withheld. He received them only when, owing to a serious shortage of priests, he was given charge of a parish; this made the exercise of full faculties necessary.

Father Anthony's championship of Frater Solanus' aspiration to the priesthood was one of the old scholar's last important acts. His health had been failing for several months, and the end came one morning toward the middle of February, 1903, when Frater Solanus and another cleric were praying at his bedside. He had frequently remarked—"When I can no longer give my classes, I shall die." He had prepared his classes up to five days before his death, and even on his deathbed he continued to teach. In semi-delirium he would quote from Hurter's textbook on theology, and from St. Thomas and St. Augustine. Then he would turn to Fraters Solanus and John, and ask them: "Habt ihr das verstanden?" —"Did you understand that?" And no doubt Frater Solanus regretted that he had not understood the great teacher's German explanations of theology more thoroughly.

Not long after Father Anthony's death, word came to Frater Solanus of the death of Rebecca Tobin. At the bottom of one of his class notebooks he records the fact under date of June 21, 1903.

"Today," he wrote, "for the first time in 7 years, I heard about Rebecca. R. I. P.—O queer world and uncertain."

Rebecca had died when thirty-three years old.

At the left of the note are the words, "Deo Gratias!" Before this exclamation of thanks to God he drew the flaming, thorn-encircled symbolic Sacred Heart of Jesus.

Was the "Deo Gratias" a thanksgiving that Rebecca had died well? Or a thanksgiving for having realized a religious rather than a matrimonial vocation? Do the words—"O queer world and uncertain"—indicate that Frater Solanus was thinking of the possibility that it was only her mother's "No," that had stood between him and marriage to the lovely young girl whom no doubt he would always remember in his prayers and Masses?

Sometime between the day Frater Solanus wrote this note about Rebecca, and July, 1904, the seminary superiors met to pass finally upon the fitness for the priesthood of each member of his class. It is probable that at this meeting they definitely decided to withhold from Fraters Solanus and Damasus the faculties of formal preaching and administration of the sacrament of penance.

It would seem that in arriving at this decision as it related to Frater Solanus, his grades were not the chief factor; they were only a little less than average. At the end of the last semester—in June, 1904—he was still fifth in the class of six. But his grades from September, 1902, to June, 1904, had been average. Unlike their classmates, neither he, nor Fraters John and Damasus, had taken liturgy in their last two semesters. Inasmuch as they were in the lower half of their class in scholastic standing, it may be that they had been relieved of this study in order to devote additional time to subjects considered more important.

During the four last semesters, Frater Solanus' marks in dogma were somewhat below average. With equal grades in a medical or engineering or law college, he could have been awarded a diploma. But a candidate for the priesthood is not approved for ordination solely on his scholastic record. And even after his ordination—in Frater Solanus' time—certain faculties of his priesthood could be withheld for various reasons. Rightly or wrongly, Frater Solanus' superiors might have been concerned about his judgment in both doctrinal preaching and in the confessional. Even if they deemed his knowledge sufficient, that fact in and of itself would not guarantee his good judgment. On whatever grounds their decision was taken, they may well have been mistaken in arriving at it. But whether mistaken or not, they had to vote according to conscience.

The end result was to prove fortunate for the tens of thousands who were to depend upon Father Solanus' counsel and compassion during his long priestly career. Most of these would never have come to know him had his daily routine been that of a Capuchin exercising all the faculties of the priesthood.

What was the effect upon him personally of his limited ministry? A Capuchin who observed him over a period of years believes that his lack of faculties was a humiliation and a cross. "It brought forth in him," says this friar, "a greatness and a holiness that might never have been realized in any other way."

Another Capuchin has remarked on the probability that Father Solanus would have made a most impractical confessor.

"With his disregard of time," he said, "and his boundless compassion, he would probably have heard only one penitent's confession in the space of time another priest would have been hearing ten. Moreover, his horror of mortal sin was such that I am sure some confessions would have caused him almost unbearable shock and sorrow."

Frater Solanus was ordained to the priesthood in Milwaukee's Capuchin St. Francis Church. It was a Sunday, July 24, 1904, and Archbishop Messmer, brother of his old novice master, officiated.

For all eternity, the Frater who had now become Father Solanus would carry the indelible mark of his consecration. He was a priest forever—but in this life his ministry would be sharply restricted. Throughout his career he would be forbidden to hear a confession, unless a penitent were at the point of death with no other priest available. He could preach only informally or inspirationally; he could not deliver sermons on Catholic doctrine. This meant he would not be permitted to conduct missions or retreats. He was a "sacerdotus simplex"; a simplex priest, more commonly known as a "Mass priest."

Yet to be the channel through which God the Son descended upon the altar to become food for souls—this was, to

Father Solanus, the great thing. It is quite probable that at his ordination he did not fully realize what it would mean to be deprived of the other faculties.

He offered his first Mass in St. Joseph's Church, Appleton, Wisconsin, on Sunday, July 31, with his parents, and his brothers Jim, Maurice and Edward among the congregation. Maurice had been transferred to the railway postal service in Chicago; Edward was still a seminarian. Jim—now head of a numerous family—was living in Superior, as were his parents. Most of the family had moved to the state of Washington.

It was the first time since joining the Capuchin Order eight years before that Father Solanus had seen his mother.

After the Mass, and dinner in the friary, Maurice pulled Father Solanus aside, for he desired a private talk with him. Several months before, he had disclosed that he was thinking of resuming studies for the priesthood; it was this idea that he now wanted to discuss.

As they strolled in the friary garden, Maurice talked—as much to himself as to Father Solanus—remembering events of his seminary days and of the twenty years that had gone by since he had given up his studies. He referred to those two decades as if they had merely interrupted his own progress toward the priesthood.

"By George, Barney," he exclaimed at last, "I think I'll have a try at it once again!"

If he returned to his seminary studies it would be another seven years before he could be ordained, but this prospect did not discourage him.

Chapter 10

A Simplex Priest

Shortly after his ordination, Father Solanus was assigned to the Sacred Heart Friary in Yonkers, New York.

The parish which the friary served could have benefited from the coming of a full-facultied priest of Irish blood, for the once Germanic community was becoming more and more Irish. Unfortunately, Father Solanus could not take his turn in the confessional, nor instruct classes in religion, nor deliver doctrinal sermons. He could not even be sent on a sick call that might require the hearing of a confession.

To the Friary's Father Guardian, he thus presented a problem—a problem that, in a sense, the Father Guardian had brought on himself. For the Guardian at the Sacred Heart Friary was now the same Father Bonaventure who had admitted Barney Casey to the novitiate six years before.

In 1904 Father Bonaventure was in his seventy-third year, and he had chosen the Yonkers Friary as his home. He was both superior of the friary and pastor of the surrounding parish, which he had founded thirteen years before.

The best duty Father Bonaventure could think of for the new arrival was the position of sacristan—usually entrusted to a Brother. Father Solanus' work thus confined him to sacristy and sanctuary. He must see to it that the supply of linens was ample, that they were laid smoothly on the altar, that altar breads and wine were provided for each Mass celebrant, that altar vestments were kept mended and clean, that altar boys were scheduled for the various Masses.

He was also given charge of the Altar Society—a group of women who met once a month and who raised money for altar flowers, and other requirements of the sanctuary.

These simple duties could have taken only an hour or two of the day to perform. He must have been brought to full and painful realization of what it meant to be a faculty-deprived priest. He was thirty-four years old—an age at which every normal man is filled with desire to achieve. He had devoted more than ten years to studies and disciplines calculated to fit him for the priesthood. And now he faced a life devoted to services so comparatively trivial that most men contemplating such a future would have thought themselves doomed to futility.

He was by nature outgoing, adventurous. He had hoped to be—as he revealed in a letter to his brother Maurice written years later—a missionary in far lands.

He loved people; he had a genius for friendship. His simplicity, his generosity, his sweetness of disposition, drew others to him. Deep down, he must have been aware that through such attributes he could be of substantial service to God and man. But now he was limited to spreading altar cloths, policing mischievous altar boys, and acting as cicerone to a few ladies at their monthly meetings.

The sense of uselessness can literally torture in that it can twist the personality, can bring on intense nervous depression, can even cause mental instability. Fortunately, Father Solanus was spiritually matured and truly humble. Instead of sinking into despondency, he accepted his slight and simple duties, and his lowly place among his brethren, without sign of complaint in either word or manner. In this, his faith and his immense love for his Sacramental Lord must have greatly helped. Years later he was to observe to a co-worker that of all duties possible to a Capuchin, that of sacristan was to be preferred. In no other capacity, he pointed out, could one live so much of his time in the presence of Christ in the Blessed Sacrament.

His brother, Father Edward Casey, evidently sympathized with his position and admired his silent acceptance of it. This he indicated in a verse entitled "The Brother Sacristan," which he sent to Father Solanus. In this, he pictures his Capuchin brother at work about the altar.—

> The God of Mercy, meek and humble, holds
>   His reign of peace in tabernacled cell:
> While spotless order quietly enfolds
>   The place where man's Redeemer comes to dwell.
>
> With reverend love a modest figure kneels
>   To pay the voiceless homage of his heart.
> Then silently from place to place he steals
>   The worship of his fingers to impart.
>
> Each object there receives his tender touch—
>   The snowy linen, flowers, burnished bell—
> While conscience whispers sweetly: "It is much
>   For His dear sake to do each duty well. . . ."
>
> "Dear Lord!" he whispers. "Dearest! Crucified!
>   Teach my poor heart in penance to repair
> In some degree, the luxury, the pride,
>   The cold neglect that leaves You lonely there."
>
> He lingers still, and fain would there abide,
>   When evening shadows fill the chapel dim;
> At last he goes, but leaves his heart beside
>   The faithful little lamp he loves to trim.

Father Solanus thought highly of these lines, as he did of every metrical line Father Edward wrote. The sentimental verse, titled "The Brother Sacristan," he submitted to a Capuchin magazine, which published it. Readers doubtless envisioned the "Brother Sacristan" as a lay brother. But when Father Edward wrote "Brother" he was thinking of a brother to whom his heart went out in sympathy; a brother even more curtailed in his priestly duties than if he had become, in body, tragically crippled.

Not long after Father Solanus had assumed his humble duties at Sacred Heart Friary, Maurice wrote him that he was now fully determined to resume his seminary studies. Since his semi-soliloquy when walking with his Capuchin brother in the friary garden in Appleton, he had given much thought to the move.

"This," he said in his letter, "is my plan; and I want you to let me know what you think of it . . . I'll try the seminary out for a year or so, and if it goes, then I'll join yours or some other holy order. If it doesn't go, I'll be a lay-brother. And if that fails, then, by George, I'll marry and go out West and be as useful to God and man as I can. A secular priest I'll never be."

Father Solanus showed the letter to Father Bonaventure, who remarked—"He has good intentions. Tell him to go ahead."

Before many weeks had passed, Maurice wrote again. He was in a seminary in Berlin, Ontario (now Kitchener). Maurice informed his brother: "I have found the peace again I looked for so long, and in this I feel amply repaid for the sacrifice it took to give up everything."

What he meant by 'giving up everything' is unclear, though he had advanced in the postal service and may have been alluding to his postal career.

The other Casey brothers, too, had been prospering. Near the turn of the century John had led a movement of some of the Casey clan to the state of Washington. By 1905, John, Pat, Tom, Augustine, Leo and Owen were in the Evergreen State, as were their sister Ellen and her husband. John had become a lawyer, Augustine was teaching, and Owen was in business in Seattle. Their parents later joined them.

In August, 1906, a new Guardian was appointed for Sacred Heart Friary. Father Bonaventure, declining all further honors and offices, had asked to be relieved of supervisory duties and to be permitted to continue his priestly ministry in the Yonkers parish. Father Aloysius Blonigen succeeded.

He immediately added to Father Solanus' duties by making him friary porter.

In his new job Father Solanus answered the friary doorbell, called to the waiting room whichever Father or Brother a visitor asked for, and accepted and recorded Mass offerings. He continued as sacristan, and Father Aloysius also appointed him director of the parish Sacred Heart League. For twelve years—from 1906 to 1918—he served the Sacred Heart Friary in these capacities.

His duties as sacristan at times presented problems, which he solved through prayer. In one of his memo books, he notes under date of December 8, 1908—"An encouraging meeting of the Altar Society. After novena—immediately— good boys asked to become servers!"

Careless altar boys tried his soul, but again the difficulty yielded to prayer. He notes in November, 1909, that he had been "anxious and fearful for altar boys. Made a little novena to Our Lady of Perpetual Help, and before I believed it or thought how it came, every one showed new zeal."

About a year later, he finds himself blameworthy for negligence toward their spiritual good. The negligence occurred during an "auto outing" for the altar boys—a rare treat, for the automobile was still a glamorous curiosity. The car sped past several churches during the outing. And Father Solanus—probably speed-dizzy and enjoying the ride as much as the servers—forgot to bid the driver stop at one of them so all could make "a little visit to Jesus." He sorrowed over his thoughtlessness.

So the years went by, and he answered the doorbell of the gray granite monastery overlooking the lordly Hudson; kept the sanctuary orderly, the vestments properly hung or folded, and directed the altar boys and the altar society. Occasionally, too, he gave devotional talks to members of the Sacred Heart League. Father Guardians came and went at the Yonkers friary, but he, as priest-porter-sacristan, stayed on to answer the doorbell and to care for the sanctuary.

In early fall, 1913, Father Solanus left Yonkers for Seattle, Washington, to join his family in celebration of his parents' golden wedding anniversary. The journey was the sight-seeing highlight of his life up to this time. On the passenger train he embraced with catholic friendliness the varied humanity of America. His Capuchin habit and long beard made him, to most of his fellow travelers, an almost sensationally interesting figure; many of them had never before laid eyes on a friar.

Not a few found themselves searching for some excuse to talk with him. He met them half-way in his simple, easy manner, and answered their sometimes startling questions with Franciscan humility and good humor. His habit—which Capuchins of that day were required to wear when traveling —had been, he told them, the dress of European peasants. When St. Francis of Assisi founded the Order of Friars Minor in the middle ages, he and his followers dressed like poor people because they were poor people. And still were. His

questioners were rather staggered to learn that he himself
didn't own even the brown habit he was wearing. And they
were surprised to find this man in medieval garb so know-
ledgeable about trains, and street cars, and farming.

When passengers alighted for their meals at the Harvey
railroad restaurants—which they did three times a day—he
was always surrounded by a little group. Even those who had
heard from childhood horrendous stories about dissolute
"monks" found themselves thinking that there must have
been something wrong with those lurid tales. For how could
those "monks" be so bad if this gentle, innocent-eyed man
was one of them?

By the time he arrived in Seattle, Father Solanus had
come to know his fellow Americans better than ever, and to
know for the first time, too, the sea-to-sea beauty and majesty
of their land, and his.

At their parents' anniversary Mass—the high mark of a
week-long celebration—Father Edward was celebrant, Father Maurice deacon, and Father Solanus subdeacon and
preacher. Father Maurice had been ordained three years, and
Father Edward two years, before.

Speaking for himself and his brothers and sisters, Father
Solanus dwelt on all that his parents' love and faith and
goodness had meant to their children. He recalled their pioneering labors and cares on the Wisconsin farmsteads, their
confidence that the Almighty would always help them if they
strove to do His will. As always, he spoke simply, but with
even more than his usual fervor. The homely story, told feelingly but with such unconscious eloquence, penetrated every
heart. The women wiped their eyes without attempting to
conceal their tears; the men also had recourse to handker-
chiefs, but blew their noses. When with the jubilarians their
sons and daughters knelt to receive Communion, they were
profoundly thoughtful.

So happy was the jubilee gathering, and so serene his parents, that to Father Solanus it seemed "like a tiny taste of heaven."

A photograph of the family taken at the time shows the ten Casey brothers as vigorous, clean-cut men; the four living daughters as feminine and lovely. Every face reflects goodness. These were the kind of people, one finds himself thinking, who upgrade the world about them and make it more pleasant and liveable.

Two men in the group wear full beards—the patriarch, Bernard Casey, gnarled and rugged, and his namesake son. Father Solanus was then forty-three years old; his hairline had already begun to recede. The face is extraordinarily youthful; the eyes, candid and innocent, seem to retain much of childlike wonder. It was an expression they were never to lose.

Youthful candor and innocence are seen, also, in the mother's face. From childhood she had worked unceasingly; had borne and reared many children amidst pioneering hardships. At the time the group picture was taken, she was seventy years old. Yet her face is wonderfully young. It is the gentle and humble and holy face of one who daily for fifty years had consecrated herself to her Creator through sacrifice for others.

Like most genuinely saintly people, she was a realist. When her children, gathered about her on this occasion, grew nostalgic about their early days on the Casey farms, she remained silently attentive. But when one remarked—"Wouldn't it be great if we could go back again!"—she spoke. Gently sighing as if remembering the trials of those days, she exclaimed in a half-whisper—"Thanks be to God, I'm glad it's over."

To her children, particularly the older, the game-rich woods and waters of western Wisconsin had become a re-

membered paradise. But hers were a mother's memories of
labors and cares and near-tragedies whose seriousness her
children had never fully realized.

The boys reveled in tales of their younger days, and
Father Solanus found himself their leading spirit. It was he
who most frequently told stories of their earlier years—and
so humorously or so feelingly as to bring laughter or tears.
It was he who started the group singing the old songs they
had sung so many years before around the family table.

After this memorable week, Father Solanus began the
long trip back to New York. He hoped for connections on
schedule at St. Paul and Chicago. Missing either connection
would make it impossible for him to reach Yonkers on Sunday in time for the dedication of the new Sacred Heart Church
next day. As both sacristan and porter, he considered it imperative that he be there for the once-in-a-parish-lifetime
ceremony. He particularly wanted his train to make St. Paul
on schedule. If it did, he would have sufficient time to offer
Mass in that city, and still catch the train for Chicago. He
was eager to do so, for he felt keenly disappointed that his
travel schedule had prevented him offering Mass the day before.

Only one who believes in the Mass as devout Catholics
believe in it can realize what it means to offer that holy
sacrifice and banquet. To Father Solanus, to re-present the
rite through which Christ offered himself; to be the instrument through whom Christ makes Himself present as the
saving victim of Calvary risen from the dead, and through
which He applies to mankind the fruits of the Cross—this
was the supreme privilege, the unsurpassable joy.

As his train drew into the St. Paul station he felt that he
should at all odds offer Mass that Friday morning, and that
his "dear Lord" would help him. Therefore, when told that

the only train for Chicago that day was due in thirty minutes, he put the matter of catching it in God's hands—as always when adverse circumstances confronted him. He then set off for St. Mary's Church in a light rain. To the assistant pastor he explained his need for haste—then offered Mass with his usual devotion and deliberation, and made his thanksgiving. He even ate a hurried breakfast. As he left to catch a trolley car to the station, the assistant hopelessly shook his head. He was sure that this queer Capuchin would miss the train by a full hour or more.

The train, however, had been delayed—a fact of which Father Solanus knew nothing until he hastened into the depot. As the Chicago-bound train began to roll, he pulled himself up to the rear platform of its last car.

All the way to Chicago rain poured down, and the train arrived five hours late. As it pulled into the city the baggage master informed Father Solanus that he would of course miss connections with the Detroit-bound train, scheduled to leave Chicago four hours before and from another station. But again the friar had the pleasant duty of thanking the good Lord for holding trains! Almost as if the train were waiting for him alone, up went the announcer's megaphone as he entered the depot, and the news blared forth that the Detroit-bound train was about to depart. It, too, was late.

Still, Father Solanus didn't rush to get aboard. He didn't want to waste money by paying full fare.

"God bless them," he said to himself. "They'll wait now until I get my clergy-fare verified."

And so "they" did.

Now he could offer Mass at St. Bonaventure's in the morning, and reach Yonkers in time for dedication of the Sacred Heart Church next day.

Two years after the golden wedding anniversary, his father died, slowly and painfully. Father Solanus, in Yonkers, wrote his mother comforting letters. He knew from correspondence with his sister Ellen that Mrs. Casey was patient and resigned, but Ellen had told him that their mother treasured every word he wrote her.

In Sacred Heart parish, Father Solanus had long since found his work scope broadening. The people had come to know him as an eloquent speaker. For, though he was forbidden to deliver doctrinal sermons, he could give inspirational talks, or "ferverinos," as the Capuchins termed them. His spiritual fire warmed and moved his auditors. As he spoke, his whole being seemed to radiate love of God and souls. His language wasn't precise, nor his theology deep, but he touched hearts.

He was given to quoting poetry in which moral values were drawn from nature—particularly his brother Edward's verse. His favorite stanza was one in which Father Edward speaks of the "sublime beauty" of the Montana mountain scenery as but the reflection of "the glory of heaven"—"eternity's breath on the ashes of time." And he would ask—"What must be the glory of the Divine Creator, and what must be His goodness and power and love? If the stars are beautiful as they reflect the light of the sun at such immeasurable distances, what will be the beauty of the saints who for all eternity and not at a distance, will reflect the divine image of God?"

In a day when many preachers chose to emphasize God's justice, the simple fact that God is love was his constant theme. To him it was an inevitable theme, for he never ceased wondering at the divine love, and being grateful for it. He loved all men because they were children of the heavenly Father, and brothers in Christ, and all the angels and saints because they were, assuredly, the eternal friends of God.

Above all creatures he loved God's mother. To him, the history of the Church was the history of the saints, and the supreme saint was Mary. To him, after Christ, she was the human, God-provided assurance to man that His all-powerful grace, which had preserved her immaculately free from sin, could save all sinners. To honor Mary was to acknowledge God's goodness, generosity and love, and proclaim one's faith in the restoration of all things in Christ.

Through her, he had learned humility, and patience in life's humdrum circumstances. From her he learned, too, that apostolic action may consist merely in waiting for God's chosen moment.

Father Solanus' devotion to the human creature upon whom the Godhead had conferred such unimaginable dignity was intensely tender; to him, the Blessed Mother was a never-ending source of wonder at the Creator's love for mankind. This led him to strongly desire more knowledge of her than the few basic facts revealed in the New Testament. It also led him to give credence to apocryphal accounts and "private revelations" concerning the Blessed Virgin, while fully realizing that none of these was of the deposit of faith.

His confidence in the Blessed Mother's intercessory powers was unlimited. For, he reasoned, how could the dear Lord refuse His mother anything she asked of Him? So he was constantly imploring her help for others.

At about this time he was urgently praying her to help one especially dear to him—his older brother, Father Maurice.

He had learned with delight of the latter's new pastorate —a vast area in Montana then under the jurisdiction of the Archbishop of St. Paul. This was missionary territory, and in earlier years both Father Maurice and he himself had desired to become missionaries.

It was also a country of scenic grandeur that from Father Solanus would have drawn exclamations of joy and wonder at the glory of creation and its Creator. Father Maurice's residence was in a little town called "Plains," one of his parish's eleven settlements, scattered more than a hundred miles along the Northern Pacific Railway.

Father Edward wrote to Father Solanus after visiting in Plains. He had fallen instantly in love with "the peaceful valley hidden in the rugged grandeur of the surrounding mountains." He had stood in the valley with Father Maurice, entranced as he raised his eyes to the majestic peaks and ranges. But all this failed to beguile Father Maurice; he was, in fact, deeply discontented.

An intensively gregarious person, he was one of the most friendly, persuasive, magnetic of men. He had a genius for instant friendship. But in this far-flung parish, he could ride for miles and not behold another human being. He sadly missed the thronged streets of St. Paul and Minneapolis. There he had been in the habit of talking religion with several people each day. He would go into a quick lunch restaurant, for example, and over a cup of coffee would at the passing of a salt shaker, establish rapport with a diner at his elbow. While stationed in Minneapolis after his ordination, he acted as a home missionary. In this activity he is said to have converted many scores of people to the Catholic Faith.

His brother's discontent worried Father Edward. Trying to lead him to see his scenic parish as he himself saw it, he wrote and sent Father Maurice a verse entitled *The Valley of Plains*. In this he recalls the magnificent scene which had met their eyes as they stood together in the valley one day during his visit.

> ". . . far, far above us (he wrote) the great mountains
> rise

Their heaven-wreathed summits now lost in the skies,
    Now tipped in the glory of sun's golden light,
Or decked in the silver of moon-beams by night."

Referring to the "sweet vale called the Valley of Plains," he
mentions that

"Around it a river majestically glides
    Caressing the scene where contentment abides;
While yon lofty peaks of immaculate snow
    Their tribute of crystalline waters bestow."

Calling himself "the traveler," he reminds Father Maurice
that he

". . . climbed a tall cliff and looked lingering down
    On forest and river, on meadow and town.

"Beneath him the homes of the vale nestled there
    Half hidden 'mid orchards of apple and pear;
The grazing herds dotted the hillsides, or strayed
    Far down on the pastures of meadow and glade. . . .

"O God, what Thy glory in heaven must be
    When its feeble reflection on earth, sky and sea
Enrobes the dull clay with such beauty sublime—
    Eternity's breath on the ashes of time."

Father Edward's versified sermon on scenic appreciation
seems to have influenced his brother not at all. No metrically
measured statements that the solitude about him was a
"dream of delight" and a "scene of contentment" could cure
his discontent. He wouldn't buy scenery, nor the little town
of Plains. He wanted city sidewalks, and in the far west he
had remained lonely, longing for more populous pastures.

Father Solanus learned of all this both directly from

Father Maurice, and indirectly from Father Edward. His brother's dissatisfaction weighed upon him. He prayed for his peace of mind.

In the latter part of April, 1918, Father Solanus received saddening news from Seattle; his mother, stricken with pneumonia, was dangerously sick. Father Edward wrote him details. He mentioned his mother's first words to him when, after his long journey from St. Paul, he entered her room. "Father Edward," she said, the words coming with painful difficulty—"did—you—have—any supper?"

It was not until after two weeks of suffering that her strong, motherly heart beat its last.

The following July, Father Solanus was transferred to Our Lady of Sorrows Friary on Pitt Street on Manhattan's lower east side. The Guardian, Father Venantius Buessing, made him sacristan and Director of the Young Ladies Sodality.

After three years he was again transferred—this time to Our Lady of Angels parish in Harlem.* In this parish there would occur the first of those seemingly inexplicable events that for the next thirty-six years were to be associated with his name. Here would begin the fulfillment of Father Anthony's prediction that Father Solanus "would be something like the Cure of Ars."

---

*In 1921, Harlem's citizens were whites of the economic middle class.

Chapter 11

The Provincial Orders
Father Solanus to Keep Notes

During his New York years Father Solanus spoke at
various devotional services on the Almighty's creation and its
wonders and His infinite mercies to man. Occasionally, too,
he contributed an inspirational article along similar lines to a
small Capuchin magazine. These he signed "Homo Simplex."
He was, indeed, a simple man as well as a simplex priest, and
quite childlike in his never-ending wonder at the Creator's
marvelous works and graces.

This wonderment became associated with personal experience in 1921 after he was transferred to Our Lady of
Angels Friary in Harlem. Here he again found himself a
porter and was also made promoter of the Seraphic Mass
Association. Though the appointment was eventually to result in his name being known to tens of thousands, there was
nothing unusual or special about it. At every Capuchin friary
it was a duty that had to be assigned to someone, and it seemed to go along very well with answering the friary doorbell.
All it required was making out enrollment cards for those
who wanted to enroll, and entering their names in a book.
And few came to enroll.

As a whole, the United States Capuchins had been rather
passive about promoting the Seraphic Mass Association,

which had been founded many years before in Switzerland.

To Father Solanus, promotion of the Mass Association was no routine task. It was a way of promoting devotion to the Mass—the central devotion of the Church.

And remarkably, the assignment coincided with an unexpected development in his life: Suddenly, people had begun to come to him with their spiritual and other problems.

This marked the beginning of his great mission as a spiritual counselor—a work which over his next thirty-five years was to affect the lives of tens of thousands.

It was precisely his assignment to a porter's duties that now brought this momentous turn in his career. At first, friary visitors to whom he opened the door mistook him for a lay Brother. While they awaited a summoned priest, the "Brother" would put them at ease with casual talk. If they seemed troubled, however, his words would turn to earnest praises of the good Lord's love and care.

Later on, when the visitor came to the friary church for Mass, he might see the porter offering it!—Splendid! One could talk with this wise and gentle priest merely by ringing the friary bell!

And ring it they did, in ever-increasing numbers, to consult this endlessly patient priest-porter, and to hear his Christ-inspired wisdom. Nearly always, he would suggest that they attend Mass more frequently, and receive Holy Communion, and give more time to prayer.

When, grateful, they desired to offer something for charity, he might suggest that they help the Capuchin missions and leper colonies by enrolling in the Seraphic Mass Association. This meant that their intentions would be included with those of others for which, every day, hundreds of Capuchin priests offered the Holy Sacrifice.

He would enroll them for a particular intention, if they so desired—for the recovery of a sick husband, wife, or child, or perhaps for a wayward son or daughter, or a friend or relative who had given up practice of his religion. And his visitors were very happy to be enrolled, or to enroll others, especially as they could easily afford the nominal mission contribution of fifty cents. When a person didn't seem to have even that small sum about him, Father Solanus would frequently enroll him anyway, and ask him to contribute his prayers for the mission's success.

Soon after Father Solanus began to promote the Seraphic Mass Association, interest in it spread with surprising speed. For after he had enrolled them, some people declared that they had experienced unexpectdly quick recoveries from sickness, or prompt and remarkable solutions of problems they had considered hopeless. Naturally, they told others, and their stories were repeated in their own and other parishes. Before long, Father Solanus found himself busy all day long, giving counsel to troubled men and women and enrolling people in the Seraphic Mass Association.

After a while these unusual happenings came to the notice of the Capuchin's Father Provincial, the Very Reverend Benno Aichinger. On one of his regular visitations to Our Lady of Angels, in November, 1923, he ordered Father Solanus to keep a record of "special favors" reported to him. That same day, Father Solanus began to do so. He used a twelve-by-ten inch ledger-type book with heavy covers and ruled pages. More than nine years after his death, this book came to light in the library of St. Bonaventure's Monastery in Detroit.

Above the first page of notes is the caption—"NOTES ABOUT SPECIAL CASES—November 1923." The first cntry records the Provincial's order. It reads: "Nov. 8th, 1923. Today Visitation Closed. Father Provincial wishes notes to be made of special favors reported as through the Seraphic Mass Association."

Following this is his first memo of a special favor. "Deo Gratias," it reads. "This P.M., Marg. Quinn, who enrolled her neighbor Mr. M----* against drink and consequent anger on October 26—and also her sister, E. Remy, of Philadelphia, against severe inflammatory rheumatism—reports 'wonderful improvement' in former,' and letter this A.M. from sister says—'Thank God and the good prayer society, I'm feeling fine.'

"Thanks be to God!"

This phrase, in English or Latin, was to appear at the beginning or the end of many scores of notes in which through the next three decades Father Solanus would record reports of favors which their recipients regarded as extraordinary.

Father Solanus characteristically includes not only petitions answered but also those of many more whose misfortunes or sorrows evidently made special appeal to his sympathy. It is probable that these notes were made as reminders to keep these people in his prayers, for he prayed constantly for all those who brought their troubles to him.

The entries give a cross sectional view of the kind of men and women who came to him in New York, and of their problems and sufferings. A mother from Danbury, Connecticut, visits the friary to enroll her son in the Seraphic Mass Association that "God may give him the grace of a religious calling and the strength and grace to accept it." Another woman who has had two "partial strokes" enrolls her irreligious husband and two sons who are "drug fiends." A distracted mother tells Father Solanus that her sixteen-year-old

---

*Names are omitted when their mention might possibly bring embarrassment to the principals or to their relatives or friends.

daughter vanished a week before, but comes the day after she enrolls her to report that the girl has been found in Jamaica, Long Island. On December 9th, 1923, a sister enrolls her brother, who has been drinking heavily for five years; on December 14th she reports that he has stopped drinking and that she is "hopeful." A couple who have "been terribly beaten up" appears at the door, and the porter brings them in and helps to heal their physical and moral bruises. Another visitor has lost the sight of her right eye; still another is suffering "a nervous breakdown."

So run the entries made between November 8th and December 9th, 1923, on the notebook's first page.

Between November 8th, 1923, and July 28th, 1924, there are ninety-six memos. Forty-one mention petitions answered after enrollment in the S.M.A. by Father Solonus.

AMONG THESE FAVORS are the following: A youngster of eighteen who had been keeping "bad company," drinking, staying out all night and upsetting his family's peace, is enrolled on December 17 and immediately gives up his wild life and returns to the sacraments. Evidently he reformed just in time to escape the "terrible and notorious misfortune of his former comrades."

A woman dying of pneumonia, whose doctors gave her three hours to live, recovers remarkably and declares her conviction that it is due to her enrollment in the S.M.A.

Another enrollee reports recovery from a heart condition and says that doctors are surprised that she is still alive.

Two days after enrollment a woman who had lost her memory because of a concussion eight years before, regains it—and her husband comes to Father Solanus to relate the fact.

Many hard drinkers after enrollment by their relatives, quickly stop drinking. Six days after a Pelham Bay man who has not been "doing right by wife and family" is enrolled, he "suddenly shows determination to do God's will."

A Freehold, New Jersey man, a patient "in an insane hospital" in Philadelphia, is enrolled on December 1, and before Christmas is able to write normally to his family. Early in March he is back at work.

Patrick Hardiman of 114th Street enrolls his crippled mother on January 14, and on February 2 reports that she "cried with joy at her recovery, and now goes shopping as she did twenty years ago."

A 54-year-old Manhattanite, "despondently nervous over a year," enrolls with his wife and recovers.

A woman facing an operation for cataracts on both eyes asks, in November 1923, to be enrolled and on the following St. Valentine's Day "returns jubilant and perfectly cured" without operation.

A Bayonne, New Jersey woman who is described as a member of the Capuchin Third Order and a promoter of the S.M.A., enrolls her cause after her lawyer tells her that a technicality prevents recovery of a legacy left her nineteen years before. Within three months those who for nearly twenty years have stood between her and her inheritance voluntarily come to her and hand her five thousand dollars.

A daughter enrolls her father that he might return to the church and within a few weeks reports that—"Papa went to confession and holy Communion for the first time in 49 years."

In most of the notes addresses as well as names are given and some of the claimed cures seem impressive to a medically uneducated layman. Such as that of Patrick P. McCue, who was enrolled by a fellow motorman on February 9, 1924, as he was being taken to Belleview Hospital. He was suffering from diabetes and a gangrenous toe and had signed papers authorizing amputation of the leg if necessary. On March 28 he was reported back at work on his two legs and Father Solanus adds that the "doctors are baffled." A Margaret Buick was enrolled on September 6 after specialists had found an optic nerve condition incurable. One month later her sight was "wonderfully restored."

No medical authentication certifies any of these reported cures, nor in later years was such authentication made even when, as on one occasion, hospital authorities offered it. Neither Father Solanus nor his superiors were interested in establishing him as a miracle man; quite the contrary. Certainly during Father Solanus' New York period no notes of the reputed cures would have been made had not the Provincial so ordered. And his purpose seems to have been, to be able to inform the diocesan authorities about the matter if and when they should begin asking him why people were flocking to Father Solanus and spreading reports of remarkable cures. Whenever anyone who had received a "special favor" attempted to thank him, Father Solanus would stop him short, explaining that any favor he might have received came through the Mass, prayer and the mercy and goodness of God. His faith in the power of the Mass was absolute and he saw nothing strange that graces should come to those who even in a small way participated in the merits of the Masses ceaselessly offered by Capuchins stationed in missions around the world. He seems always to have been more gladdened by spiritual cures than by physical ones. One detects this even in the heavily penned "Thank God!" he writes in a note about the sudden conversion of a Michael F----, whose "heart broken sister" enrolled him on June 4, 1923. Mr. F----- had been away from the sacraments nine years and from his wife four. The sister returned July 2 to report that since his enrollment her brother had been to confession and Communion three times—which indicates that he resumed practice of his religion almost coincidentally with his enrollment. His sister reported that when asked why he had returned to the Church he replied—" I do not know."

Still, the Provincial must have wondered why people enrolled by other promoters of the Seraphic Mass Association did not report such startling responses to their petitions as did those enrolled by Father Solanus. People, it is true, can become intensely excited by manifestations they come to believe are supernatural, and there can be all kinds of wild rumors. On the other hand, it was evident that those who claimed cures and other special favors were sincere and in good faith; that Father Solanus was and always had been an exceedingly spiritual Capuchin, and that he was doing an immense amount of spiritual good for those he counseled. It was only prudent, however, that the Provincial keep himself fully informed from his own observation of all that went on around his pious and simple confrere.

So it was that about eight months after Father Benno first directed Father Solanus to keep a record of reported special favors, he ordered his transfer to St. Bonaventure's in Detroit. That was the Father Provincial's headquarters.

Chapter 12

St. Bonaventure's Chief Porter Finds that His New Assistant Multiplies the Work

When Father Solanus arrived at St. Bonaventure's in the first days of August, 1924, he took up much the same duties he had been performing in New York. There was this difference, however; in Detroit he wasn't the head porter, he was assistant to a Brother Porter, whose name was Francis Spruck.

Brother Francis, whose portering work was so light that he was able also to serve as tailor for the entire Capuchin province, was Santa Claus in a Capuchin habit. Short and rolypoly, affable and witty, his merry humor made him a favorite both with the community and the public. The tailor shop was on one side of the entrance hall, the porter's office on the other; thus from either room he could hear the doorbell. Although his portering did not add greatly to his daily burden, nevertheless, he was grateful for Father Solanus' coming. Now, he told himself, he would have more time for his tailoring, and some friars awaiting return of mended garments would have less cause to practice patience.

At first, things worked out quite as he had anticipated. For a few weeks, he was able to concentrate on his sewing, while Father Solanus answered the doorbell and took care of the visitors. But soon, much the same situation began to evolve as had developed in New York. More and more frequently, the doorbell would ring two or three times instead of the customary once. Brother Francis, wondering why Father Solanus hadn't answered it, would find him in the porter's office, listening to a previous visitor. And more likely than not, the new visitor at the door would also ask to see Father Solanus. Pretty soon, this sort of thing began to go on all through the day, with Father Solanus deep in consultation with visitor after visitor, and Brother Francis answering the doorbell to admit still more visitors wanting to see his assistant. Additional chairs had to be provided for people waiting to talk with the slim, patient, friendly friar so recently transferred from New York.

Of course, Brother Francis soon learned why people were coming to Father Solanus. Visitors began telling him, as they waited to see the porter-priest, of what they considered to be remarkable favors they or others had received. One of the first such incidents that came to his ears had to do with a 37-year-old man who had been carefully planning suicide. He intended boarding a passenger boat at Detroit for Cleveland, and on the way disappear overboard. Somehow, his two sisters discovered his plan. While constantly watching him, they lived in dread that he might evade them and do away with himself.

During this critical period, their father died, and at his funeral a friend happened to hand one of the sisters a pamphlet explaining the Seraphic Mass Association. That very day—October 16, 1924—one of the sisters visited Father Solanus and enrolled her brother. On October 20, the sister returned to tell Father Solanus that her brother had suddenly and completely changed. He was no longer despondent and despairing; he was "praying, and full of hope," and planning to go back to his work.

The sister immediately enrolled another brother who was tuberculous. On April 18 she reported that all symptoms of his disease had disappeared and that he was in perfect health.

Then there was Mrs. Rose M. Moraine, who came from her home on East Grand Boulevard to tell about a remarkable result after her husband had been enrolled by Father Solanus in the SMA. That had been on December 5, 1924, and the favor she sought was that something might happen to prevent a total collapse in her husband's business, about which he was desperately worried. The following evening she returned to the Monastery, enthusiastic and cheerful. Within a few hours after his enrollment, her husband's business prospects had taken an upturn.

It was on December 5, also, that a 65-year-old man was enrolled by an older son, against whom the father nourished a deep hatred. He also hated the Catholic Church so bitterly that he had ordered his younger children taken out of the parochial school. A week after enrolling his father, the son came to the office to say that the man's attitude towards himself and the Church had undergone a complete reversal.

Many cures were reported. Some of them occurred almost before the ink had dried on the enrollment card which Father Solanus made out for all who joined the SMA. Nine-year-old John V. Slyker of Pleasant Ridge, a Detroit suburb, was taken to the Monastery February 4th, received Father Solanus blessing, and was enrolled. He was seeing double out of one eye and was blind in the other; the specialists were puzzled. On his way home from the Monastery his parents noted that his eyesight had improved; he was reading the street signs.

Deafness was also said to have been cured, as in the instance of Mrs. Anna Doyle of Detroit. On February 6, 1926, she came to Father Solanus with her husband and was enrolled, her petition being that she regain her hearing. Eight days later she reported to Father Solanus that her hearing had begun to improve on the day she was enrolled, as she was being driven home, and that she was now "perfectly okay."

Another on-the-way home improvement was reported by Stephen J. Hook, then 65 years old and living on Avery Avenue, Detroit. Enrolled August 10, 1925, he returned August 21 to inform Father Solanus that a cancerous growth on his nose began to heal after enrollment, as he was returning home from the Monastery, and that it seemed to be gradually disappearing. He came back a month later to show Father Solanus that it had disappeared leaving only a very slight scar.

People about to undergo serious operations asked Father Solanus—frequently over the telephone—to enroll them in the Mass Association. Remarkable recoveries, it was said, sometimes followed. Among them was that of Anna Schram, 30, then living on Yellowstone Avenue, Detroit. Miss Schram was first operated on for gallstones on December 18, 1926. She had not been too worried as to the outcome of that operation, but she was deeply concerned when she was taken to Grace Hospital a month later, on January twentieth—for an operation for abcess of the liver. So were the surgeons; there had been only one similar operation performed in that hospital, about five years before. The patient had died. Before the operation, Miss Schram's sister enrolled her in the SMA, and on February 17 informed Father Solanus that Miss Schram was already home.

So the notes go on, page after page. Most of them suggest stories of profound human interest, but Father Solanus seldom elaborates. On the contrary—he gives all too few details and generally fails to satisfy curiosity in various directions. Time after time one comes on a memo that indicates a tale of love and heartbreak and final triumph and joy, but

Father Solanus leaves the reader wishing he had told more. This typical note, written in the latter part of 1926, illustrates this too great brevity—

DOROTHY DETLAFF, 13393 Young Avenue, only baby after her parents had been praying for ten years to be blessed with children, is enrolled the day of her birth, then despaired of, and receives transfusion of blood same day. Three days later she received another transfusion and today after 7 months is the picture of health. The doctor (E. Robinson) a non-Catholic, wondered at the recovery as a positive miracle, declaring: "Indeed there must be a divine power behind such a cure."

A medically uneducated person can read and re-read this note and still be left wondering what Dr. Robinson wondered about. What was the disease? Who were the parents?—These are only some of the questions Father Solanus leaves unanswered in this memo.

Toward the end of 1928, Father Maurice visited him. He was still dissatisfied with his life as a diocesan priest.

Twenty-five years before, just previous to his decision to again study for the priesthood, Father Maurice had roundly insisted to Father Solanus that he would never become a "secular" priest, as diocesan priests were then known. At that time, he had planned to apply for admission to a religious order.

Yet, for whatever reason, he did become a diocesan priest. At this time, he had served several discontented years as pastor in the western missions.

It is probable that during his 1928 visit to St. Bonaventure's, Father Maurice discussed with the Capuchin superiors a desire to join their ranks.

It is probable, too, that when he left for the west after this visit, he was eagerly looking forward to returning in July of the next year for the celebration of Father Solanus' twenty-fifth anniversary as a priest. For not only brotherly affection now moved him, but also a lively interest in joining him in the Order.

Five or six weeks after the anniversary celebration—he had acted as deacon at the Solemn High Mass—Father Maurice returned to St. Bonaventure's. Accompanied by Father Solanus he went to the new St. Felix Friary in Huntington, Indiana, to which the novitiate had recently been transferred. On September 10 he was invested as a Capuchin novice, Father Solanus assisting at the ceremony.

Thus at sixty-two years of age he entered upon a severe and restricted life—a kind of life which seems to have been foreign to his freewheeling disposition.

Observing him during his novitiate year, the superiors evidently did not become thoroughly convinced that he possessed a Capuchin vocation. He was admitted, not to the Regular or First Order, but to the Capuchin Third Order. This entitled him to wear the habit, but without the capuche or hood, and to bear a "name in religion," as did Third Order members. He would, however, take part in choir services and carry out the duties of a Capuchin priest.

Actually, during all his years with the Capuchins, he would be the Order's guest. Such status was extremely rare.

Sent to New York, he was to serve ably several years in Capuchin parishes.

Happy that Father Maurice Joachim—as was now his way of referring to his brother in family letters—was at long last enjoying peace of mind, Father Solanus continued daily at his desk in St. Bonaventure's. Daily he listened to a score or more of troubled souls, now and then hurriedly penning a note to be referred to at the Wednesday services.

Among the notes were a few lengthier ones that give us a glimpse of the principals' reactions. One such note is the following.

APRIL 3, 1930.—Phyllis Blake, 7, (of 1138 Nottingham Rd., Grosse Pointe Pk.) contracted measles about a month ago. Two weeks later her ears started to run. Last Saturday, March 29, was screaming from pain when mother phoned to have her enrolled. Improvement followed, but Doctor pronounced double mastoid. She was taken to St. Mary's Hospital 30th March. Yesterday, two doctors and two nurses came in to prepare child for operation. Little head shaved and all ready, Mother pleads: "Don't cut her." And today Phyllis brought to Monastery smiling on her way home from hospital. Mother and grandmother came last night and had her name once more inscribed in Mass Association, promising perpetual enrollment if operation were not necessary.—Sobs and tears last night, of sorrow; this a.m., tears of joy.

While this memo is more complete than most Father Solanus wrote, it still conveys little of the real life drama concealed in so many of his notes. How little, is realized when we listen to the first hand account of a mother in a situation that paralleled in considerable degree that of little Phyllis Blake. It is related by Mrs. Gladys M. Stork, formerly Mrs. Coppiellie, who in the 1960's still operated the Alter Road Hardware, 14840 Kercheval Avenue, Detroit, founded by Mr. Coppiellie about fifty years before.

About 4 p.m. on a day early in May, 1932, the then Mrs. Coppiellie entered the Monastery office carrying her eight-months-old son, Raymond. The infant was suffering from mastoiditis in both ears. She had come directly from Harper Hospital, where Dr. Milton Robb, a recognized authority in aural medicine and surgery, had been brought into the case. In an attempt to save the child's life, he had ordered an operation performed the next morning. This would necessitate boring a hole through the bone back of each ear to establish drainage* and getting at the infection. Long sickness had reduced the infant to skin and bone. His temperature was 108 degrees.

Since the previous October, Raymond had been under a physician's care. He was so pitifully thin and weak that Mrs. Coppiellie was sure he would die during the operation.

Scarcely knowing what she was doing, she suddenly lifted the child from its bed, and fled the hospital.

MY BROTHER CYRIL was waiting in our car—said Mrs. Copiellie. I told him to drive home. But as we drove along, the thought of Father Solanus came to me. We had to pass the street on which the monastery stands. Some years before I had attended services at the monastery church, and I had heard reports of cures through Father Solanus' intercessions.

Now I asked myself why I hadn't gone to him before about Raymond. When we reached Mt. Elliot Avenue—on which street the monastery faces—I asked my brother to turn toward the friary. Arriving there, I walked in the office holding the baby in my arms, and straight over to Father Solanus at his desk. He was alone.

He stood up and held out his arms as if he instantly understood, and I placed Raymond in his hands.

I told Father Solanus about Raymond, and the operation that had been ordered, and that without the doctors' permission I had just taken him away from the hospital. And I said —"Oh, Father, help him."

Father returned the baby to me, and talked with me a

---

*Today, antibiotics have largely eliminated need of this operation.

little. He asked Raymond's name, and inscribed him—without me asking him to—in the Seraphic Mass Association. He told me to put all my hope in Our Lord's infinite kindness and mercy—to have confidence in Him, and that He would not fail me. He prayed over Raymond, silently, for a moment, and raised his hand and blessed him. Then he blessed me.

"Take Raymond home now," he told me. "He'll be better by morning." He walked with me to the door. Almost as an afterthought, he added—"And don't worry. He won't need an operation."

These were the first hopeful words I had heard in many weeks.

I arrived home with Raymond before 5 o'clock, and went directly to our apartment upstairs over our store. As I put the baby in his crib beside my bed, I held my hand several inches above his head, and could feel the fever's heat. He was still whimpering with the pain, but weakly.

I sat on the bed and, utterly spent, lay my head on my pillow for just a moment. I must have fallen asleep instantly. I awoke with a start, and at once looked at Raymond. He was as still as death. I grasped him to me; he was stone cold. I could feel no heartbeat.

For a moment my own heart stopped beating. Then I could feel him breathing, very lightly, but regularly; not fitfully, as with fever. He was in a deep sleep.

I laid him down again and rushed downstairs, calling to my husband to come and look at Raymond. He felt his forehead, and said—"He has no fever. The inflammation must be gone. That means he's cured! Let's kneel and thank God for this wonderful mercy."

I returned to Father Solanus at 7:30 and told him of Raymond's sudden recovery. He didn't seem at all surprised. When I tried to thank him, he told me to thank God, and talked a little about man's duty of gratitude toward God for all His blessings, and about the power of the Mass. He seemed totally unconscious that he himself had had anything to do with the baby's cure. Despite the terrible financial depression of that period, we had a little cash, and I pressed a ten dollar bill on him for the Capuchin missions.

Next morning, when Dr. Theisen took Raymond's temperature, it was about the same as when we had taken it the night before—about two degrees below normal.

At noon, I took his temperature again. It had risen a degree. By 6 o'clock that evening, it was normal, and remained normal.

Since that time Raymond has never had as much as an earache. He is now a brawny six-footer, served in the Navy during the Korean conflict, and is assistant principal at Detroit's Myra Jones Elementary School. He is thirty-four years old and the father of five children.

Father Solanus was always particularly sympathetic with physically afflicted parents whose children needed them. Mrs. Mary Wasner was one of these. When she told the following experience in 1963 she was living on Birwood Avenue, Detroit.

IN THE 1920's—Mrs. Wasner said—I was living in the neighborhood of the Capuchin church on Mt. Elliott Street, and had formed the habit of going to confession there. Early one Wednesday afternoon after having been to confession I went to the office next door to talk with Father Solanus, of whom I had heard, though I had never met him. I thought it might be helpful to have his counsel in some family trouble that was worrying me.

It didn't occur to me to ask his help in a physical trouble I had—an inner goiter so large that it choked me when I stooped to pick anything from the floor. In fact, I didn't know at this time that Father Solanus was credited with helping the physically afflicted.

I had, of course, been to doctors. They had told me that if I were to obtain relief from the goiter, I must be operated on. My husband was strongly opposed to an operation.

So I was surprised when, after Father Solanus had counseled me about my family problems, and I had risen to take my leave, he touched his fingers to my neck where the goiter was, and asked—"What's that?" I told him it was an inner goiter, that it was becoming worse, and that the doctors recommended an operation.

Father said—"You don't need an operation. You say you have never been to the Wednesday services. Well, this is Wednesday. Services start in another half hour. So go to them and get the blessing for the sick. Come to the services every Wednesday. And if you earnestly pray, and believe that God will help you, He will."

I went to the services, and continued to go for many Wednesdays thereafter. Each time, Father Solanus blessed me with the relic of the cross as with others I knelt at the altar railing.

The second Wednesday, my goiter felt better, and I noted continuous improvement. Finally, it disappeared altogether; I don't know just when. I have never been bothered that way since, and I have no goiter today.

Not long after this—it was in the spring of 1926—I became arthritic. My joints swelled. I was becoming a helpless cripple. Dr. George Walters at the North End Clinic, after examination, said I could expect to lose my ability to walk.

At this time, I had a daughter six years old and a son four. Yet I could not even do my own housework. When I grasped a broom, my fingers locked. They seemed to go out of their sockets. And my toes! Most people wear out their shoes at the bottom—my toes were so bent I wore out my shoes at the tops.

I did not go at once to Father Solanus about this afflction. I stayed that summer with my children at the home of my mother, in Cloverton, Minnesota. When I returned in the fall, and set out to consult Father Solanus, a neighbor accompanied me; I had to be helped in and out of the taxicab.

Father Solanus suggested that I come three Wednesdays in succession to the services for the sick, and assured me that I would not be crippled for life.

I went nine Wednesdays, being able to do so because the arthritis was getting better. So much so, that the last two Wednesdays of the nine, I walked to and from the church— a distance from my home of six or seven blocks.

Both my thumbs are still crooked—but I was certainly not crippled for life, as the doctor told me I would be. For twenty-two years after this I was able to make a living for myself and my children—working seventeen years at Siegal's downtown store and five at Kern's department store in Detroit.

Among the many who were warm friends of Father Solanus was William Riley, an employee of Charles J. Rogers, Inc., one of Michigan's largest excavating and paving contractors. In August of 1935 Mr. Riley hurried to the monastery to ask the friar to pray for the young son of the president of the company, Charles J. Rogers of Warwick Avenue, Detroit. Mr. Rogers relates the experience.

IN 1935—said Mr. Rogers—during a polio epidemic in Detroit, Charles, our twelve-year-old son, fell sick, and before we were aware, the sickness became serious. He experienced headaches and stiffness of the neck, which later extended to arms and legs, and still later, began suffering spasms.

One of Detroit's leading specialists in polio at that time was Dr. Ronald Athey, and on August 9th—it was three days before the boy's birthday—we called him in. Dr. Athey diagnosed polio and ordered him to the Herman Kiefer Hospital. I delayed—and for this reason: An employee of my company —Bill Riley—had just enrolled Charles in the Seraphic Mass Association. Father Solanus had told Riley—"Don't let that boy go to the hospital. He'll be fifty percent better tomorrow, and he will be all right."

The next morning Charles was better. I 'phoned Dr. Athey the news. He told me: "I know better. I've handled a lot of these cases all through my medical career. What you tell me is impossible. I insist that you take that boy to the hospital."

When I insisted in my turn that Dr. Athey come again to the house and examine the boy, he became rather angry with me. But finally he agreed to do so.

When he arrived and went into Charles' room, he took off his coat, pulled the bedclothes down, and instructed Charles to put one hand against his hand, and push as hard as he could. Then he ordered him to repeat this with the other hand. The boy was able to push back with what seemed to us the usual force of a well boy of his age. Then Dr. Athey said: "Brace yourself and put your foot against my chest and push —give it all you've got." Charles pushed Dr. Athey almost through the wall. This test was repeated with the other leg with similar results.

This seemed to stimulate Charles. The bed clothes had been drawn over him again, but he threw them off and jumped out of bed. Then Dr. Athey had him do a little walking.

Upon this Dr. Athey went into the next room, motioning me to follow. He said: "This is a miracle. You did more than pray."

(Interviewer: "Did Dr. Athey use the word 'miracle?' Medical men generally avoid that term."

Mr. Rogers: "Yes, he said 'miracle.' ")

We went downstairs and sat down and I told the doctor about Riley going to Father Solanus and what the latter had said about the boy's being "fifty percent better" the next day —which was the day on which we were then talking. Dr. Athey replied that he had never before in all his experience seen anything like it—that it surely was a miracle. I don't know what Dr. Athey's religious conviction was—I am quite sure he was not of the Catholic faith.

He ordered Charles to rest, but we could hardly keep him in bed. Within the week he was out on the farm, chasing horses.

Charles is now forty years old, married, with a family of nine children. Four years later, in 1939, when our daughter Joanna, then nine years old, took sick, Dr. Athey diagnosed the sickness as infantile paralysis. He said: "We are not sending these cases to the hospital any more. Keep the girl quiet."

Within a few days she became worse. She was suffering spasms. When I saw this, I went into the next room and telephoned Father Solanus, telling him her condition. He said—"I am going to the chapel now to say vespers, and she will be all right."

I returned to Joanna's room at once. The spasms had ceased. She was holding a newspaper—the "funnies"—in her outstretched arms, and the arms were perfectly steady. Dr. Athey had been visiting her regularly, and he came again that afternoon. He said: "This surely is a miracle. I was afraid to tell you, but your daughter had infantile paralysis of the throat, which few if any recover from. Didn't you do more than pray? You must have made some offer." Under his orders Joanna rested for a week and then was up and as well as ever.

Mr. Rogers is evidently self-trained in saying only what needs to be said, and in saying it precisely. He was as coldly objective in talking about his experiences with Father Solanus as when—a telephone call interrupting—he talked with an employee about the terms of a large earth-moving contract in which a miscalculation would have meant a major financial loss.

In the foregoing instances, as in others, an attempt was made to contact the attending physician. Most of these attempts failed; the physician had moved and could not be located, or had died. In the Rogers instance, Dr. Athey was located through the Wayne County Medical Association. To a letter from the author he responded on March 30, 1965, on the letterhead of the Department of Health of Midland City and County (Michigan). He said that he "remembered these cases, but not in detail," and added—

I AM PLEASED to be remembered by Mr. Rogers. It would be hard to forget his great concern for the welfare of his family. I know that he was a man of great religious faith and see no reason to question his belief that prayer had an effect on the favorable outcome of these cases.

Many physicians knew and loved Father Solanus; he himself had high respect for medical men and their science. When sick himself, he would, in obedience to superiors, place himself under doctor's orders and try faithfully to follow their directions. Frequently, he would ask those who complained of sickness whether they had consulted a doctor, and would urge that they do so. His assurances of recovery, or gentle predictions of death, might conflict with, but were never in rivalry with medical opinion. His emphasis on prayer and God's power and goodness were on a plane above and apart. After all, many who consulted him did so only because their physicians had given up hope.

He seemed to possess prescience. Frequently, he foretold that a sick person would, or would not recover. And his predictions came true. Sometimes the prediction of a recovery would be indefinite as to time. The assurance would be merely—"Don't worry, he'll be all right"—or some such phrase. In other instances, it would be specific as to time.

It was specific when he predicted the recovery of Harry Downer, a son of Detroit surgeon Dr. Ira Downer. The boy, sixteen or seventeen years old, was stricken with infantile paralysis in 1940. Sympathizing with the deeply concerned father, his office nurse, Mrs. Mary Doyle, asked her husband to stop in at St. Bonaventure's and enroll Harry in the Seraphic Mass Association. Late that afternoon, Mr. Doyle telephoned his wife, still on duty in Dr. Downer's office, that he had seen Father Solanus.

"Father Solanus said that Doctor Downer needn't worry," he told her. "He said: 'Tomorrow afternoon by 3 o'clock the boy will begin to improve.'"

Mrs. Doyle wrote this assurance on a prescription blank and left it on Dr. Downer's desk, where he found it the next morning, before he hurried off to his son's bedside in Herman Kiefer Hospital.

That afternoon, Harry began to improve. He made a full recovery, served in the Armed Forces, and received several decorations, including the Purple Heart.

Calling on Father Solanus to thank him for his interest in Harry, Dr. Downer became greatly drawn to the Capuchin friar. He told this narrator, several years later, that he had found consolation and strength in further visits. On the day of Father Solanus' burial he was one of the hundreds who stood patiently in line for a last farewell. Dr. Downer is not of the Catholic faith.

Most frequently, Father Solanus did not specify the time-interval before recovery could be expected. He might merely say—"She'll be all right." This he said of Elizabeth, infant daughter of Mrs. John Frederick Fanning of 821 North Melborne Avenue, Dearborn. Three or four days after birth in August, 1938, a red birthmark appeared on Elizabeth's neck, and a thick, red-colored growth on her cheek. A pediatrician prescribed a series of radium treatments which were given at Woman's Hospital. Growth of the birthmark stopped; the cheek growth disappeared. But the child's hair ceased to grow and she remained small. Specialists diagnosed leukemia; one advocated operation to remove the spleen. Other specialists at the Mayo Clinic in Rochester, Minnesota, confirmed the diagnosis, but warned that the child was too weak to stand an operation.

OUR FAMILY DOCTORS—said Mrs. Fanning—stopped charging me fees, telling me that Elizabeth would die. To lessen the shock of her expected death, they warned me that I could expect to find her dead in her crib. By this time she had a large, protruding stomach, and skinny arms and legs, like children who suffer from malnutrition. I was feeding her liver soup about eight times a day, according to the doctor's instructions. She was sensitive to the touch and cried when I moved her.

Sixteen or seventeen months went by. Sometime in the spring of 1940, my aunt, who belonged to the Third Order of St. Francis at the Capuchin Monastery, suggested that Elizabeth be taken to Father Solanus.

My husband and I did so. I carried her in my arms all the way. She was listless and inert and could not walk.

Father Solanus talked to her, and said simply and matter-of-factly—"You are going to be all right, Elizabeth."

Then he gave her a piece of candy.

Driving home, we noticed that Elizabeth was alert and watching everything. She sat up. She smiled. She was more active than she had ever been before.

Surprised and happy at this quick change in her, we felt like celebrating. We stopped at a restaurant. The place was crowded—and Betsy— who only an hour before had been lying in my arms as limp as a rag doll—immediately became the "life of the party." She waved to the people about us, jumping up and down. She was full of life.

She continued to improve, and started to walk.

When I brought her back to the doctors, they were incredulous. She looked so different—healthy, lively, and her once wispy, lifeless hair was now curly.

"That's not Betsy!" they exclaimed. "Why, she's walking."

Today, Betsy is strong, tall and healthy.

Many mothers credited Father Solanus' intercession for safe deliveries. A representative instance is related by Mrs. Mildred Boyea of Golfcrest Drive, Dearborn, Michigan.

IN 1930 I WAS EXPECTING my first child. At that time, we were living in Toledo. The doctor I consulted examined me, and then informed me that I would require more expert care than he could give me. He suggested I consult a specialist. I went to Detroit, stayed with my mother, and went to Dr. Wayne A. Yoakam in the Fisher Building.

As the time of my delivery grew nearer, Dr. Yoakam— who was exceptionally forthright and blunt—informed me that of the hundred and fifty pregnant women then under his care, I was the only one he had to stay awake nights worrying about. The reason was, that I had the toxemia of pregnancy—eclampsia. This can be extremely dangerous; it causes convulsions and coma, high blood pressure and edema.

I told the doctor that I would prefer to go to Providence Hospital, but he insisted that I must go to Ford Hospital.

On Saturday, February 1, 1931, he said that he felt he must tell me that it was doubtful whether I could successfully bear a child, that he was very concerned about me and could promise nothing. He instructed me to go straight from his office to the Hospital, and stated that if I did not go into natural labor by the end of the week he would have to induce it, or take—I think he said "force"—the baby.

I was very upset and asked if I could go back to my mother's till the time came. He agreed, provided I remained in bed.

As my husband and I left the Doctor's office, I asked him to take me to Father Solanus. Protesting against what he thought my recklessness, he did so.

I said to Father Solanus—whom I had met five or six years before—"I am pregnant but the doctor says I am not going to have the baby, and that there is nothing he can promise me,"—for the doctor had said he would be thankful if he could save me.

Father Solanus said—"Have faith, child—and we'll start remembering you in our prayers."

"Father," I told him, "I haven't that kind of faith."

"You must have that kind of faith," he answered. "You must. Now go home, and have confidence."

Then he said—"You will have a beautiful baby. And you will be all right."

I returned to my mother's, and about 11 o'clock that night I went into natural labor. I was taken to Ford Hospital and the baby was born about 3 a.m.

Early in the morning my doctor came through the swinging doors and said—"I've heard about the Guardian Angels you damn Catholics have hanging over you, but you had more than angels last night."

We named the baby Thomas. He is now (in 1966) thirty-four years old, and the father of seven children. He is an engineer at the Ford Motor Company.

The persons relating the foregoing incidents were personally interviewed by the author. These are but a small fraction of those who have detailed reports of cures and extraordinary answers to various problems. In turn, all these first-hand accounts taken together are but a fraction of the total "favors" reported.

Were all the reports of remarkable events associated with Father Solanus to be included in a single volume, it would have to be hundreds of pages longer than this biography. The limited number here set forth are representative rather than comprehensive. To make them more fully representative, a wider variety of such incidents in Father Solanus' life are presented in the following chapter.

The deep spirituality of Father Solanus
impressed the minds of all who saw him
and remained in their memories.
As he became more frail the spiritual
seemed to transcend, increasingly, the physical.
His love of God and man spoke silently
and became a lasting impression.

Father Solanus was baptized at St. Joseph's in Prescott on December 18, 1870. Above is the record as inscribed in the Baptismal Register preserved at St. Patrick's Church in Hudson, Wisconsin. The Latin reads: "On the 18th day of December, A.D. 1870, I baptized Bernard Francis Casey who was born on the 25th of November A.D. 1870, the son of Bernard Casey and Helen (Ellen) Murphy. The sponsors were Thomas Mannion and Catherine Mannion."

Christian A. Verweyst

The first St. Joseph Catholic Church at Prescott Wisconsin, built in 1868. The occasional visits of the Pastor from St. Patrick's Church in Hudson, Wisconsin, to this little Mission at Prescott saved the Caseys several bumpy miles over rough roads.

Home on vacation while a second-year student
at St. Francis de Sales Seminary in Milwaukee,
Barney Casey posed with his parents
and his nine brothers and four sisters,
for this family portrait. Top row—Edward,
Leo, Bernard (the future Fr. Solanus),
Jim, Ellen, Patrick (Pat), Owen, Augustine (Gus)
and Maurice. Bottom—John, Margaret,
Mrs. Ellen Casey (Mother), Genevieve, Mr. Bernard Casy
(Father), Grace and Tom.—the photo, taken at the Casey
home in Superior, Wisconsin, is dated, August 14, 1892

This enlargement of Bernard Casey's face
reveals the 22-year-old seminarian as a mature
but notably gentle and unassuming young man.

At the Stillwater,
Minnesota State Prison
a few miles from his Wisconsin home,
Bernard Casey at 16 years,
served as relief guard and handy man.
Conversing with prisoners
—among them notorious bandits
including Jim and Cole Younger
—he learned compassion for the miserable,
whatever their own responsibility
for their condition.

As a newly ordained Capuchin priest, Fr. Solanus was assigned to Sacred Heart Friary in Yonkers, N.Y., a suburb of New York City. The Friary Church then occupied the first floor of the left wing. Here Fr. Solanus became noted for his fervent sermons on the love and mercy of God. In 1906, he was assigned the Porter's duties and spent most of his days at a desk near the Monastery entrance (near right).

During his fourteen years at Sacred Heart, Fr. Solanus saw the building of this impressive edifice, completed in 1913.

Among these acolytes of Sacred Heart Church—all appearing appropriately solemn—are some of those "careless altar boys" who "showed new zeal" after Fr. Solanus (back row, far right) made a novena to Our Lady of Perpetual Help. Fr. Anscar, the Superior, is at far left.

Clear-eyed and oak-like strength speak in wordless eloquence from this photograph of the Casey family. It was made in 1913, during the parents' golden wedding celebration. Left to right: 1st row, Mrs. Thomas (Ellen) Traynor, Bernard Casey, Sr., Mrs. Ellen Casey, Father Solanus (Bernard, Jr.,); 2nd row, Mrs. Frank (Margaret) LeDoux, Mrs. Patrick (Genevieve) McCluskey, Mrs. Bernard (Grace) Brady; 3rd row, James Augustine, Patrick, John, Leo, Tom, Father Edward, Father Maurice, Owen.

From July 1918
to October, 1921,
Fr. Solanus served
at Our Lady of Sorrows Friary,
Pitt Street,
on Manhattan's lower east side,
mainly as Sacristan
and Porter.

From October 25, 1921, to August 1, 1924,
Fr. Solanus was stationed at Our Lady of Angels in Manhattan's
Harlem—then populated by middle income New Yorkers.
Here as Porter and Promoter of the Capuchin Seraphic Mass
Association, parishioners began to seek his counsel. And here, too,
those consulting him began to witness the spiritual conversions
and physical cures they considered direct answers to prayer.
It was here that the Fr. Provincial directed Fr. Solanus
to keep a record of the answers to prayer
through the Seraphic Mass Association.

In St. Bonaventure
Monastery on Mt. Elliott
Avenue, Detroit,
Father Solanus lived
and labored more than
twenty years. The white
shelter leads to the door
through which scores
daily passed, seeking
his counsel and prayers.

At his desk day after
day for forty years
as friary porter in
New York and in
Detroit, Father
Solanus listened to
countless problems
and sorrows, and
inspired new faith
and hope in the
discouraged and the
despairing.

Above—Father Solanus and his two priest-brothers in their prime—Father Maurice on his right, Monsignor Edward on his left.—Right: As a Capuchin Franciscan, Father Solanus devoted his life to helping others, materially and spiritually. But his life, as that of all Capuchins, was also contemplative. He devoted untold hours to prayer and meditation. For devotional reading, the monastery garden was a favorite locale, as *The Detroit News* photo indicates.

Even in old age, Father Solanus enjoyed trying his hand at any game that offered, including tennis and volley ball. Here he is playing scrabble with Father Multerer. . . . He loved children as he reverenced innocence. Children, in turn, felt strongly drawn to him. For them he always carried candy or some other little gift.

So wholesouled was Father Solanus' desire to please as he bowed his violin, that even listeners with an absolute sense of pitch enjoyed his somewhat erratic playing, and joined in singing with him the hymns he loved.

Father Solanus thought that the newspaper photographer was taking a full length picture, but Frank Lyerla was focusing on his arthritic hands.

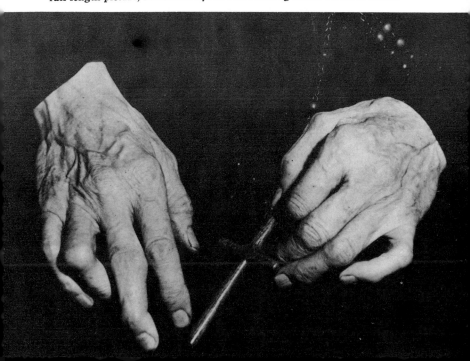

To thousands, Father Solanus was a spiritual storehouse from which they drew new measures of faith and hope. Loving all men as his brothers in Christ, striving constantly to bring them closer to Christ, he gave them all his life, even to his last heartbeat.

At his burial, friends of Father Solanus crowded the little Capuchin cemetery beside the Monastery; it could contain only a fraction of the crowd. Here the mourners are seen approaching the gate in the wall that surrounds the burial ground.

Father Solanus' grave is in the foreground. Near it rises a bas relief depicting St. Francis of Assisi, with words from his Hymn to the Sun: PRAISE TO THE LORD FOR OUR SISTER BODILY DEATH. At the base are carved the words that have lived in the hearts of every spiritual son of St. Francis down through the centuries: MY GOD AND MY ALL. . . . The seasons 'round, visitors make pilgrimage to the grave of the porter of Saint Bonaventure's.

Chapter 13

Father Solanus' Notebooks

It wasn't long after Father Solanus came to Detroit that he found himself conducting the services for the sick every Wednesday afternoon in St. Bonaventure's Chapel. The blessing of the sick, with a relic of the true cross, had been introduced at St. Bonaventure's many years before. As Father Solanus' fame increased, so did attendance at the services.

Generally, long before the service was scheduled to begin, the Monastery office was crowded with people wanting a few words with Father Solanus. This created a weekly problem, especially for Brother Francis, who had taken over as a kind of manager of operations. By nature, he was highly efficient, and he tried his best to make up for what appeared to him to be Father Solanus' easy inefficiency and disregard of time. On Wednesday afternoons, one of Brother Francis' self-appointed tasks was to get Father Solanus into the Chapel on time for the 3 o'clock services. And if he seldom succeeded, it wasn't for lack of trying—or, for that matter, any lack of good will in the matter on the part of Father Solanus.

Brother Francis kept his eye on the big clock on the wall. As the clock's hands moved closer to the hour, he would ask himself why Father Solanus didn't watch the clock too, and speed up his consultation with his current client. But Father Solanus never hurried anyone.

About fifteen minutes before three, Brother Francis would commence a countdown. "It's quarter-to-three, Father," he would announce . . . . "It's ten to three, Father" . . . . "It's five to three, Father." Then, finally, and much more urgently— "Father, *it's three o'clock.*"

All this was uttered a little louder than sotto voice, with Brother Francis looking straight ahead as if unaware that Father Solanus was talking with a visitor. To all warnings except the last the priest seemed deaf. When he finally did rise, the visitor nearly always had one last word that had to be said, or a question that had to be asked. At last, Father Solanus would graciously bid farewell and hurry through the connecting corridor to the chapel, while Brother Francis' sigh of relief could be heard across the room.

In the chapel the sick, crippled and infirm awaited to hear his sermon, to venerate the relic of the true cross, and to receive the blessing. Many had arrived early—some on crutches, some in wheelchairs, some leaning on the more able-bodied. Not a few people carried babies and small children—children crippled from birth, or with the sadly enlarged craniums of the hydrocephalic, or doomed by leukemia. Their faith had brought them there and now drew them together in the fellowship of suffering. Here they prayed for one another and were brought to realize that love for others was the measure of their love for God. Whatever their sickness or affliction, their faith in God's love was too great to limit hope.

During these devotions they were strengthened in their faith by Father Solanus' informal talks. The Capuchins called such sermons as his, ferverinos; little talks delivered with glowing ardor. Father Solanus' talks were always about God's infinite, all-embracing love for men, and man's debt of love and gratitude to God. His words frequently were like outbursts of flame from a soul on fire. To many, his sermons seemed impregnated by the power of the Holy Spirit. They often dealt with the passion of Christ; of the ways in which nature reflected God's love and wisdom and care for men; of penance; of patience in trials, misunderstandings and sickness. He was particularly given to marveling at the mysteries of the Redemption. Frequently he spoke of how God had honored man through the glories and privileges He had bestowed upon the Blessed Virgin, and he would dwell on her love for sinners.

The desires and needs that brought people to Father Solanus in a never-ending stream were as varied as humanity's aspirations and miseries and misfortunes. Many came to receive his blessing—especially on Sundays after chapel services. Many deeply religious people came to consult him on spiritual matters. Young people conferred with him about their choice of a calling in life, particularly when they were considering a life in religion. Not a few sought his advice and prayers in serious domestic troubles. Every week scores came to enroll sick relatives or friends in the Seraphic Mass Association. Some brought sick children and adults to the Monastery that he might bless them and pray for them. A great multitude came burdened by some kind of failure—a failure in health, in the loyalty of friends or family, in business, in themselves. All profited from the warmth of his love and compassionate friendliness, his common-sense, his practical advice, and often a spiritual wisdom that helped them realize failure's redemptive meaning. After talking with him they would leave St. Bonaventure's with their burdens lightened; go out comforted, and strengthened in faith and hope. They would leave his presence feeling less insignificant and helpless in this immense, complex, speeding world, and that world itself would seem less cold and less unfriendly. For they had talked to one who had accepted them as friends and fellows

in the love of Christ, their Brother and his. They felt that he
would never fail them; that he would always walk that extra,
scriptural mile with them if need be. As he talked to them in
his low, thin voice about their infinite value in God's mysterious plan, they grew in spiritual stature.

He would concentrate on the person in the chair beside
him as if he were the most important individual in the world
—as indeed, to Father Solanus, he was. For to him all men
were of infinite value.

When charity could be better served by going out to
others in their homes or in hospitals, he would do so. He
would join in their festivities, also—though instances of this
are rare. In one note he writes: "Oct. 20, 1931—Today
(p.m.) went to Mt. Vernon Memorial Park; had supper with
colored folks in Dexter [about forty miles from Detroit].
Too bad someone cannot go to them regularly for service . . .
a good field."

By 1928 pressure on the Monastery office and on Father
Solanus had become constant and at times overtaxing. Brother
Francis' ability to keep the office running smoothly was regarded as essential. Therefore, when it was decided that year
to move the tailoring shop to the new St. Felix Friary in
Huntington, Indiana, the Brother—excellent tailor though
he was—remained at St. Bonaventure's. He sat at the rear of
the room, at a desk, and when not busy with his own work
was forever doing something to help out Father Solanus or
his visitors. Both of their jobs were now made easier, also, by
a little sign above the doorbell which read, Walk In.

Walk in they did, endlessly; mornings, afternoons, even-
ings; day after day, seven days a week. Some wanted to talk
with Brother Francis, or with one of the other Brothers, or
Fathers, but most by far came to see, to talk with, to listen to
Father Solanus. Seated at his desk they would pour out their

griefs, sufferings, longings, blasted hopes. Listening to the pitiable or urgent, Father Solanus would take a pocket size notebook out of the center drawer of his desk, and jot down a note. At the Wednesday services for the sick, he would take the little book from a pocket of his brown habit, and referring to the note and others he had made during the previous week, ask special prayers for these unfortunates.

In this way, Father Solanus during his twenty-one years at St. Bonaventure's filled seven notebooks with more than six thousand notes. To between six and seven hundred of these notes he has added a sentence or two to state the person mentioned had reported being cured of cancer, or lukemia, or tuberculosis, or diphtheria, or arthritis, or blindness, or other malady; or had been converted, or had received a favorable answer to some domestic or business problem. Perhaps many, like "the other nine" in the Gospel, did not return to report favors received. Or perhaps they did, and Father Solanus—who was not keeping a record for posterity—just didn't write notes on their reports.

When scores of people were interviewed after Father Solanus' death regarding special favors they said they had been granted after he had enrolled them in the Seraphic Mass Association, it was found that the names of only two or three of them were mentioned in the notes.

The notebooks do, however, suggest concretely the variety of human needs, misfortunes and physical afflictions which brought people to him in such numbers seven days a week for more than two decades.

Inasmuch as the memos were reminders to himself, they contain far less information than if he were writing them for others. If the Provincial had called on him for a report, he would probably have expanded the memos greatly, and corrected the spelling. This is archaic, and as uncertain as spelling frequently is when intended only for the note-maker's own eyes. With spelling corrected for easier reading, here are typical notebook entries for a week,—the week of September 7 to 14, 1938.

Sept. 7—Hugh S.-----. Enrolled (evidently by a friend or relative) for grace to go back to the sacraments. (A later addition)—He did go back before death last November.

Sept. 7—Lawrence Howey—40—Vanished Aug. 23 on way to work with car. Believed to have been waylaid. Has not been seen since. Now two weeks.

Sept. 7—Robert Piscopink—5—a twin. Leakage of the heart. In bed now three months. His twin sister started to school—bright child.

Sept. 8—Louis Laboe—46—fractured skull, broken back—in auto accident. Is able to be around in harness . . . but asks prayers for improvement. Helped him in—four men helped him in.

(After this note follows another dated five weeks later.)

Oct. 14—Here today—a new man—perfectly healthy—working since Sept. 21st. (Father Solanus evidently considered some amplification desirable, and his memory having been refreshed by the second visit from Mr. Laboe, he writes a more complete memo.)

Oct. 14—Louis C. Laboe, 46, of 308 Michigan Avenue, Monroe, Michigan, came here Sept. 8th last—carried (almost) in by four men—with broken back and skull healing from fracture. Comes today in perfect condition. He tells he walked out of the monastery that day (September 8) without assistance. He has been working since Sept. 21st.

Sept. 8—A----- about 40—phones first and then is silent. Finally tells of temptation to "end it all."

Sept. 10—Baby Mary Shriner—four days old—a bleeder. Enrolled today as against further loss of blood. Parents have lost three little ones so far and now ask prayers.

Sept. 11th—. Elsie H.—wayward.

Sept. 11th.—June VanWert of Bay City—16—Cancer-like growth, very threatening. Oct. 10.—Improved . . . But . . . Enrolled today.

Sept. 13. — Nicholas Kobane — 20 — shot accidently six months ago. Still very low and "in balance."

Sept. 13.—Thomas Carney—7—Cross-eyed since year ago.

Sept. 13.—Bracken (John)—48—Plymouth. Heart, etc.

Sept. 13.—Hattie Snider—45—inward cancer—has three children.

Sept. 13.—Mrs. Doherty—Marysville.

Sept. 14th.—Ronald Stephen McD-------, twin, 7—When a year [old] was given up by specialists who said he'd never walk or talk. He does both perfectly, but is slow mentally. Enrolled today as perpetual member.

The memos leave questions unanswered. Was Lawrence Howey found? Did A------- commit suicide? Were there any recoveries other than that of Louis Laboe among those mentioned in the notes? And what would his physicians have to say about Louis Laboe's sudden ability to walk?

Such inquiries would hardly have occurred to Father Solanus. He knew that the infinitely loving Creator of man could cure man supernaturally; could set aside the laws of nature which He had made. He had seen the blind suddenly recover sight; the crippled instantanously recover their power to walk; ugly exterior cancers and huge goiters speedily disappear. And such cures had been coincident with enrollment in the Seraphic Mass Association, through which the victims of these maladies had joined themselves with thousands of priests and tens of thousands of laymen, offering the Mass and praying for all the others.

Because Father Solanus' faith in God's goodness and power and in His graces flowing from the holy sacrifice of the Mass was absolute, he didn't anxiously go about asking medical scientists for their opinions. To him the facts, even in the Louis Laboe instance, were plain. Laboe had sustained a fractured skull and "a broken back." He couldn't walk. Four men had more than half-carried him into the Monastery. And he had walked out "without any assistance." He had returned to work in less than two weeks, and less than three weeks after that had appeared at the Monastery "in perfect condition"—evidently to thank Father Solanus.

Fully recognizing the general efficacy of medicine and surgery, he would still point out that God was the Supreme Physician.

He was chiefly interested in the reported cures and other benefits insofar as they demonstrated God's power and goodness. Himself he regarded as a mere witness on the sidelines. Many said that Divine Providence must have selected him as a special channel of supernatural aid to men; to Father Solanus himself, such a thought would never occur.

"If people were cured before his very eyes," a Capuchin Father said, "those eyes would fill with tears, and he would seem utterly amazed at the power of the Mass, and fully convinced that their cure had no connection with him, and was entirely due to the power of the Mass."

His belief in the authenticity of the cures was both positive and undiscriminating. He knew God could not fail, if the cure was according to His designs.

As has been said, he thought of himself in relation to the reported cures as an onlooker. Had anyone suggested to him that some of the reports might have resulted from the excited fancy of the afflicted one, or that doctors might have mis-diagnosed a case, he undoubtedly, in his gentle and easy man-ner, would have admitted such possibilities. But he would never have doubted the power of prayer and of the Mass, nor that many of the reported cures were the result of that power.

He was never overwhelmed by surprise when one of those he had enrolled in the Seraphic Mass Association reported a favorable answer to his petition; such signs of God's love were to be expected. This assurance is indicated in the matter-of-factness of most of the memos, as illustrated in the follow-ing.

MARCH 8, 1925—Mrs. Stella Sherwin—47—312 DeSoto Ave., McKeesport, Pa., suffering from gall stones when, on Feb. 10, her daughter, living in Detroit, enrolled her in S.M.A. and sent her the certificate. The time of her cure cor-responded with that of the issuance of the certificate.

JUNE 25, 1925—Leo Krivick, 22, 4479 Cadillac. Overcome by heat and unconscious for 5 days—is enrolled June 11th. Today reported as having recovered almost immediately after enrollment. Gets up same day and showers. Deo Gratias.

DEC. 6-16, 1925—Telegram rec'd from Seattle, Wash., Dec. 6th to enroll Mrs. Ella Traynor in S.M.A. as against opera-tion of Dec. 9th for cancer of the breast . . . Today letter from patient—same Mrs. Traynor—reads thus: Seattle, Wash., Dec. 10, 1925 . . . "I was to have gone to Providence Hospital Dec. 9th. While receiving Holy Communion on the morning of the 7th the pain all left me and I felt well." Sub-sequent letters assure us of positive return of health without further treatment. Thanks be to Jesus in the Holy Mass. [Note: Whether "Ella Traynor" is Father Solanus' sister Ellen Bridget Traynor, is uncertain. She was generally called

"Nell." At this time she would have been 61 years old, and living in Seattle.]

MARCH 27, 1926—Mrs. Marg. Rabedeau, 44, of Grosse Ile, staying at 1646 W. Gr. Blvd. Enrolled last Wednesday for curvature of spine after doctoring for years. On Friday—yesterday—spine snapped back into place and she is here in perfect health today. Sept. 3rd—Mrs. Rabedeau, still in perfect health, enrolls wayward relative today.

JULY 26, 1926—Russell Jay, just 17 years old tomorrow and 49 inches tall is enrolled in the S.M.A. today (non-Catholic). Asks Fr. S to "make me grow." He will sign his name. [After this appears the name "Russell Jay." This is the first and only time throughout Father Solanus' thousands of notes that anyone signed his name. Possibly Russell Jay suggested it.]

JAN. 2nd. 1927—Today Russell Jay reported he grew 4½ inches—1st change in 12 years.—Now developing normally.

MARCH 29th, 1926—Mildred Kirchoff (25) of 5737 Seminole, had a bad fall when 9 years old. Four years later it began to affect her spine, leaving her badly deformed and paralyzed. After doctoring and suffering for seven years she enrolled in S.M.A. in May last year. Today, a picture of health, she is teaching in physical training school. Thanks be to God!

JULY 7, 1926—Bertha Smith, 59, 239 McDougall, of Windsor. Examined for cancer of stomach in Windsor Hospital and four times on the operating table at Ford's, is enrolled three weeks ago—June 17—in the S.M.A. and is declared entirely cured July 2 without actually having any operation. P.S. Found cured at said 4th examination at Ford's.

OCT. 12, 1931.—Mrs. Mary E. Reynolds, 59, of Clinton, Ont. 17 years with epileptic fits. Enrolled about July 25th. Has not had a shadow of an attack since. Deo Gr.

JUNE 21, 1932—Joann Gietzen, 15 months old, seemed paralyzed. Had never tried to stand or use her legs. Enrolled with promise of father to enroll her perpetually as soon as improvement was noticed—and weekly instead of monthly Communion for one year (also promised). One minute after these promises were made she stood alone on mother's lap . . . [a later note adds] next day started to walk.

JULY 29, 1932—Jean Dorothy Wards—6—had convulsions since 3 months old, till 2 yrs. ago—as many as 20 a day —when taken here and enrolled. Since that time [two years before] has not had a spell.

DEC. 9, 1932—Doraine Innes—8—of Montreal—At 4 had meningitis of brain—then paralysis and curvature of spine and cross-eyed. Enrolled in 1930. Since day of enrollment has been able to walk without crutches.

OCT. 17, 1933—Arthur Alders, 39, Episcopalian—Abcess of liver—very low. Enrolled perpetually at 10 p.m. Oct. 17 by non-Catholic wife. —At 7 p.m., Oct. 18th, wife phones thanks: "Mr. A. much better." —Oct. 19—wife comes to show appreciation:—"Husband continues improving." Nov. 8—Husb. "expected home soon." Nov. 22—Home and well. —Jan. 18 (1934) Comes to Monastery. O.K.

APRIL 17, 1934—Vincent Welch—about 30. Mastoid operation arranged for tomorrow—enrolled about 9:50 p.m.— Came back to Wed. devotions next day. On 18th phones. Wed. 25th, improving fine. Sunday, 29th, enrolls perpetually. Drs. astonished. No operation. Mastoid quite healed by itself. Deo Gratias.

MAY 5, 1934—Maurice O'Connor, 56. Thank God, is well without question—gall stones. He had taken anesthetic and O.K. for knife. Drs. ? ! ? ! ? ! ?

[The exclamation and question marks are Father Solanus'

shorthand for saying that the doctors were astounded and mystified. Evidently, a second, just-before-operation diagnosis revealed that Mr. O'Connor did not require an operation.]

JULY 7, 1934—George D----, 46, had lost memory four years ago. Six months later lost his job on that account. Was enrolled in Ser. Mass Assoc. day before yesterday. Had been away from sacraments 2 years (about, he thinks). Yesterday, —1st Friday—went to Communion and is happy. Memory restored at same time. O.K. Asks prayers now to go back to work.

AUG. 14—Dr. F. X. Zinger, 51, enrolled July 22, for cancer of the stomach. Operation started Aug. 1st, but abandoned as hopeless. Enrolls again Aug. 4th, perpetually. That was Saturday. Monday 6th—Dr. Z wonderfully improved, wife and nurse report.

AUG. 8, 1935—Floyd McSweyn, now 24, of Merrill, Mich. In May, 1933, fell 18 feet to cement floor, received to all reckoning fatal skull fracture. His mother, sick at time, got out of bed and phoned to have him enrolled. —She tells us today that Fr. assured her "the boy will be better inside of five hours." [The boy was] blind and dumb and totally paralyzed at time mother 'phoned.—Asked for a smoke after. He has completely and perfectly recovered—save hearing in one ear.

[The "Fr." means "Father Solanus".—He seems to have had no recollection of having assured the mother that her son would improve "inside of five hours," but quotes her to that effect, as if becoming aware of the prediction from her lips. If he had arrived at the prediction through a deliberate mental process, it seems probable that he would have remembered it.]

DEC. 29, 1937—John Charles Kulbacki—6—blind since 3 weeks old; was enrolled in Ser. Mass A. 6 weeks ago. On Xmas Day when at "Crib" here in Church, was almost frightened as he exclaimed—pointing to the lighted "crib": "Look, Mama." Deo Gr.

NOV. 19, 1938—Thanks—Marlene—6—was inward bleeder, day before she came hither. —A year ago was prayed for and enrolled—had five hemorraghes day before—has never bled since. Deo Gr.

JULY 12th, 1939—Eva St. Ours—38—of Escanaba, Mich., cured of blindness. One eye completely blind, [sight in] the other almost gone. Enrolled in Seraphic Mass Association and promised a novena to Sacred Heart. Completely cured that day—sight 100%.

THANKS—AUG. 23—Rose Marie Platkowski, 10, for 35 days continuously in convulsions.—Enrolled perpetually. Convulsions stopped and none since enrollment.

OCT. 27, 1943—Patrick McCarthy—44—very threatening lip cancer. Threatened starvation.—Nov. 9—Dr. Wm. Koch calls up—concerning a cancer patient—fearfully threatening ten days ago. Dr. hardly able to speak from emotion at wonderful improvement. We asked your prayers for the patient, Patrick McCarthy, two weeks ago. [The last sentence is evidently to be directed to the Wednesday congregation at the blessing of the sick.]

MARCH 12, 1944—Mrs. John Shaughsany (Shaughnessy?) called last night—Thursday night—to enroll her husband in Ser. Mass Assoc.—Very serious operation scheduled next a.m. —kidney was to be removed.—No operation necessary. Instead her husband came home that afternoon. This was the second big favor [evidently, for Mrs. Shaughsany] over phone.

AUGUST 6, 1944—James Lee Kiser—6—in Highland Park Gen. Hosp.—diagnosed as infantile paralysis and brain tumor. Operation was to take place yesterday. Mother 'phoned day before when child was on way to the hospital. A 2nd x-ray showed nothing wrong. Child home and O.K. Deo Grat.

JAN. 7, 1945—Robert Hamilton—44—Enrolled last Wednesday expecting brain tumor operation on Friday. Drs. who had x-rayed his head were astounded at finding no tumor at all. However, they now predict blindness to follow! Patient still in Ford's (Ford Hospital).—Feb. 25th, 1945—Patient here today 100% well—save healing scar on side of head. Deo Gr.

All the extraordinary material and physical favors reported must have had powerful spiritual impact, for their recipients, and witnesses to them, looked upon their source as spiritual. But also among the notes are reports of favors that are directly spiritual. Here are a few such reports representative of many.

JUNE 4, 1924—Michael F------. Once a student [possibly Father Solanus means seminary student] Married 24 years. Tomorrow, away from Sacraments 9 years; and from wife 4, July 2nd—Thank God! has been to confession and Communion 3 times (since enrollment on June 4). Asked why he went into church first time after such an absence, answered: "I don't know."

SEPT. 27, 1924—Leo W----, consumption, in Marine Hospital. Refuses this p.m. to listen to talk of going to confession —angry at proposal of his sister that he do so. Enrolled in S.M.A. after fruitless efforts [to induce him to go to confession] lasting a year. [Added note] Oct. 1, happy and appreciative, receives everything [that is, the sacraments of Penance, Holy Communion and Extreme Unction]. Happy death, Oct. 4, Feast of St. Francis of Assisi.

MARCH 29, 1926—Joseph G--------, 24, reported hopelessly sick and dying in Providence Hospital with complications— kidney trouble principally—is enrolled on St. Joseph's Day by his chum, Edward K-----, at the time a Russellite [later known as Jehovah's Witnesses]—who promises to do something specially pleasing to God if his friend is spared. Two days later he 'phones that the patient is back to consciousness and able to talk. A week elapses and he 'phones that his friend is actually reading the newspapers and feeling fine. Next day makes profession of faith, abjures heresy and returns after 7 years to reception of the Holy sacraments. Thanks be to God . . . Both young men come to Monastery today, healthy and happy. Thanks be to God.

While Father Solanus always attributed such "special favors" as those described in this and Chapters 11 and 12 to the graces flowing from the Holy Sacrifice of the Mass, he himself seemed to possess, in some instances and to some degree, the charisma of foreknowledge.

Instances of this are described in the following chapter.

Chapter 14

The Predictions
of Father Solanus

To many of the troubled who came to him, Father Solanus gave assurances which were also predictions.

To a mother whose soldier-son was fighting in a battle in which thousands were being killed, he said—"In a couple of days you will receive word that he has been injured"—accompanied by the positive declaration that he would not be seriously injured.

To the husband of a dying woman, he promised . . . "She will find relief before night."

To a woman whose sister was dying . . . "There will be a change at 9 o'clock tonight."

To one whose husband had been pronounced permanently blinded in an accident . . . "Worry not—he will see."

To a desperately sick woman whose case had long mystified specialists . . . "You'll feel better tomorrow morning."

These assurances that God would answer a person's prayers within a certain time and in a specific manner were made, generally, in the most casual manner.

They came true, even to the hour.

His predictions were confined to the question of whether prayers would or would not be favorably answered.

Sometimes he would find it necessary to inform relatives or friends that one for whose recovery they were earnestly praying would not recover. Or, to inform an earnest young man or woman that his or her calling was not, as the inquirer thought, to be the priesthood or to a religious order, but to marriage.

At times one finds himself wondering whether Father Solanus' help to a client was in the physical, the mental or the spiritual order, or in all three. For example, alcoholics came to him for counsel, and some, after having talked with him, never took another alcoholic drink. Did Father Solanus, in helping them, act through their minds or their souls? That he did employ an innate knowledge of psychology is revealed in the experience related by Luke Leonard, once well known in Detroit real estate circles. He says that he was at the end of his rope and felt that he was about to let go when he called on Father Solanus.

IN JUNE of 1941, says Mr. Leonard, I was living in a rundown hotel, an alcoholic bum. Induced by friends, I had made a spiritual retreat and had then joined the Third Order of St. Francis. At the services I attended, I heard Father Solanus give his little talks. He didn't preach, but frequently approached his subject in a gently humorous way.

Although I prayed for strength, I knew it was impossible for me to quit drinking. I had tried to do so by tapering off; it hadn't worked. Now I tried quitting cold—while entirely convinced that it was impossible for me to do so.

The Sunday after I had decided upon the impossible step of quitting alcohol cold, I left my hotel and started to walk Detroit's streets, as I had been doing for the several days since I had stopped drinking. I had been suffering tortures. Delirium tremens came and I would see horrible monsters. I was miserable and hopeless.

That Sunday morning I walked miles, consumed by inner heat. I had the shakes so badly that when I stopped in a soft drink place for a glass of gingerale, I couldn't raise the glass to my lips. A woman standing by did that for me.

I started walking east, toward the Capuchin Monastery. When I reached there, I went into the office. Father Solanus must have seen that I was desperate. He asked me to wait for a moment or two, said farewell to a couple with whom he was talking, and then beckoned to me. I told him I had to talk to him privately. He led me into an adjoining room, closed the door—and I talked. . . Two or three times a friar came in to remind Father Solanus that others were waiting—some from out of town. He'd say—"Ask them to wait a little longer," and continue to listen to me.

I didn't realize it then, but he was certainly giving me psychological therapy, just by letting me confess my weakness.

Finally he said—"When did you get over your sickness?"

His assumption that I had actually conquered my slavery to alcohol astounded me. So did his use of the word "sickness." This was before research had done so much to establish alcoholism as a kind of sickness.

I replied: "You mean my drunk, Father?"

He laughed; it was a gentle, encouraging kind of laugh.

I went out from that talk with Father Solanus strengthened and with a free, elevated spirit.

I never again took an alcoholic drink.

Among the alcoholics who declared they owed their ability to resist alcoholic cravings to Father Solanus was one who had ridiculed friends when they urged him to have a talk with the friar. As he admitted later, he didn't desire help, and he scouted the notion that anyone could influence him. When he finally went to Father Solanus, it was because a friend charged him with fearing to do so. And because he was at the moment full of alcoholic courage. Emboldened by John Barleycorn, he allowed his friend to introduce him to Father Solanus. The friend promptly left them, saying that he would wait for him in the monastery chapel.

When the alcoholic finally came to the chapel, he was sober in more than a physical sense. He never took another drink, was devoted to Father Solanus throughout the latter's life, and was for years prominent in furthering Capuchin charities.

How many people Father Solanus cured of spiritual afflictions is unknown. Most people, understandably, prefer to keep their spiritual sicknesses confidential; physical recoveries they are generally eager to relate. And so it is that, however numerous may have been the spiritual cures atributed to Father Solanus' prayers and counselings, relatively few have been recorded. For this reason, Father Solanus must be seen largely through the eyes of those who feel that his prayers have brought them physical health.

Even when a person confines his story to description of a cure or other material benefit, it is evident that he considers the entire experience rooted in the spiritual. John Sullivan is one of these. As a twelve-year-old, he admired the sainted heroes of the Church far less than the members of the Detroit Tigers baseball team. In 1940, his studies as an eighth grader in St. Mary's School in Detroit's Redford district were entirely incidental to the far more important business of knowing the batting and fielding averages of those peerless athletes. For Johnny felt himself virtually a member of the team. Charlie Gehringer, the Tigers' great second baseman, was his next door neighbor. And Charlie had introduced him, on an intimate, neighborly, man-to-man basis, to all the Tiger players who frequented his home.

So when his beloved Tigers won the American League

pennant in 1940, Johnny's cup of pride and joy was almost brimming over. Almost, but not quite. They still had to lick the Cincinnati Reds for the "world's" championship. Eventually, it didn't turn out that way. But when his father got two tickets from Charley Gehringer and took Johnny to the fifth game of the series on Sunday, October 6, the series was tied at two games each. And Johnny agreed with a lot of sports writers who said that if Detroit won the fifth game, it would probably go on to win the series. The game was what is spoken of as "crucial."

It was an 8 to 0 victory for the Tigers, and gave Johnny plenty to cheer about. He was a chunky, vigorous lad, and he went all out in rooting for every Tiger who came to bat, or got on base, or fielded a ball. He shouted encouragement every time Bo-bo Newsom, the Tiger pitcher, threw the ball. He shouted loudest of all for his special hero, Charlie Gehringer—telling him, each of the four times he came to bat, to "knock the cover off the ball."

It was a great triumph—and it left Johnny with practically no voice at all. He left the stands so hoarse his voice could have been mistaken for a bullfrog's. Still, at first, even his mother wasn't too greatly concerned. Everyone thought his voice would return to normal in a day or two.

Only it didn't. Several days passed, and Johnny still sounded like a foghorn. His mother took him to the family physician, who treated him without result, and finally referred him to a throat specialist. The specialist also treated him for a period, then he too gave up. He might, or he might not recover his voice, said the specialist. Time would tell.

All this consumed five months, at which point Mrs. Sullivan brought Johnny to Father Solanus.

"He talked with me about the ball game at which I had lost my voice," said John Sullivan when talking about Father Solanus in 1966. "Finally, he told· my mother, 'Don't worry.

There'll be a change in Johnny's voice before you get home.'

"There was a change. By the time I entered the house, I was talking normally."

In December of 1944, Mrs. Sullivan went to Father Solanus in worried concern about her son Bill. She knew that he was fighting in the Battle of the Ardennes Bulge. She asked Father Solanus' prayers.

To her surprise, Father Solanus answered—"Just don't worry about Bill. In a couple of days you will receive word that he has been injured. But don't worry. He'll be all right."

Two days later, Mrs. Sullivan received a telephone call from Le Havre, France. A former classmate of Bill's was on the line. He was in the army medical corps, and had happened to talk with Bill as the latter came through that port while being invalided to England. Bill's injuries, he informed Mrs. Sullivan, while not major, made it advisable that he be hospitalized several weeks.

In a few days, an official telegram arrived, to the effect that Bill had been wounded.

"My mother," said Mr. Sullivan, "naturally showed no concern, as she had known the facts for several days. The messenger, a gray-haired man, couldn't understand her attitude. He went down our walk shaking his head, convinced, I am sure, that he had just encountered the coldest hearted mother in the United States."

Sigmund A. Zech was another who could speak from personal experience of Father Solanus' love for children. As a boy he often accompanied his father, a German baker, when the latter brought day-old bread to the Monastery. Mr. Zech was a great friend of the Capuchin cook, Brother Hugo, and the three would sit at the kitchen table while the two men discussed the ways of the world. Frequently, Father Solanus would stop by and join in the conversation.

After a few minutes Father Solanus would say to Brother Hugo—"We ought to have some refreshments." This was a suggestion that the Zech lad was happy to hear, for like most boys he was nearly always hungry.

Then Brother Hugo would bring some bread, or cake or cookies, and the others would eat. Father Solanus would just nibble at a heel of bread, saying it was the best part. Excepting on Sundays. Then he would eat a little of everything, including the butter, which otherwise he never touched at these in-between-meal snacks. Sometimes he would bring out the refreshments himself, including a glass of wine or beer for the adult guests, and generally he'd produce an apple or some other extra treat for the boy.

When Sigmund grew up he, too, became a baker. One day he ran a pastry tube through his thumb. After trying home remedies, he finally went to a doctor. After three treatments, the thumb was turning black; the doctor spoke of amputation. Now greatly worried, Zech went to his old friend Father Solanus.

He blessed the thumb, and told Sigmund to go about his work, adding—"The Lord will take care of it for you."

"The pain left that day," said Zech. "The blackness disappeared and the thumb got better, though I still have a scar."

Knowing how greatly he loved children, some named theirs after him, as did Mr. and Mrs. John O'Connor of Alter Road, Detroit. Mr. O'Connor got to know Father Solanus well when, a lonely newcomer from Ireland, he visited him in 1929, seeking counsel. He found, also, friendship. A little later, he began suffering great pain from severe sinus infections. Several operations gave him no permanent relief. His physician finally advised him to move to Arizona or New Mexico.

When he informed Father Solanus, the friar said—"You

will be all right. And in thanksgiving, receive Holy Communion once a week for a year."

Mr. O'Connor's sinus condition cleared up completely, and never recurred. The O'Connors named a son "Casey."

A similar prediction was to change an apparently hopeless outlook and bring joy to the Joseph F. Droste family. Mr. Droste's wife became sick with diphtheria during the Christmas season in 1928. On December 28, the family doctor informed Mr. Droste that she could not last till midnight. When the stricken husband telephoned Father Solanus, the latter assured him that his wife would "feel better before night." By 7 o'clock that evening her physician reported that Mrs. Droste was out of danger and recovering.

"The abcesses in my wife's throat simply disappeared," said Mr. Droste. "This puzzled the doctor."

Diphtheria had also attacked the Droste's daughter, Mildred. Two days after her mother's recovery, the physician advised Mr. Droste that the daughter had but a few hours to live. She received the last sacraments.

Again—it was New Year's Eve—Mr. Droste telephoned Father Solanus.

"You and your family," the Capuchin assured him, "will have a Happy New Year." The next day Mildred, also, began to recover.

Another family whose members frequently consulted Father Solanus was that of John Uller. After one of several operations on Mrs. Uller, the doctors informed him that his wife could not live.

When he consulted Father Solanus, the latter told him— "Don't worry, Johnny, your wife will get well. You go and visit her this afternoon, and you will see. She will be better by the time you arrive."

When Mr. Uller entered his wife's hospital room that afternoon, she cheerfully greeted him with an "Hello, Dad." She lived several years.

These and many other such predictions by Father Solanus were certainly not based on medical knowledge; in the scientific sense, he had none. He generally knew as little about the sickness of a person whose recovery he foretold as he did about that of Albert McCarthy. The latter was in Blaine Hospital, Detroit, but his family had no intimation that his condition was serious. One night, as his wife was leaving the hospital after visiting her husband, a doctor asked her to remain. He told her that Mr. McCarthy might not live through the night, and she was assigned a bedroom.

Mrs. McCarthy asked her nephew, who was waiting to drive her home, to go instead to Father Solanus and ask his prayers.

"Tell Almira not to worry," the Capuchin told the nephew. "Albert is going to be all right."

Given this assurance, Mrs. McCarthy ceased to worry. And at six-thirty the next morning the nurse came to her room and informed her that her husband had passed a critical point in his sickness.

Such firm belief in Father Solanus' predictions was common. It probably saved the life of John Joseph Tighe, in 1939. Mr. Tighe, suffering from a malady which for some time had puzzled doctors, finally went to Mayo Clinic in Rochester. There he was informed that he was cancerous and had no more than sixty days to live. The Mayo surgeons were positive that an operation would be useless.

Mr. Tighe remembered, however, that Father Solanus had assured him he would "be victorious" over his sickness. He insisted on an operation.

The surgeons were amazed to find no cancer present.

They discovered, instead, a slight blockage of a bile duct. This was removed, and Mr. Tighe's recovery from the large exploratory incision was unusually rapid.

At times Father Solanus' predictions were precise even to the hour of recovery.

Mrs. James Moran of Grosse Pointe Park, Michigan, received word that her sister was near death following an operation in Toronto. Mrs. Moran, however, was very sick herself. She telephoned Father Solanus, asking him to pray for her sister, and in the course of her conversation told him how deeply she regretted not being able to go to her.

"You don't have to go at once," Father Solanus assured her. "I'll pray for her, and enroll her in the Seraphic Mass Association. There will be a change at 9 o'clock tonight. She is not going to die. She is going to get better, and you'll go on Sunday to visit her in Toronto."

He suggested to Mrs. Moran that she come to the Monastery on Saturday, so that he could bless her.

Shortly after 9 o'clock that night—it was a Good Friday —Mrs. Moran received word that her sister's condition had improved. Her own sickness passed, and she went to Toronto on Sunday. Her sister recovered fully.

Father Solanus was seldom required to reiterate his assurances, but when the occasion demanded he could become most positive in his predictions. Mrs. T. J. Holland testified to this. In 1941 she was keeping house for the Immaculate Heart of Mary Sisters in a mission convent at Wayne, Michigan. The convent's superior, Mother Irma Elizabeth, was stricken with pneumonia. Her physicians said they had little hope for her recovery. A priest anointed her, then telephoned the Sisters that death was but a few hours away.

Mrs. Holland called on Father Solanus that afternoon after attending Third Order services in the monastery chapel.

"Father, Mother Irma Elizabeth is dying," she informed him.

"I know her," he replied.

He sat with head inclined, in deep thought.

"I don't know what else I can tell you," said Mrs. Holland, thinking that the few details she had supplied about the superior's condition had failed to impress. "But I'd like to enroll her in the Seraphic Mass Association."

"Yes, of course," Father Solanus said. And added, quite casually—"She'll be all right."

"But you don't understand, Father," Mrs. Holland insisted, quite certain that he didn't realize how grave Mother Irma Elizabeth's condition was. "She's dying."

Father Solanus lifted his head and looked at her.

"Now you go home and take care of *yourself,*" he told Mrs. Holland. "Mother Irma Elizabeth is going to be all right."

Returning to the convent, Mrs. Holland found one of the younger Sisters weeping inconsolably. To distract her, the housekeeper suggested that a Sister telephone the hospital for the latest news.

"Mother Irma Elizabeth is improving," came the answer.

She recovered, and when Mrs. Holland related this experience, had been teaching twenty years since her near fatal illness.

At times, in answer to a relative's insistent questioning, Father Solanus had to predict that a person would die. He made such predictions only when they seemed inescapable, and then gently, frequently by indirection, and accompanied by urgent counseling of resignation to God's will.

"If God wants to take this beautiful, innocent soul to Himself, you wouldn't want to stand in His way, would you?" he would say to a sorrowing parent begging him to intercede for her young daughter.

This was his indirect way of informing the parents that

their child could not live; that it was useless, therefore, for him to pray for her recovery.

Such predictions were always made with reference to God's wisdom and goodness, and the minor importance of this life's duration compared to eternal life.

Many of those who asked his prayers, or for whom prayers were asked, were not facing death, but an affliction they felt was almost as bad. One day a young man named William King told his superior Richard Bette, an executive of the Grand Trunk Railway, that he was suffering from serious eye trouble. Mr. Bette, a Catholic, knew that young King daily passed St. Bonaventure's Monastery on his way home. Although Mr. King was a non-Catholic—he was a Protestant clergyman's son—he suggested that he stop in and ask Father Solanus to pray for him. Mr. King did not act on the advice at once.

His condition grew worse, and blindness threatened. When his doctors informed him that to save the sight of one eye they would have to remove the other, he decided to heed Mr. Bette's suggestion. At this point, he had to be led; his wife guided him into Father Solanus' office.

Father Solanus suggested that he defer the operation a little while; that if necessary, the eye could be removed a little later.

He then reminded the couple that they were asking a favor from God, and that they must "do something for Him in return."

"Do you go to church on Sundays?" he asked, the couple having informed him they were not of his faith.

"Once in a while," the young husband answered.

"How about you?" Father Solanus said, turning to his wife.

"I go when Bill goes," she answered.

Father Solanus then asked them to promise that they would attend church every Sunday.

Mr. King's sight returned. He went back to work. In subsequent years, he not only had the use of both eyes, according to Mr. Bette, but the eye the doctors had planned to remove was his better eye.

Mr. King was one of a number whose eyesight had been seriously threatened, and who felt they owed much to Father Solanus. Among these was Mrs. Jennie Oliver, of St. Clair Shores, a Detroit suburb. She came to him with cysts on both eyes, with swelling and infection that extended to her cheek bones. Lancing had brought no relief.

After talking with her, Father Solanus said, "I will give you a special blessing."

She knelt and he placed both hands over her eyes as he blessed her. As soon as he touched her eyes, Mrs. Oliver felt an absolute conviction that they would be better. Two days later, they were completely healed.

Mrs. John J. Regan relates that in 1929 her husband, in charge of the monotype department of the Detroit News, was working on a monotype machine when hot casting lead blew up in his face and burned his eyes. By the time she reached Harper Hospital, a Doctor Robb had operated. Her husband's head was covered with bandages. She rushed to the floor supervisor's desk, at which a nurse was seated. The nurse was writing and did not look up or answer her questions immediately. Before she got around to doing so, Mrs. Regan saw a form on the desk headed, "Regan." She picked it up and read—"John Regan, permanently blinded." She fainted.

When revived, she saw her brother-in-law looking down at her. She asked him to drive her at once to Father Solanus.

Before she had said a word, the friar, touched by her grief, sought to calm her.

"My child," he said gently, "what's the matter?"

"My husband has been in an accident. He is blind," Mrs. Regan answered.

He blessed her, and assured her.

"Worry not," he told her. "He will see. He has not lost his sight. I will have a Holy Mass offered tomorrow morning."

Mrs. Regan sought out Dr. Robb, and questioned him. He told her that he did not expect her husband to see again; that he would be fortunate if he were able to distinguish between light and dark.

Approximately two weeks later, the bandages were removed from her husband's eyes. He said to the doctor, "I see you."

Mrs. Regan said that the astounded Dr. Robb told surrounding nurses—"If ever I saw a miracle, this is one."

A few days later, Mr. Regan's vision was tested, and found to be excellent.

Another experience revolving about Father Solanus involved not only sight, but mental derangement, and—with no association intended—romance.

Mrs. Martin Wachinger of Harper Woods, a Detroit suburb, in 1936 was caring for a relative who, following brain surgery, was blind and mentally incapable. A doctor confided to Mrs. Wachinger that an optical nerve had been severed. She was informed that her relative would never see again, would never recover sanity, and probably wouldn't live much longer than six months. The woman had to be declared legally incompetent, and a guardian appointed.

When her charge was able to walk, Mrs. Wachinger started to bring her to the Capuchin chapel on Wednesday afternoons for the blessing of the sick, "given," Mrs. Wachinger emphasizes, "by Father Solanus."

"I continued to do this for six months," said Mrs. Wachinger. "Gradually, my relative's physical and mental health returned. Sight came back, too—first in one eye and then in the other. She recovered her mental powers, and her legal rights were restored.

"Though more than forty years old at this time, she took a secretarial course, then started to work at a Detroit manufacturing company as a secretary. While working there, she met a man who became her husband. They were married when she was forty-nine, and at the age of sixty-five [Mrs.. Wachinger related this experience in 1961] she was running her own home and has continued in good health."

This was one of many cures reported that came without personal contact with Father Solanus, but after attendance at the Wednesday services for the sick.

Nor did great distance and entire lack of contact with a sick person seemingly diminish the effectiveness of his prayers.

Traveling in Wisconsin, the Bettes previously mentioned visited a nineteen-year-old girl so seriously infected through eating diseased corn that she was unable to take even liquid nourishment. She had become a virtual skeleton.

When the Bettes returned to Detroit, Mrs. Bette told Father Solanus about the case. He gave Mrs. Bette a small bottle of water blessed in the name of St. Ignatius.

"Send this to the girl's mother," he said. "Ask her to administer it to her daughter by spoon. At first the girl will be unable to retain it, but after a while she will. I suggest, also, that you ask the girl's parents to make a novena to St. Fidelis* for the girl's recovery." "Why," said Mrs. Bette, in surprise, "that is the name of the parish to which the family belongs!"

She did not ask Father Solanus why he had suggested a novena to that particular saint. He merely said—"I know this girl is going to get better."

---

*The Saint was a Capuchin priest martyred in 1622, and called during his lifetime the "Advocate of the Poor."

The five doctors who had been in consultation on treatment of the girl's disease and who had declared they could do nothing to help her, said her recovery was a mystery to them.

Father Solanus' assurances of recovery were sometimes in direct conflict with professional opinion. Nevertheless, he sincerely respected the healing art and those who practiced it. One of those testifying to this is Mrs. Patrick Murphy of Ellsworth Avenue, Detroit. In 1933, a mysterious disease prevented her swallowing food. At Ford Hospital, examinations and tests failed to reveal a cause for her sickness. She was wasting away, and was finally anointed.

Mrs. Murphy was ready for death, but her husband decided to bring her to Father Solanus. He had to carry her into the monastery office, where she reclined in a chair and told the friar of the six small children who needed her.

He blessed her, and said, "Now, go home. You will feel better tomorrow morning. But return to the hospital for further examination, as your doctors advise."

The next morning, something of a foreign nature was evacuated from her body, and she began immediately to gain strength. Improvement was so rapid that she saw no reason for returning to the hospital. Later, while telling Father Solanus of her recovery, she mentioned that she had not gone back to the hospital. He reproved her, saying that she should have done so.

Father Solanus did penance continuously, and continuously prayed for the afflicted who came to him, but few realized how ardently and untiringly he prayed. His self-disciplining and sacrifices and humble supplications were part of his interior life, and little can be known about them. Here and there may be caught a glimpse of the fervor with which he besieged Divine Providence for others. Some idea of the

earnestness with which he prayed is conveyed in the story of
the recovery of Sister Mary Joseph.

In 1935, while Sister Mary Joseph was on duty in St.
Joseph Mercy Hospital in Detroit, a severe streptococcus infection on the right side of her throat sent her temperature to
105 degrees, and her neck became rigid. She began to slip into
a coma, with heavy choking spells. Her doctor informed
Sister Mary Philippa, a hospital supervisor, that the infection was spreading to the other side of the patient's throat.
He ordered a tray set up, preparatory to doing a quick tracheo-
tomy if needed.

At this point, Sister Mary Philippa telephoned to Father
Solanus, who said he would come at once. When he entered
the sick Sister's room he went directly to a stand at her bedside, seemingly oblivious of others. Taking a book from his
pocket, he started reading prayers, slowly and quietly, though
the Sister was in the midst of a choking spell. Almost immediately, Sister Mary Joseph's choking stopped.

While reading the passion and death of Christ from the
gospels, he several times blessed the Sister with a relic of the
True Cross, and placed it to her lips and throat.

Thus for two hours he read and prayed, while three
Sisters, kneeling, joined their prayers to his.

Then he closed the book, and said, "Sisters, it won't be
necessary for me to return. Sister Mary Joseph will soon recover and join her community."

As he was walking down the corridor toward the elevator,
accompanied by the hospital chauffeur who was to drive him
back to the monastery, a man who seemed well acquainted
stopped him. He asked Father Solanus to come to his wife's
room and give her his blessing.

After he had done so, the man walked with him to the

elevator. Calling him by his first name, Father Solanus counseled him to be resigned. His wife, he told him, would not recover.

Shocked, the husband exclaimed, "Father, her operation wasn't serious—why do you say this?"

In answer, the friar talked to him as the chauffeur stood by, urging him to place his wife's soul in the arms of God, and to pray for strength to accept his cross.

On the way to the monastery, he did not speak, and seemed to the driver to be praying.

When the driver returned to the hospital, he went at once to Sister Mary Philippa, and repeated the conversation between Father Solanus and the man who had stopped him in the corridor.

"The man's wife died," the sister informed him, "shortly after you left the hospital."

Sister Mary Philippa is one of the few who, telling of cures, was able to describe them in professional terms. In recounting attributed recoveries most of those quoted merely repeated in their own way what they had been told, or thought they had been told by physicians.

Most of the reported cures occurred before the "wonder" drugs of today had come into common use. Penicillin, for example, though discovered in 1929, was not employed generally till 1941; sulfanilamide, not till 1934; terramycin, 1950; neomycin, 1949.

Cures attributed to Father Solanus soon became so common that the friars of St. Bonaventure's came to expect them almost as everyday occurrences. Some were interested; some rather indifferent. A few were annoyed that the world's pressure on the Monastery office sometimes disturbed their semicontemplative lives. All wondered, of course, at the remarkable favors reported, but none seems to have discussed with

Father Solanus such reports in any depth or detail. In this, their attitude was formed by faith. If the reported cures and other favors were of God, then God would use the works to His purpose without anyone's assistance. The people spoke of Father Solanus as a saint. But the friars realized that if in its inscrutable designs Divine Wisdom desired their brother in religion to be recognized as of heroic sanctity, then there would be cures through intercession to him after his death.

No attempt was made to scientifically authenticate the reputed cures; to the friars, such a course would have been unthinkable. Inevitably, it would have put them in the position of trying to establish that God had favored one of their number with miraculous powers. Even when a Catholic Detroit hospital's staff, impressed by the inexplicable cure of a patient who had been blessed by Father Solanus, offered to supply the patient's medical history and x-ray plates, the Capuchins made no move to take advantage of the offer.*

Nevertheless, events they happened to witness in the Monastery office at times startled the friars—Father Marion amongst them. It was Father Marion who had been the local superior in 1936-39 when the hospital's offer of medical authentication had been made.

"One cure," says Father Marion, "remains vividly in my mind. It was the cure of a crippled child who had not walked in years. She was held in the lap of an adult, sitting at some distance from Father Solanus' desk.

"Father Solanus enrolled the child in the Seraphic Mass Association, and blessed her. Then he told her to walk over to

---

*If they had been disposed to set up a scientific bureau for authentication of cures, its establishment would have been impossible because of economic and other reasons. Outside of the world-famed Lourdes, medical experts could hardly have been found to devote the time necessary to such a task.

him. She immediately got to her feet, and walked, going straight to his desk. The youngster's parents were almost hysterical with joy."

To relate the story of Father Solanus' life without including such things would be impossible; they happened and they happened to him. Not that any of these occurrences is scientifically authenticated, as are the miracles of Lourdes; nor is there the slightest intention of so equating them. For some, perhaps for many of the cures credited to Father Solanus' intercession there were, quite possibly or even probably, natural causes—however unusual those causes might have seemed. Increases in medical knowledge would enable today's physicians to explain cures that baffled the medical profession forty or fifty years ago, or even more recently. Some of the claimed cures, however, seem to have no explanation, as do the event-substantiated predictions, and the answers to prayer that did not involve cures.

The attributed cures and other, non-medical, benefits that petitioners believed resulted from the power of the Mass and Father Solanus' intercession, certainly must be somewhere in the thousands. It is obvious that by far the greater number are unrecorded and will remain unknown. Of those of which there is some record, only a fraction are noted in this book.

Father Solanus' intense love of God, expressed through his love for and service to people, wholly governed his existence. His mission on earth, as he saw it, was to bring himself and others ever closer to the holiness of God. He experienced deep happiness when, in his eyes, God responded in immediately recognizable ways to the prayers of His children; this was faith-building evidence to him and to them of the good Lord's love.

Most of those who came to him expected no such evidence; they came for spiritual reasons alone. Many sought him simply because they were basically good people, drawn by his goodness, his warmth of selfless love, his spiritual light and joy and strength. It was this that chiefly attracted men, women, young adults, and children of all religions, races, and degrees of culture. It was this that bound to him individuals, and whole families; that won to him the most unlikely persons. Somehow, through knowing him, these people found their lives changed—sometimes radically—to their own astonishment and the wonder of their friends and relatives.

His spiritual influence was as gentle, as warming, as unhurried as sunlight—and frequently as powerful. The following chapter, relating the story of his quite casual, accidental, and incidental contacts with the members of one family, reveals his mild but potent influence at work.

Chapter 15

Father Solanus
Asks for a Ride

Though he entered few homes, even to visit the sick, Father Solanus was an intimate spiritual presence in many families. The majority of those who loved and reverenced him had never been recipients of physical cures. They thought of him mainly in terms of his evident goodness and its influence in their lives.

Of such was Edward Karber, one of three partners who owned and operated Shuman & Karber, Incorporated, in the 1920's and 30's a nationally known manufacturer of men's hats. Mr. Karber managed the firm's sales, making his headquarters in Detroit.

Tall, dark, impressive, he counted his friends by the score. Possessor of a fine bass voice, he made one of a celebrated quartet that hundreds of thousands of radio listeners enjoyed. He was a devoted family man, an excellent business man.

Outside of these spheres, all his activities centered about his Masonic affiliations. He loved the Masonic brotherhood; Masonry was to him both a religion and a cherished fraternity.

Children had not come to the Karbers, but in 1916 they inherited, as it were, two sons and two daughters. The children had been orphaned by the death of Mrs. Karber's sister, who had died six months after her husband.

Mr. Karber, a compassionate man, readily agreed to the children's adoption—on one condition. They were not to bear his name. The reason was the children's religion—they were Catholics. They could, he agreed, go to Catholic schools, but if they were to be brought up as Catholics, they could not be known as Karbers.

Though his wife was a Catholic, Mr. Karber had never permitted religious pictures, or crucifixes, or anything that might have been considered symbolic of Catholicity to be displayed in his home. Nor could he bring himself to drive his wife—and later, his wife and adopted children—to the front door of a Catholic church. A kindly man, he would drive them most of the way. But he would always stop a block short of the church. He observed a like precaution whenever he drove the children—whose family name was Ufford—to St. Brigid's school.

His attitude remained unyielding when the older Ufford girl, Catherine, informed her foster parents that she desired to join the Sisterhood of the Immaculate Heart of Mary. Her uncle firmly reminded her that, until she was twenty-one, he was her guardian.

"When you are twenty-one," he said, "you will be able to do as you please. But until then, I refuse my consent."

In 1930, having celebrated her twenty-first birthday, Catherine entered St. Mary's Convent at Monroe, Michigan, as a postulant. At this time, in accordance with custom, she was given a thorough physical check-up. The medical report showed her to be "exceptionally healthy."

To honor her uncle, Catherine upon completing her postulancy and entering the novitiate, took the name of Sister Edward Marie.

Her Uncle Ed's conversion was her most ardent desire. She was sure that faith in the Eucharistic Christ would bring him something of the peace and joy her own heart knew. To that end, she solemnly asked God to accept her as a sacrifice in whatever way His inscrutable wisdom might decree.

In September, 1932, she underwent a purely routine physical check-up. An x-ray picture revealed a half-dollar size spot on one lung. The young lady whose health but a few months before had been pronounced perfect, had become a victim of tuberculosis.

Mr. Karber of course knew nothing of his niece's sacrificial offer. But about the time she made her heroic act an unusual circumstance brought her uncle into contact with Father Solanus. Business being at an all time low, he had added to his duties for his own company the management of the Men's Store of the Crowley-Milner Company, a large Detroit department store. In this capacity, the man who wouldn't be seen driving his family to a Catholic church found it necessary to visit the Capuchin Monastery. His business there had to do with a Crowley-Milner contribution to the Capuchin Soup Kitchen.

At the Monastery, Mr. Karber met and conversed with Father Solanus. In the words of his younger niece, whose name at that time was Ann Ufford, here is what came about thereafter.

MY UNCLE—said Sister Mary Solanus, the former Ann Ufford—was irresistably attracted to Father Solanus, who treated people of all religions and of no religion as fellow children of God. We knew nothing, at the time, of the impression Father had made on him.

To our surprise, Father Solanus 'phoned my Uncle one day not long after their first meeting. Would it be convenient, he asked, for Uncle Ed to drive him to a hospital, where he wanted to visit a sick man? Incredibly—to us—Uncle Ed said he would. —Perhaps I should explain that at this time the Capuchins had no motor car transportation of their own; therefore, Father Solanus had to depend on friends.

From the first, however, Uncle Ed laid down conditions. First, Father Solanus must always sit in the back seat; there his Capuchin habit would be less conspicuous. Secondly, he must promise never to mention religion. Uncle Ed told Father he would talk politics with him, or economics, or sports, or anything—but NOT religion!

Uncle and Father Solanus started getting together in this way rather frequently. Sometimes, when Uncle Ed couldn't spare the time, I would drive Father—that is, when I was home from convent boarding school.

After graduation, I came home determined on only one thing. Never, never would I become a nun. Convent life, I informed everyone, was not for me.

Nevertheless, the possibility was all the while quietly present at the back of my mind. While driving Father Solanus, I would sometimes ask him whether he thought I should be a Sister.

He'd always reply, with a twinkle in his bright blue eyes that were so innocent and yet so wise—"Oh, you'll have to wait till you're converted first."

From this I gathered that if I were ever to become a Sister, my faith and my love for God must deepen and strengthen.

After my graduation in 1933, Uncle Ed took me into Crowley-Milner's to train for an executive position. In the meantime, he continued to drive Father Solanus at irregular intervals.

When Uncle had a press of work at the office, he and I occasionally ate dinner at a restaurant. One day in the fall of 1933, Uncle Ed—instead of driving us straight home—asked me to dine with him.

During dinner, Uncle Ed said—"Ann, I am about to become a Catholic."

I gasped and almost fell off my chair.

"How did that happen?" I finally managed to ask.

"Oh," he replied, with a big grin, "it's that damned Irishman, Solanus."

He said that he had been taking instructions in the Catholic Faith, that I was the first to know this, and that he wanted it kept secret. Particularly from my Aunt, who was a somewhat emotional and take-charge person. Uncle Ed didn't want anyone managing him at this spiritual crisis in his life.

"How," I wanted to know, "in view of your insistence that Father Solanus never mention religion, did you ever come around to taking the first step toward instructions."

"Father Solanus never brought up religion," he explained. "But I did. He just answered my questions."

On Christmas Eve, my uncle drove my aunt and me to midnight Mass at St. Bonaventure's. My aunt suspected nothing, though she must have thought it strange that Uncle Ed came into the church with us. Never before had he gone that far. The fact that Father Solanus was to celebrate the Mass may have struck her as the reason.

My uncle sat on the aisle side of the pew. At Communion time, he arose to let my aunt and me out. As we walked toward the Communion rail, he followed and knelt beside my aunt.

She was horrified—and panic stricken.

"Ed," she whispered desperately, "you go back! Ed, you can't do this! Ann, take your uncle back to his seat."

We both tried to tell her it was all right, that he had become a Catholic and was making his First Communion. She was too agitated to comprehend.

Then Father Solanus came down from the altar with the ciborium, holding the Host in the fingers of his right hand. As my Uncle was a First Communicant, he went directly to him, and gave him Communion.

Next he stopped in front of my aunt. She was still so upset that Father Solanus had to pause. He gently called her by name.

"Delia," he said, "Delia."

By that time she had begun to realize what had happened, and she received our Lord, tears coursing down her cheeks.

After this, my sister's health grew worse.

I still insisted that the thought of entering a convent was preposterous. But the idea came and went. It wouldn't go away—and once in a while I'd ask Father Solanus his opinion.

One day I said to him, very seriously—"Father, do you think I have a vocation? Do you think that's possible?"

This time he didn't put me off with the usual—"Oh, you'll have to be converted first."

Instead, he said—"Well, God does queer things."

"Well, what do *you* think about it?"

He answered my question with another.

"You don't *want* to be a Sister, do you?"

"No," I answered, "I don't want to be a Sister."

"Well, then, why are you thinking about it?"

"I'm thinking about it because I think that maybe that's what God wants me to be."

"And who," he asked, "is going to win out in this?"

"Well, for the present, I think it will be me—because I don't think I could make a go of it."

"Yes," he said, "He can die on the cross for you, but you can't give up the pleasures of life for Him."

Then he switched to some other subject.

After that, I talked to him several times about the possibility of a religious vocation. Each time he let me go just so far, then he'd turn our talk to something else.

His psychology was perfect—but I am certain that he prayed that I might realize my true calling in life.

I am sure, too, that his prayers were effective. In 1934, I entered the Immaculate Heart of Mary Order as a postulant. At my investiture I asked for and received the name, "Mary Solanus."

During my first year in the convent, Father Solanus came to see me and my sister. By that time, she had been suffering from tuberculosis two years. She was now isolated in the infirmary.

Sometime before, she had told me about her self-offering. But I had an idea that, because she had suffered this long, she would now be restored to health.

As I talked with Father Solanus, before we went in to see my sister, I asked his opinion of my thinking in the matter.

"Whatever God's will is, is best," he said. "We know that God wants only our good."

This was his compassionate way of refusing me the assurance I so desperately sought. The response was characteristic of him; his gentle way of predicting continued suffering, or death.

We went into my sister's room.

She asked Father quite directly whether he thought she would recover. And his answer was almost as direct—but not quite.

"God's will," he told her, "is that you suffer for seven years."

"You think I am never going to get well?"

"You are well. You are well in mind, and in soul. But you will suffer physically."

My sister was then twenty-five years old.

Her tuberculosis had been discovered in September, 1932.

She died in September, 1939. She had suffered seven years.

During those seven years, my Uncle had financed her stay in various sanitariums, and her treatment by eminent specialists. It was all useless.

From the day of Uncle Ed's conversion to the Catholic faith till his death several years later, he was a daily communicant.

He was killed in an automobile accident while driving to Chicago to address a businessmen's convention.

Sister Mary Solanus is Director of the nationally known Speech and Hearing Clinic of Marygrove College in Detroit, and of the college's Special Education Department.

The story of her family's close ties with Father Solanus is typical of his equally close and beneficent friendships for a multitude of families. Most of us have room in our hearts for only one or two such friendships; Father Solanus' love embraced all with, seemingly, the same deep and singular love. All had the strong conviction that he was, in a special way, their special friend. His capacity for selfless and compassionate interest in the lives and problems of others seems to have been boundless.

Yet he was not without his critics, both in and outside the Order.

Chapter 16

A Free Man

Incoming Capuchin novices had all heard of Father Solanus, and solemnly looked forward to their first glimpse of him. This came when, gathered in choir chapel, they saw a slim, ascetic figure enter and make the low bow with which Franciscans greet their Eucharistic Lord in the tabernacle.

Respectful curiosity sometimes gave way to supressed laughter as the sweeping obeisance sent pieces of hard candy popping out of Father Solanus' upper pocket and rolling across the floor. There were questioning side-glances, and one could almost hear the novices asking themselves—"What kind of a friar is this?—a between-meals candy muncher?"

Later, they would learn that he always kept candy about him for his young visitors.

They had more solid reason to be scandalized when, gathered in the choir loft to sing the eight o'clock high Mass in the public chapel, they watched as Father Solanus entered to celebrate the Mass. Generally the organist—a grizzled, choleric layman with Teutonic regard for order—bustled into the choir loft at the same time. Hurriedly taking his seat at the organ, he would throw two questions about the day's liturgy at the novices.

"Ist der a Gloria?" he would ask. "Ist der a Credo?"

Pointing to Father Solanus, a novice would answer— "Ask him."

"Ach, der wieder!"—"That man again!" the organist would moan, knowing from experience that Father Solanus might sing the Gloria, or the Credo, or both, when the Mass of the day included neither.

Of liturgical detail he could at times be unconsciously unobservant. But he was keenly observant of the number receiving Holy Communion. When communicants were few, he was saddened; when many, he was happy.

He generally offered to celebrate Mass at an hour his confreres found less convenient to them. He was a good community man, always helping where and when he could. Whenever he had a few spare minutes, he would help the Brothers on kitchen duty. While wiping dishes he would start the Brothers singing one of his favorite hymns. He loved music; loved to play a violin, and when asked, would give a "concert" at recreation. This he always introduced by playing the opening phrases to "Oh Mary, Sweet and Fair," a hymn to the Blessed Virgin.

Even musicians enjoyed his sweet desire to please, when they could only tolerate his renditions, for he was a violinist of considerable mediocrity. Yet his playing was always an act of love—sometimes of adoration. Particularly before Christmas Midnight Mass. Then he would steal into the balcony and stand at an opening looking down on the Christmas crib. There, thinking himself alone, he would play Christmas hymns for the Christchild in the manger.

At times he seemed to carry his cooperation with the community to unwise excess. His choir stall was next to a draughty window, and he was subject to colds. Yet he never suggested that his place in choir be changed, and it never was.

All his virtues as a community man could not, in the minds of some of the friars, balance the troubles he sometimes was accused of bringing on the friary. Now and then a Chancery official would telephone the Father Guardian, and ask embarrassing questions. These generally involved Father Solanus' alleged counseling of Catholics who had attempted marriage with divorced persons, or who were themselves divorced.

Was Father Solanus making new marriage laws for the Church? the Chancery official would ask. He would explain that Father Blank had reported that a couple had come to him, saying that he must be mistaken about not being able to marry them in the Church. They had seen Father Solanus, and, they declared, he had told them exactly the opposite.

The Chancery person would add that he realized, of course, that Father Solanus had been misinterpreted. But he would also add—"Will you please ask him to avoid creating such misunderstandings?"

Both Chancery officials and the Chapuchin superiors knew that it was impossible for any priest to counsel hundreds weekly without being misquoted by a few. People can give amazing twists to plainest words, particularly when the twist serves their heart's desire. In all good faith they can even infer a meaning diametrically opposite to that which the speaker intended. It would have been surprising had Father Solanus, who was not exactly a precisionist in language, and extremely compassionate, had not been a victim, ocassionally, of misinterpretation.

Understandably, such happenings disturbed his superiors. To some of the friars, also, the constant stream of visitors to Father Solanus, itself became a trial. As followers of St. Francis of Assisi they were devoted to the contemplative life as well as to an active apostolate. The outside world seemed to be invading the friary's innermost precincts; the walls were not proof against it. They afforded even less protection against long distance telephone calls for Father Solanus from

Chicago or San Francisco or other cities, sometimes at un-
earthly hours. The call was always from one who felt that his
life, or some relative's or friend's life, had reached a crisis—a
crisis Father Solanus alone could help him meet.

It would have been strange if some friars had not been
upset by such intrusions. After all, when one's day begins at
4:45 a.m.* a good night's sleep becomes man's most needed
friend.

Nor in some minds was this faculty-deprived priest an
intellectual ornament to the Order. People came from miles
away to hear him talk, and his fervor touched their hearts.
But his little "fervorinos" had no carefully developed theme,
illuminating exposition, compelling logic, or convincing
climax. His more intellectual confreres agreed with the
celebrated pulpit orator who, visiting the monastery, asked
to hear Father Solanus preach. It was a Wednesday afternoon,
and as usual, Father Solanus was in the public chapel, about
to talk at the services for the sick.

His simple fervor failed to impress the formidable preacher, professionally skilled in logic and the art of eloquence.

"Why," he commented, "he merely repeats the simplest
truths over and over again." It was in a similar vein, perhaps,
that early Christians may have questioned the preaching of
St. John the Apostle, who in every sermon would repeat—
"Little children, love one another."

Whatever they may have thought of his sermons, most of
the friars realized that in what one called "Father Solanus'
apostolate of friendship" he was literally a Godsend to thousands of people. And they realized that this apostolate was
made possible by that lack of priestly faculties which prevented his functioning in many of the ordinary duties of the priest-

---

*Now later, according to the needs of the particular friary.

hood. He brought peace and spiritual renewal to a multitude, but he was never merely sympathetic and comforting; he constantly sought to inspire his clients to a fuller spiritual life.

After listening to a visitor's story, he would give simple, sound advice. Then he would ask, perhaps—"When were you to the sacraments last?" If the answer was "Every month," he would suggest the petitioner try to go every week. If the reply was "Every week," he might suggest twice a week.

His method was simple. Always he would find some good in the visitor; then he would build on that. Whether he was Catholic, Protestant, or of no religious denomination, Father Solanus would try to make him aware of Christ's love.

To a person who professed no denominational belief, he might say—"Do you believe in God?

"Yes," would be the probable answer.

"And you believe in Jesus Christ His Son, don't you?"

"Yes."

"And so do I. And if we both strive to do what He wants us to do, we will be all right."

From there, having established something of a foundation for faith, he would go on to give spiritual counsel based on God's love for men.

With a non-too-ardent Catholic he might take a more direct course.

"Do you go to confession?" he would ask.

"Yes."

"How often?"

"Oh, it's about a year now."

"Don't you think you could go a little more often?"

"Well, I suppose so."

"Then why not try to go once a month?—Now, don't say —'I'll do so if you cure my boy' "—or whatever might have been the visitor's petition—"Leave that to God. You show God more love, and He'll help you and your boy."

Conferences with those seeking help sometimes took a turn that startled the petitioner.

In the early forties a supposedly practicing Catholic bachelor came to him at the suggestion and in company of a devout Catholic couple with whom he boarded. The young man desired prayers for his father.

"My father is a very good Catholic," he informed Father Solanus.

"Yes, he is—but you are not," came the friar's blunt response.

The man flushed, and the couple who had brought him objected.

"Why, Father!" the woman said in surprised annoyance. "We know Michael goes to Mass faithfully every Sunday."

The young bachelor began to perspire.

"He has not been going to Mass," Father Solanus said. "And he has not been to the Sacraments in the last five years."

At this, the young man admitted that Father Solanus' statements were facts. The bachelor promised that he would return to the sacraments at once.

As were nearly all conferences with Father Solanus, this meeting was in the monastery's combination office-waiting room. Other visitors sat along two walls, yet only the couple who sat at the desk heard Father Solanus disclose the young man's duplicity. For his voice was always so wispy that one had to be quite close to him to understand his words, and he never raised his voice. Occasionally, when the caller seemed greatly disturbed, or when it seemed that counseling would require much more time than usual, Father Solanus would take him to a room adjoining the office. This was done to avoid interruptions as well as to enable the visitors to feel more at ease.

He gave his time so freely that generally he was late for meals. Often, the Father Guardian would send a Brother for him, to take him to the refectory; otherwise, he might have missed the meal.

He interrupted his labors during 1936 for a visit to Father Maurice Joachim in Manhattan. The occasion was the observance of the latter's twenty-fifth year in the priesthood. He was now sixty-nine years old, and stationed at Our Lady of Sorrows on New York's lower east side.

Father Solanus doubtless welcomed the opportunity to talk with his brother, for Father Maurice had again entered upon a winter of discontent. Both Father Solanus and Father Edward had become aware of this a few months before.

He had sent a strong letter of complaint to Father Edward, then in the Philippines. In this he accused his Capuchin superiors of coldness toward an ingenious idea he had conceived for promoting piety. They evidently considered it somewhat fanciful and its exploitation outside the proper Capuchin field.

In response, Father Edward wrote him a psychological masterpiece—a rhyming letter in prose form in which he counseled patience, saying—

YOUR PLAN may prove to be sublime, if you'll await God's own good time: We cook up plans but turn them ill with too much flavoring of self-will. If this idea comes from Heaven, be patient: it will grow like leaven.

God condescends to use our powers if we don't spoil His plans by ours . . . We do God's work best when we obey, and crucify self-will each day.

We know this well. Then why refuse? Why balk at orders? Why abuse? The cause is clear—our vain self-will insists on acting, good or ill. We fear men won't appreciate the wisdom *we* might formulate.

We seek God's glory, not our own? Then let us honor Him alone. No matter if I preach or pray, or sweep the floors or mow the hay, the angels watch, to recompense my loving, prompt obedience . . .

Father Maurice Joachim seems to have been sufficiently contrite about his stubbornness to have shown this gently reproving verse to at least one of the friars.

Father Solanus assisted at the anniversary Mass and visited with Father Maurice Joachim ten days. He found that his brother had made a multitude of friends during his seven years in the same parishes in which he himself had been a worker several years before. But Father Maurice Joachim's popularity did not blind him to the fact that he was a disturbed and unhappy man.

Shortly after the jubilee, the Capuchin Provincial Chapter was held. In the list of transfers decided upon at the Chapter was Father Maurice Joachim's name. He was assigned to St. Anthony's Monastery in Marathon, Wisconsin.

Evidently, his superiors judged him no longer able to carry on pastoral work, and Father Solanus seems to have agreed. He expressed himself later as considering the transfer "providential."

At the time of his transfer, Father Maurice Joachim visited with Father Solanus a few days at St. Bonaventure's.

When he left for Marathon, he took a round-about way and stopped off for a week to renew acquaintances in the old Casey territory in northwestern Wisconsin.

Transfer to the Marathon seminary failed to cure Father Maurice Joachim's discontent. He began to contemplate certain moves, and wrote about them to Father Solanus.

In a letter written immediately after his arrival in Marathon, he also mentioned that the three Casey priest-brothers would probably be invited to take prominent parts in the seventy-fifth anniversary celebration of their old parish of St. Joseph in Prescott, Wisconsin. Prescott had been one of the towns he had stopped in on his trip to Marathon, and the parish priest there had urged him to participate.

At this time, neither he nor Father Solanus thought it probable that Father Edward would return from the Philippines for his own twenty-fifth anniversary as a priest, the following June. The Prescott pastor, however, had been in touch with him. Sometime later, he was able to inform Fathers Maurice Joachim and Solanus that he had invited Father Edward to be celebrant of the parish's jubilee Mass, and that he had accepted.

To take part in the celebration of both the parish jubilee and that of Father Edward, Father Solanus left St. Bonaventure's on August 11, 1937. Old friends met him at the Chicago depot and entertained him at dinner. In Milwaukee, he had time to visit the Capuchin houses and to talk with his fellow Capuchins working there.

The Capuchin rule having been changed, he wore, instead of his habit, a black suit with Roman collar. Because his beard concealed the collar, he wondered, as he boarded the Prescott-bound train in Milwaukee, whether his fellow passengers would not mistake him "for a venerable rabbi, or something else more or less ideal." Any question in passengers' minds was settled with dramatic suddenness when Father Maurice entered the train at New Lisbon. As the brothers greeted each other Father Maurice noticed twenty nuns in the car. He stopped, astonished, and in a clear voice called out—"Glory be to God! Look at all the Sisters!"

The three brothers were reunited when Father Solanus and Maurice met Father Edward in St. Paul. They stayed at the College of St. Thomas, where Father Edward had been rector in earlier days, and visited relatives and friends in the Twin Cities. Later, they went to Superior, where a host of friends greeted them. Here, on the Feast of the Assumption, a Sunday, Father Edward celebrated his silver jubilee Mass in their old parish church. Father Maurice served as deacon, and Father Solanus as subdeacon.

The following Sunday, August 22, they were to help celebrate the seventy-fifth anniversary Mass of St. Joseph's parish in Prescott. During the whole, glorious intervening week the brothers traveled about, meeting friends they had not seen in decades, and visiting scenes that recalled memories of younger days. They crossed the St. Croix River to Stillwater—where, Father Solanus recalled, he had learned to run the trolley cars. Then they recrossed the river to visit Burkhardt, New Richmond, and other towns and familiar countrysides.

The Saturday night before the Prescott jubilee, the two older brothers slept in the parish house at St. Mary's, Big River, in the Trimbelle territory. Here intimate, warming, small boy memories flooded back; these were surroundings hallowed by childhood wonder at a world whose colors were for the moment again as bright as those of sixty years before. Here they offered their Masses early Sunday morning before leaving for Prescott. And here Father Maurice in his sermon talked of earlier days with a tender nostalgia.

At the Jubilee Mass in Prescott, Father Solanus was the preacher. His sermon moved the people, crowded into the old church. But when, at Communion time, not a single parishoner came to the altar rail to receive his Eucharistic Lord, he was shocked and greatly saddened, but characteristically expressed himself as hoping that they had received at earlier Masses.

"But what a crowd"—he recalled years later—"was waiting outside! Old friends we'd not seen in fifty or sixty years! One Manion family [the patriarch of the Manions had been his father's bosom friend] after another, and outstanding among them all the still hale and hearty 93-year-old 'Bill' Betzill, who always drove the horses in threshing. His wife, 87, wanted to see us, and wept."

Father Edward remained in the United States several
months on behalf of the Philippine missions, and in April of
1938 he came to St. Bonaventure's where he visited with
Father Solanus for three weeks. This gave the brothers ample
opportunity to discuss Father Maurice and his unrealistic
dreams, and the difficulties they were creating. His discontent
and restlessness had become more pronounced. He had written fully to Father Solanus about his unhappiness, and his
hope of becoming re-established in the St. Paul archdiocese.
In December of 1938 Father Solanus wrote him at length,
reasoning with him, and hoping he was "trying, at least, to be
contented." No one at this time seems to have understood
that Father Maurice's restlessness was entirely incurable;
that is was symptomatic of physical breakdown. Not knowing this, Father Solanus suffered deeply with his brother,
prayed for him, and tried to console and counsel him.

"I offered my rosary this morning out in the crisp, moon-
light air," he writes, "for your intentions and your guidance.
I am confident that though, like the rest of us—poor children
of Eve—you have your difficulties, your temptations, your
falls even, and your occasional little triumphs, our dear Lord
will keep you from serious blunderings.

"But dear Father Maurice Joachim: I hardly know what
to say or to think of your proposition to write back to your
old diocese, to a prelate you've possibly never met, and who
had possibly never heard of Father Joachim. Naturally, you
would hope to be received with open arms—dreaming as you
do, of some cozy little place just smiling across the Wisconsin hills at you. Ah, dear Father Joachim! You may be sure,
such would be only dreaming. Your age and your experience
should rather exclude such dreams as belonging to the long
ago. This we might think, especially considering your years of
dreaming when and how you might get away from the world
to a monastery. Think of it, dear Father Joachim . . .

"Dear Brother, you've long since wanted to be a real missionary. So has your brother [himself]. When are we to start?
Where shall we turn to find a field wherein our zeal will be
profitable to souls and appreciated? Shall we go to the ends
of the earth, or shall we—convinced that Charity, rightly
ordered, begins at home—shall we begin right in our own
hearts?

"Ah, dear Maurice; if 'what we do for our own souls is
100 percent for the glory of God,' then surely we don't need
to go far for mission work. After all, we have just one soul—
and only one—that we must save.

"O, Brother Dear! Why are we all so stupid? We are all
alike in a way. We worry our heads and our hearts about
many things, like Martha, and almost totally undervalue the
invitation—most beautiful of all—to 'learn of Me because
I am meek and humble of heart.' Mary the Penitent understood it, and Jesus praised her for her appreciation . . . It seems
to me that, were we only to correspond to God's graces, con-
tinually being showered on every one of us, we would be able
to pass from being great sinners one day, to being great saints
the next.

"I am enclosing a copy of the rhyme-letter you gave to
Father Ex-Provincial two years ago. It will do you good to
read it over whenever you are inclined to play 'the blues'."

Several months later there came what Father Solanus
described to Father Edward as "the final break." Writing to
his younger brother, now serving in the Philippine missions,
he said—

FATHER MAURICE had been suffering for quite some time
from a fearful carbuncle on the back of his neck—enough to
set many a man crazy. The Marathon doctor found nothing
positively wrong with his mind. The superiors sent him,
therefore, to the hospital in Fond du Lac, Wisconsin, where

his case was believed to be hardening of the brain-arteries or something of that nature.

Not knowing him as he ought to be, the authorities of said hospital seemingly made little of his case, and let him go by himself. He 'phoned me from Chicago asking to speak to Father Provincial . . . I positively failed to recognize his voice.

The next Father Solanus heard from Father Maurice was when Father Charles E. Coughlin of Royal Oak, a Detroit suburb, telephoned him to say that Father Maurice was there. Father Maurice came on the telephone, and again Father Solanus could not recognize his voice. He consulted Father Clement Neubauer, the Provincial, who asked him to go to Father Coughlin's residence and see what might be done for Father Maurice. He did so, and found an ally in Father Coughlin. The latter appealed to Father Maurice to return to the monastery and talk with Father Clement. He complied. At the end of the interview, Father Maurice was no longer associated with the Capuchin Order. Evidently at his request, Father Clement gave him a "letter of exit," as Father Solanus alludes to it, and Father Maurice took a plane to Chicago. Father Solanus naturally assumed he was on his way to the St. Paul archdiocese, or would perhaps go to Seattle for a visit with the Casey clan before approaching the St. Paul authorities. "However," he tells Father Edward, "he had seemed so little his real self that my heart was heavy. All I could do was hope and pray on."

Thinking that Father Maurice was in the west, Father Solanus was intensely surprised, a few days after his brother had left Detroit, to receive a telegram from the rector of St. Mary's Seminary in Baltimore, saying that Father Maurice was there, and sick. He had said Mass with some difficulty, and then had insisted on going on to New York City.

A few day later, a telegram from the Father Guardian

of St. John the Baptist Monastery in New York informed
Father Solanus that his wandering brother was there. He forwarded the telegram to the Provincial, who was on a visitation to Capuchin houses in Wisconsin. By the time the latter
could wire instructions to the New York superiors to hospital-
ize Father Maurice, he could not be located. Heartsick at disappointment after disappointment in seeking relief, he had
turned his steps again toward Baltimore. There, on appeal to
the diocesan authorities, he was sent to a hospital for treatment of the carbuncle. After treatment, he wanted to return
to Chicago. The Baltimore chancery officials, however, were
convinced that he was in no condition to be traveling alone.
They sent him to Mt. Hope Sanitarium in Baltimore.

"I am convinced," Father Solanus informed Father Edward
at that time, "that he could hardly have landed in a better or
a more providential place. We at the monastery looked upon
his going thither as an answer to prayer and as evidence that
he was in God's guidance."

The St. Paul Archdiocese assumed financial responsibility
for his care.

In July, 1940, his superiors sent Father Solanus to Baltimore to visit Father Maurice. He remained two weeks. After
his return, he wrote him encouraging and consoling letters.

DO NOT BLAME poor Father Chaplain—he counsels Father
Maurice—if he seems unduly exacting. If he were not a con-
scientious priest he would hardly be in such an extremely
trying position.

Rather, continue to pray for him—and for all concerned
with the institution. They all have their difficulties and there
is none of them without defects. Who is to blame? . . . God
could have established His Church under supervision of
angels that have no faults or weaknesses. But who can doubt
that as it stands today, consisting of and under the supervision

of poor sinners—sucessors to the "poor Fisher-men of Gali-lee"—the Church is a more outstanding miracle than any other way?

Quite the same might be said of any charitable institution. So keep up your prayers and patience and resignation for God's blessed sake; and be sure He is watching all and will never be outdone in generosity. Nor will He ever fail in what He assures: "He that humbleth himself shall be exalted."

Fraternally in Corde Jesu . . .

As time went on, it would become plain to Father Solanus that Mt. Hope, insofar as his brother's further improvement was concerned, belied its name. When he became convinced that the sanitarium did not provide the therapy Father Maurice needed, he would, through a patient and passive insistence, bring about his release. Before that day, he would walk with his brother, in spirit and in grief, every step of the latter's via dolorosa.

So little time did visitors leave him that he had little left for relatives who came long distances. His sister-in-law, Mrs. Owen (Martha) Casey, whom he had never met, came to visit him in 1940. He showed her into the conference room, and talked with her briefly. Then he explained that some people were waiting to have a few words with him, and asked her to excuse him. Shortly after, a Brother came in and introduced himself; Father Solanus had evidently asked him to entertain his sister-in-law until he returned. Mrs. Casey asked the Brother if the office was ordinarily so crowded. He replied that it was. She inquired as to how many called on Father Solanus during the day. The Brother said that he had never kept count, and explained that many only came to receive the priest's blessing, which took but a moment. Including these, he estimated that the daily number of visitors to Father

Solanus was between one hundred and fifty and two hundred. Of these but a fraction came for consultation; possibly between forty and fifty.

After his last visitor had gone, Father Solanus had trays brought in—it was the supper hour—and visited with Mrs. Casey in one of the conference rooms. But between bites, he would be called to the office—another late-comer would be calling for a few words with him.

"Father," said his sister-in-law, a woman used to managing personnel, "why not have Brother tell them to wait until you have finished your lunch?"

"Oh, I don't like to keep anyone waiting," he answered. "I can always wait till the next meal, or get something from the kitchen. My personal needs are of no importance. God sends people for consolation, and I feel I must see everyone when they want to see me."

Then he brought out his violin, and soon had the dignified matron—whom he had never met before—singing hymns with him as they ate.

Young people were particularly attracted to him. One of these—now Father Gerald Walker—later entered the Capuchin Order and became its Provincial.

"When my parents had problems," Father Gerald said, "they'd run over to Father Solanus, taking me in the car with them. The help he gave them, and his unfailing compassion, made a lifetime impression. If one suffered headache, or from sickness, or was worried, Father Solanus seemed to feel that ache or sickness or worry with them. After talking with him you left with the feeling that you would be able to accept whatever God willed to send you.

"Upon me, as a boy and a youth, his love for God and for all men, his complete negation of self, undoubtedly acted through my unconscious as well as my conscious perception. I know its effect was deep and powerful, for it was, most certainly, the reason why, when I was considering a religious vocation, I applied for admission into the Capuchin Order.

"He seemed to be unaware of the effectiveness of his example and presence and of his immense popularity. There was never a sign that he took the slightest satisfaction in being sought after, or in what seemed to be the direct effectiveness of his prayers and blessings. Even when, after enrolling a person in the Seraphic Mass Association, and blessing him, he would see him walk away cured, his reaction was that of an objective spectator. Tears would course down his face, as he extolled God's love and mercy and the power of the Mass."

His day began at 4:45 a.m. and continued for eighteen or nineteen hours. Nine to ten hours of that time were his "working hours," during which he sat at his desk, endlessly counseling all who came to him.

Certainly the lightest and most enjoyable part of his day was the four hours given to prayer and meditation and worship. After morning prayers and contemplation came Prime and Tierce, chanted at 6 o'clock in the choir chapel. The community Mass was at 6:15. Then he celebrated his own Mass and went to breakfast. The bells for Sext and None called him to chapel again before 12 o'clock dinner. From 5:30 to 6 p.m. there were Vespers and Matins and night prayers came in the evening.

These chapel devotions, with their ancient, noble psalms of praise and adoration, must have rested and calmed and strengthened his spirit. He needed such periods of peace and praise. For nothing saps nervous energy as quickly and completely as continuous counseling of the troubled, the unhappy, the emotional.

His confreres wondered at the way he stood up under the demands made upon him; his frail appearance was a cause of continuous concern.

He was, indeed, often weary, but the hundreds who sought him out each week detected no hint of it in his face or manner. Not even in his later years, when he was to write to Brother Leo, his fellow porter, that at times he found daily counseling almost unbearably monotonous.

Doubtless much of the capacity to be so unfailingly patient and kind came to him through his hours of prayer before the Blessed Sacrament. Often, after his long day, he would go to the choir chapel. There he would pray until exhaustion overcame him. Sometimes Brother Sacristan, entering the chapel a little before 5 o'clock in the morning to prepare for services, would in the darkness stumble over his prone body as he lay before the tabernacle. Overcome by weariness, he had laid down "for a moment" and fallen asleep.

Once the sacristan remarked—"That's a pretty hard bed you were sleeping on, Father."

And Father Solanus, pulling himself to his feet and with a smile breaking on his face answered—"Well, it's not so bad. I was sleeping on the soft side of the boards."

These vigils were extras, probably devoted to prayer for those he was counseling. His eighteen hour day was a matter of course.

Frequently, he slept considerably less than five hours in the twenty-four.

"I get very little sleep myself," he once told a visitor who complained of insomnia. "It's amazing how little sleep some people need to get along."

Many well-to-do people sought to express their appreciation of him in tangible ways. One man wanted to pay his expenses on a tour of Europe—an offer that Father Solanus noted, obviously with astonishment, in one of his notebooks. Occasionally a devoted friend did find some acceptable means of showing his regard. In 1926, the Father Guardian, Father Capistran, desired to add two wings to the public chapel.

Father Solanus spoke to a wealthy friend, and the money was forthcoming. At that time, he had been in Detroit but two years, yet a small army of admirers were eager to help him in any possible way.

It was fitting that Father Solanus should have been the one to produce the money for the chapel's enlargement; his overcrowded Wednesday afternoon services had helped to make the addition necessary. The crowds at these services created problems. Two years after the wings had been added, a priest had to be assigned to act, as the friary's day-to-day chronicle phrases it, as "traffic cop."

Thus he labored through the days and prayed through the nights, doing penance for "Solanus, a sinner"—as he sometimes signed his correspondence—and for his fellowmen.

Not one of the hundreds who sat at his desk and poured out his miseries suspected that this simple friar, so deeply absorbed in his trials and sorrows, was close to exhaustion with the bearing of his brothers' burdens. He never betrayed it, not even when those whose complaints against life and their fellows were petty, selfish, and drearily like those voiced by scores who preceded them. They were God's children, and for that he loved them, and tried to bring them around to being a little more generous with their Creator and with others.

Long since, he had come to know the Christ-taught truth that pure love of God and one's fellowmen as children of God are in the final event all that matter. Living this truth ardently and continuously had made him, spiritually, a free man— free from slavery to passions, from self-seeking, from self-indulgence, from self-pity—free to serve wholly both God and man.

Chapter 17

Friar-about-Town—
and Countryside

The Detroit to which Father Solanus was transferred in 1924 was fast-growing, fast-stepping. As in all boom towns and boom times, its people seemed always in a hurry. It was as if they were trying to keep pace with the space-conquering automobiles and motor trucks whose manufacture centered in their city.

These people were members of a pluralistic society at its most pluralistic—a vast conglomeration of all religions, races, colors. They had come from all over North America and Europe and the Near East, and they were still coming. They came to earn twice, thrice, ten times as much money as ever they had earned before. They mortgaged their future to buy cars, homes, furnishings, clothes—and the ever-rising "securities" of the stock market.

In the autumn of 1929 the fascinating game of money-making was called on account of darkness—the panic-striking darkness of Black Friday, October 29th. The financial collapse brought ruin and hardship both to the hot-eyed profit-seekers, and to less materialistic people who had preferred to seek peace of mind and soul. Many of the latter had habitually cultivated this peace in the Capuchin chapel on Mt. Elliott Avenue. Now they found themselves joined by a host of others praying for help in a suddenly chaotic, frightening world. A world in which the delightful dream of two chickens in every pot and two cars in every garage had given way to the hard, bitter reality of closed factories and closed banks.

The Capuchin chapel of St. Bonaventure was a home-like, friendly place. In its confessionals you could consult a brown-robed priest at any hour throughout the day. And in the Monastery office next door, there was always the brotherly Father Solanus. Always, when you talked with him, it was as if he had been waiting to talk with you, so deeply was he interested in all you had to say.

He was a good neighbor you could depend upon to bind up your wounds of the spirit and help restore your weakened hope and confidence. Or, if you had strayed off the straight road and had got yourself lost, he'd help you find your way back by assuring you that God was waiting for you with His infinite love. No matter how greatly you might blame yourself, he would never blame you. But if you had been leading a foolish life you realized it more keenly than ever before after talking with him. And from that bare room in which he sat you'd go out again with head up, and a lighter step. Sometimes Brother Francis would ask those who had come solely for Father Solanus' blessing to kneel in a group, and Father would bless them, not using Latin, but American words they could understand. Somehow, that sign of the cross he made over them seemed to lighten the cross each one carried.

At times he would be faced with problems demanding for their solution deep wisdom and theological insight. In handling such problems, he astonished his confreres. Father Blaise, a fellow Capuchin who acted as his secretary when Father Solanus was quite old, noted this in the latter's correspondence.

"His spelling was atrocious," said Father Blaise, "but his thoughts and ideas always hit the problem exactly. His answers would give you, too, a new sense of the depth of his love.

"Most of his answers were short, but his words penetrated to the heart of the matter. Many of the problems presented immense theological difficulties—so difficult, that I was happy he did not ask me to answer the letters detailing them. But he solved them with great theological insight and apparently with little effort."

On the evening of January 25, 1929, as Father Solanus was about to lock the Monastery doors for the night, a Western Union messenger came up the steps with a telegram. It was addressed to him. He opened it to read that his brothers John and Thomas had been killed in a motor car accident. The two lawyers had been driving from Tacoma to their homes in Seattle after trying a lawsuit.

This personal tragedy introduced a year, and a decade, during which more stricken people than ever were to seek Father Solanus' counsel. The stock market collapse made thousands suddenly poor. As economic paralysis set in, many poorer people—and not a few who had been well off—found themselves virtually paupers, with no place to turn for the next month's rent, or the next day's food.

The Capuchins, too, were poor, and because of their status as mendicants, they had to depend largely on the charity of others for support. Yet, like all Franciscans down through the centuries, they fed any who came to their door. And so the penniless came to St. Bonaventure's, and Brother Francis or Father Solanus would show them into the office and give them whatever food the friars themselves were having that day.

As the industrial wheels slowed, more hungry men came to the monastery. Soon Father Solanus and Brother Francis found themselves operating an almost constant food supply service between kitchen and front office. All who came ate at the Monastery; some also carried food away with them for their families.

A more adequate method of dispensing food was needed. Father Solanus and Brother Francis discussed new ways and means with Father Capistran Claude, the Guardian, and Father Herman, who was director of the Third Order of St. Francis.

In solving this problem, Father Herman became key man. The Third Order included hundreds of truly charitable men and women, and Father Herman appealed to them. They went to work. In their Third Order Hall, they established a restaurant known as the "Soup Kitchen," though its chief dish was a big bowl of hearty hot meat stew that could keep a man going all day long. At the depression's depth in the early thirties, Third Order members under Father Herman's direction were feeding more than a thousand men a day. They also carried food to many homes.

The Soup Kitchen, later supported by people of all religions through the Capuchin Charity Guild, became a large and permanent activity. Thirty-five years later, it was still feeding scores of old, ailing and homeless men each day.

Religion was never mixed with the Soup Kitchen's stew. Only one change having to do with religious practice was made: The friars obtained from the Chancery, dispensation of Catholic Soup Kitchen diners from Friday abstinence. On a Friday the serving friars could always spot the Catholics— they were the ones who carefully spooned meat from their stew, placing it beside the bowl on the plate. Then a Capuchin would tell them, "Eat that meat—we're dispensed here, just like soldiers in war time." They realized that these underfed men needed the protein.

They also realized that many of their guests were bitter and angry men, who might mistake any forced attempt at friendliness for condescension. So only those Capuchins went to the Soup Kitchen who were helping in the work—excepting Father Solanus. Frequently, he would join the long line of men waiting for tables in the Third Order Hall, and eat with them, and the men accepted him as one of themselves. Sometimes he would rise from his place at a table and talk to them as one warm friend to another, hoping to build their confidence that somehow, someday, they would see better times.

To help solve the constant question of food supply for the Soup Kitchen, the Capuchins went "questing" for vegetables and meat and flour and fruits. Whenever he could, Father Solanus would mount a truck and go along with the layman or Capuchin driver. They would be bound for farms whose proprietors might donate needed potatoes, cabbage, carrots, or other vegetables.

One October day in 1934, Father Solanus accompanied a man named Ray Garland on a begging trip in the vicinity of Ruth, a little town in the Michigan "thumb," about a hundred miles north of Detroit. Mr. Garland, a real estate man and father of a large family, was one of the friar's innumerable friends. Mr. Garland had rented a truck, and in this the two set off in the early morning, huddled in their overcoats. The thermometer was registering such an uncomfortable low, the layman envied Father Solanus his ample, wind-blown but protecting beard.

When they reached their questing territory, Mr. Garland drove into a rectory driveway. The pastor was a friend of his, and the three visited briefly. As they were about to leave, the priest produced a bottle of brandy. Pouring two glasses, he said—"This will confirm you against pneumonia"—using the word in Latin sense of *confirmare*, "to make firm." Father Solanus, who hadn't tasted hard liquor in years, joined his friend Garland in gratefully drinking down the warming liquor.

The questing was highly successful. As darkness fell, the two men were Detroit-bound, their truck loaded.

The cold increased. Father Solanus, regarding his shivering companion, suggested that they again stop at the rectory. The house was dark, but in answer to the doorbell the pastor opened an upstairs window.

"Who's there?" he called down.

"We've come for a second confirmation," answered Father Solanus.

Soon, fortified with another pneumonia preventive, they resumed their homeward journey.

One of their gifts was a mammoth rooster, a veritable king of the barnyard, now miserably cramped in a too-small chicken crate. Father Solanus solicitiously removed it. To protect it from the cold, he held it under his arm. As they drove into the Monastery yard just before 2 a.m., chanticleer suddenly extended his neck in a silence-shattering cock-a-doodle-doo.

"Here, here, calm down, calm down," pleaded Father Solanus, gently patting the bird. "You'll wake the whole house. Calm down."

The rooster subsided, and Father Solanus found it a secure roosting place in a shed. Then he helped Mr. Garland with the unloading. He would not allow him to depart until he had served him hot coffee and toast. He himself couldn't partake; offering a morning Mass then required fasting from midnight.

To one farm, about forty miles northeast of Detroit, Father Solanus went questing more than once. Its owner, Earl J. Egan, had suffered from what he believed was stomach cancer.

One of Mr. Egan's eight children became Sister Mary Cecilia of the Sisters of Charity. She relates that when eleven years old she accidently overheard her father, in the next room, say to her eighteen-year-old brother—"I don't have much longer to live, Mart. You take care of your mother and your brother and sisters; you are the oldest." For several weeks Mr. Egan had been unable to retain solid food.

A few days later, he had a friend drive him to Detroit to see Father Solanus, about whom a neighbor had told him. He was far too feeble to drive himself.

The friar assured him he would get well and strong again, and over several weeks he made a complete recovery.

On his first visit to the Egan farm Father Solanus was introduced to the family—all, that is, excepting Dorothy, the future Sister Mary Cecilia. Her name wasn't mentioned because her mother knew that Dorothy had just come in from play, was barefoot and disheveled, and would be embarrassed.

Seeming to sense that someone was missing, Father Solanus asked whether all the children were present. At her mother's urging, Dorothy then came down the stairs. The friar made the barefoot girl feel perfectly at ease, and she looked upon him as a great friend from then on. It was natural, then, that he should come to mind when at the age of seventeen she suffered constant racking pains in her side. She asked her mother to drive her to the Monastery, though during the journey the pains were almost unbearable.

After she and her mother had talked with him, he asked Dorothy to kneel, blessed her, and gave her a little slap, saying—"Go into the chapel and pray, and let's see what the good Lord wants." She suffered no more pains from that time.

In later conversations with her, Father Solanus predicted that she would enter a religious order.

Mr. Egan attributed his recovery to Father Solanus, and was eager to contribute what he could to Capuchin charities. Besides, he regarded the friar as a fellow farmer. Father Solanus had demonstrated his farming background when a truck on which he was a passenger drove into the Egan farmyard as

Mr. Egan and a helper were sacking potatoes. Father Solanus, then about sixty-two, jumped lightly down from the truck seat.

"Let me help you," he said. "You know, I was raised on a farm."

The seemingly frail friar surprised the two farmers by expertly tying the bags with a twist and a pull of the cord, then tossing them into the truck. Mr. Egan noted that he hadn't forgotten the knack of lifting loads, and that he was wiry and much stronger than he looked.

Father Solanus had especially ready sympathy for young couples. He was particularly interested in the Ryans when they came to him in 1932. Handsome Daniel Ryan had been a dispatch runner for the Irish patriots when they were fighting the Black and Tans. Clare Ryan, his young bride, was very sick. Intense stomach pains had tortured her for months; she was unable to retain solid food. Skeleton thin, she was taken to Harper Hospital, and there tested and x-rayed over a six-week period. Nine physicians conferred, but failed to agree on a diagnosis. Six advised an exploratory operation; two were against it. Her personal doctor was neutral, and her sister, a trained nurse, opposed it. The disagreements left Mrs. Ryan uncertain, and she therefore refused an operation. After consulting another doctor, she later entered Ford Hospital for further tests. Various diets failed to improve her condition, and the Ford doctors were unable to determine the cause of her sickness.

It was about this time that her husband heard of Father Solanus. He drove Mrs. Ryan to the Monastery, stopping the car about every half-mile to help her, because she was doubled up with pain and retching.

When they arrived at the monastery, Father Solanus brought Mrs. Ryan into a small room, left her for a few minutes, then returned with a relic of the True Cross, with which he blessed her.

"After that," said Mrs. Ryan, "the pain and retching stopped. They never returned and I got well and strong."

Several years later Mrs. Ryan was stricken with acute arthritis, for which she was hospitalized several weeks. She was so crippled that she had to be carried to a car to be driven to Father Solanus. He came to the curb, in front of the monastery, his stole around his neck, and blessed her with the True Cross relic. After the blessing she slowly recovered. The Ryans continued devoted to him, and after his death to his memory.

It is difficult for generations which did not experience the great depression of the 1930's to imagine the helplessness and hopelessness and desperation of millions who lived through that economic blight. It was experienced at its worst in Detroit.

During those years, Father Solanus brought new hope to a multitude. Representative of his ministrations is an experience of the Nardi family, which during the thirties encountered troubles typical of the period. Mr. Nardi, just before the financial collapse which brought on the depression, had purchased a house and grocery at St. Paul and Townsend Avenues in Detroit. As the depression developed, income shrank, and payments were missed, and both store and home were about to be lost.

Mrs. Nardi prayed and somehow conceived the idea of having the home blessed. Inasmuch as her pastor was too busy she obtained his permission to have Father Solanus do so. Accompanied by another friar, he went through the house, blessing each room. When he came to a closed door, Mrs. Nardi explained that her husband was in the room, sick. Father Solanus entered, and blessed him.

After Father Solanus left, Mr. Nardi's 104 degree fever

left him; he described himself as "feeling real good." The next morning he felt as if he'd not been sick at all. Moreover, he was soon able to borrow money to meet the property payments. Even the man from whom he was buying the property surprised him by loaning him $300.

With other priests of the monastery, Father Solanus went to various parishes, particularly on weekends, on what were known as "help outs." He would offer one of the Sunday morning Masses, and preach with his usual fervor on God's love for men. After Mass, it was common for the rectory to receive inquiries; nearly always someone, and sometimes several, wanted to know the name of the friar who had spoken at the Mass.

To Detroiters, he was "Father Capuchin." He frequently represented his Order at Requiem Masses for distinguished citizens. From time to time, also, he was asked to deliver the commencement address at academies and high schools. When he attended a crowded meeting of the National Union for Social Justice at Detroit's huge Olympia Stadium in April of 1935, he was recognized as he passed through the great auditorium, and received a tremendous ovation.

His fellow Capuchins saw nothing incongruous in this public acclaim of the simplex priest and friary porter. Of the seven Capuchins who had been canonized and of the eleven who had been beatified, some had been brilliant intellects; others were as ungifted as St. Conrad of Parzham, Germany. Forty-two years of the last century Brother Conrad, too, had been a porter.

Three weeks after his ovation at Olympia Stadium, Father Solanus sang the friary's High Mass, as seemed fitting, in honor of St. Conrad. The following day, he offered still another Mass in honor of the sainted porter.

His confreres saw certain similarities between Brother Conrad and Father Solanus. Both were deeply devoted to the presence of Christ in the Holy Eucharist, and to His mother. Both were enormously patient and utterly selfless in the performance of their duties. Both were revered by the scores who came each day for their counsel.

Father Solanus, although deceptively casual in manner, drove himself to the limit. This caused the friars concern, and they sometimes resorted to expedients in attempts to safeguard his health. Late one afternoon, for example, a layman came to drive him to a parish church where he was to assist at evening devotions. A Capuchin Brother took the layman aside and suggested that inasmuch as there was ample time, he stop off at his home, and there invite Father Solanus to sit down to a meal.

"He's been fasting all day as a penance for some favor he wants very much for someone, and he needs food," explained the Brother. "At table he pretends to be eating, but I have been watching him, and he has eaten very little today. If you offer him a meal, I think he'll eat it out of politeness."

Alerted by telephone, the layman's wife had ready a hearty supper. Father Solanus, too courteous to refuse his hostess' cooking, ate, and was strengthened for the evening's assignment.

He contiued to go on food questing ventures into the country surrounding Detroit, experiences which must have brought back to him memories of his youth on the Casey farms. A typical load collected for the Soup Kitchen on such a trip would include upwards of fifty bushels of potatoes, thirty bags of beans, and quantities of various other vegetables.

All through the 1930's, begging journeys into the countrysides went on. They ceased only toward the end of the bitter decade, when good times returned—ironically, through war material demands—and more people could afford to contribute money to the Capuchin charity.

World War II came, and the seventy-year-old friar read of men, women and children degraded, tortured and destroyed by their fellowmen. Later, the war brought the Bomb, and he wondered how the world could be saved from men so armed for wholesale destruction.

"When shall we be delivered," he asked, "or how free ourselves from the dreadful nightmare of these decades? What is to be done? For what nation is there now that is not in fear of an international war of such dimensions as was never before dreamed of?

"And yet, if men would only stop to think, and to learn the lesson of history, they would know we get nowhere without God. If nations and governments and all humanity would only listen to reason and faith and know God—what a different look society would at once put on! What hope—what faith—what charity would be man's life here on God's footstool!—this privileged vestibule to a happy eternity for appreciative, grateful souls.

"But alas, for our want of faith, and consequently for our lack of appreciation of the wide difference between physical and spiritual values and between the momentary and the eternal. Well, therefore, do the words of Jeremiah the Prophet apply to any people or power or individual with little or no such appreciation: 'With desolation is all the world made desolate, because none thinketh in his heart'.

"Like a vast school of supposed-to-be philosophers, that elaborate their days and go into eternity blowing bubbles, so is that generation that fails to foster gratitude to God."

Man's ingratitude towards his Creator never ceased to puzzle and sadden him. He himself marveled endlessly at God's beauty and wisdom and care for men as seen in His creation.

Sitting in the monastery garden during a recreation period, he would exclaim over the delicate design and color-

ing and construction of a flower, a bee, a bird or a leaf. He
was in love with all nature as the work of the Almighty. He
saw the world as given to man to be cultivated as a garden,
and cherished as the place of preparation for man's eternal
life. And his heart was heavy as he saw man's hatred and
greed threatening to turn it into a wasteland. He himself
loved all men—was the firm friend of people of all races and
faiths, including Jewish rabbis and ministers of various Protestant denominations. His practical ecumenism always expressed itself simply, and sometimes in unconventional ways.

One evening around 9:30 or 10 o'clock Father Ralph
Diederichs returned to the friary, dark excepting for a lamp
at Father Solanus' desk. The latter was not, as was his custom
at this hour, looking over his daily mail. Instead, he was
playing his violin, and he was evidently playing to someone
listening on the telephone, for the receiver was off.

Father Ralph paused for one astonished look, and passed
on. The following morning he said to Father Solanus—"I
beheld a new concept in the staging of concerts last night."

Father Solanus explained that he was playing into the
telephone at the request of a Methodist minister. The minister, sick and bedridden, had asked his wife to call Father
Solanus and request him to play a hymn or two for him on
his violin.

Only those who appreciated his simplicity and childlike
desire to please valued his violin renditions; the minister
must have known and loved him well. Perhaps the clergyman
appreciated the fact that Father Solanus' musical attempts
sprang out of an impelling desire to express the spiritual joy
that possessed and sustained him even when his crosses were
heaviest. One of these crosses, whose weight he felt for many
years, was the sickness and misadventures of his brother,
Father Maurice.

Chapter 18

Suddenly, an Eastern Address

When Father Solanus heard that his brother Maurice had become chronically dissatisfied with life in the Capuchin Order, he began to pray for him in a manner quite individual to Father Solanus. Others might think his form of praying unusual, but he was used to it, having prayed in this way for many years. The manner of his praying was this: He knelt with a devotional book before him, reading and meditating. The book might be the Bible, or some such work as the autobiography of St. Theresa of the Child Jesus. Often it was one of four volumes titled *The Mystical City of God,* written by a Spanish nun in the seventeenth century.

The work's stilted and archaic stlye did not seem to lessen Father Solanus' attachment to it. Father Cuthbert Gumbinger, a Capuchin who was later Archbishop of Ismir, Turkey, wrote: "He would spend hours at a time in chapel reading and meditating on Mother Agreda's work—and always on his knees! I have often watched him on such occasions. At times, he seemed entirely lost to the world. Gazing at the Tabernacle, with tears in his eyes, he would kneel motionless for long stretches of time . . .

"If anyone discovered a new beauty in the work, or pointed up something that he had not sufficiently noticed, he rejoiced and would literally weep for joy when told of it. To those who opposed this work, he was courteous, but would not argue. He simply pitied and prayed for them."*

Many theologians have been highly critical of *The Mystical City*. They would endorse the opinion expressed by Hilda Graef in *Devotion to Mary*: "a mixture of the apocryphal legends and of Mary d'Agreda's own unbridled fancies." Nevertheless, Father Solanus, along with many others, found that reading the work was spiritually helpful—and to him that was doubtless its chief recommendation. In the early 30's, the publisher presented him with a large carton of four-volume sets. Father Solanus gave these to whomever he especially desired to read them.

When his supply was exhausted, he turned to his friend Ray Garland, and asked him to write to the publisher and have himself appointed *The Mystical City's* Michigan representative. Mr. Garland did so, and for fourteen years devoted his spare time to promoting the books. His widow—he died in 1953—reports that he sold an average of about two hundred and fifteen sets a year over this period, and that he made no monetary profit. Mrs. Garland says that he sent the publisher checks for the full amounts taken in. The fact seems to be that the book promotion was in no way a commercial endeavor, and that the publisher, Louis W. Bernicken, did not profit from the books.

To Father Solanus' amazement, his own whole-hearted advocacy of Mary of Agreda's work eventually brought embarrassment to his superiors. This resulted from the lack of understanding of a few who came to him seeking help in their troubles. To some petitioners he would suggest that they promise to read *The Mystical City*—or at least one volume of it—and go to Holy Communion often. Occasionally one

---

*From an article by Father Cuthbert titled "Father Solanus Casey, Capuchin Agreda Devotee," *The Age of Mary*, Jan.-Feb. 1958.

of these felt, after pricing the books, that he could not afford the set—though originally it was only ten dollars, and later twelve. It may have been that some who complained were extremely poor. It may have been also that the price—which was actually reasonable—may have seemed exhorbitant to those unused to buying books at all.

Had the disaffected brought their complaints to Father Solanus, he would have advised them to do some other good work to show God gratitude for the favor received. Instead, they grumbled to others, and word of their discontent reached the Archdiocesan Chancery Office. Perhaps only one, or two, complaints came to the Chancery's notice—but that would have been sufficient. For in such matters Chancery officials act quickly and decisively.

The Father Guardian at St. Bonaventure's in 1936-39 and again in 1942-45, was Father Marion Roessler, and it was he who had to answer the questions of the Chancery authorities. It was he who had to inform Father Solanus, whom he loved and revered, that some of those he had tried to help, were reproaching him for urging them to possess a devotional work whose reading he believed would promote their spiritual growth. He had to warn him, also, that he must be extremely cautious that nothing he might say lead anyone to feel that he was obligated to purchase *The Mystical City.*

Poor Father Solanus! His innocent enthusiasm for the writings of Mary of Agreda, and the obtuseness of a few— perhaps only two or three—had betrayed him. They were his friends in Christ, and he wanted them to learn from *The Mystical City* how to come closer to his and their "dear Lord." He wanted them to learn—to quote typical passages from the work—"how to resign themselves entirely into the hands of their Creator." To realize that "man's sole duty is to live in obedience to and in the love of God." To learn to "cast them-

selves securely into the arms of the provident God and Lord."
—He had thought only to have them absorb these and other inspirational urgings of Mary of Agreda.

By this time, another complication had developed. A number of people caught fire from Ray Garland's glowing ardor for Mary of Agreda and *The Mystical City* at meetings Mr. Garland called or at which he was a speaker. These were held in various residences.

After a while it seemed apparent to some clerical observers that a Mary of Agreda cult, or formal devotion, was being established. Mimeographed prayers for group devotions in her honor appeared. One pastor found that without his permission the devotees had made his Church their headquarters.

The friends of Mary of Agreda, who were offering earnest prayers for her beatification, were mystified as to why her cause for sainthood had come to a halt three hundred years before and had not advanced since. Perhaps many were unacquainted with the fact that the Vatican's Congregation of Rites had long since found *The Mystical City's* authenticity highly questionable.

While the Capuchin superiors realized that Mary of Agreda's twentieth century partisans were pious and well-meaning, they were strongly adverse to Mr. Garland using Father Solanus' name and prestige in the movement's promotion. They therefore requested him to cease visiting the Monastery—which meant, visiting Father Solanus. To this he agreed. But they had reckoned without considering the telephone's penetrating power. Sometimes Mr. Garland, in the midst of a Mary of Agreda meeting, would call Father Solanus and ask him his blessing, over the telephone, of those present, and Father Solanus always complied.

So the superiors' concern continued, for they thought that —to quote Father Marion—Mr. Garland was, however innocently, "misusing Catholic practices." "Father Solanus never participated in this," adds Father Marion. "He was just too simple and trusting to be able to stop the abuse."

This situation developed over a period in which the Capuchins' superiors were becoming increasingly solicitous about Father Solanus' health. Early in the 1940's, varicose veins in the lower part of his legs began to cause recurrent torture. Theodore J. Becker, former prefect of the Detroit Capuchin Third Order Fraternity, frequently served Father Solanus' Masses, generally at 6 a.m. He observed that the aging friar, now in his seventies, could at times hardly hobble to the sacristy. Every dragging step seemed to be taken at the cost of pain. But as he emerged from the sacristy in his priestly robes, a marvelous change would come over him. He would ascend the altar steps so smoothly that the worshippers in the pews never suspected his condition.

Though he considered Mr. Becker a close friend, he never mentioned his leg trouble to him. Not even when Mr. Becker informed him, about 1940, that he himself suffered from painful ulcers on his legs between ankle and knee.

"Don't you go to a doctor about them?" Father Solanus asked.

"I've doctored for years," said Mr. Becker, recalling that his affliction had started about fifteen years before. "Treatment hasn't done me a bit of good. Dr. William Mayer treated me with salve. Several boxes did me no good, so I stopped the treatment."

"Don't you have some of Dr. Mayer's salve left?" asked Father Solanus. Mr. Becker thought he had part of a box left.

"Bring it when you come again," Father Solanus instructed.

Next day, when Mr. Becker handed him the box of salve, he blessed his legs and the salve.

"Apply the salve again as the doctor directed," he said.

When Mr. Becker again entered the Monastery office, Father Solanus greeted him with a king-size smile.

"How are the legs, Ted?" he asked in a tone that seemed to indicate he was confident of the answer.

"The sores have disappeared," answered Mr. Becker.

For several years Mr. Becker—who worked as a truck driver until he was 74—remained free from leg ulcers. In his later years, sometime after Father Solanus' death, fluid developed in his legs and sores appeared. Whether this condition was a recurrence of the former trouble, Mr. Becker could not say, but it yielded to medical treatment.

Mr. Becker sometimes drove Father Solanus to a physician's office, and he was sure that the priest went there for treatment of his legs. But Father Solanus would never say a word about it to him. He was never known to refer to any sickness he might have, unless it made carrying out his duties impossible. Generally, the friars became aware that his varicose vein condition had become very bad when they noticed drops of blood on the hall floor. Then Father Guardian would order him to a doctor for treatment.

In September of 1942 influenza struck him down. The attack was so severe that he was hospitalized, and his physicians feared for his life. A rumor that he had died spread through the city, and telephone calls swamped the monastery. For some weeks he remained in the hospital, secluded from visitors. This stay enabled his physicians to thoroughly treat the varicose veins.

He was still weak when he returned to St. Bonaventure's. To assure his uninterrupted rest, he was sent to St. Felix Friary on the outskirts of Huntington, Indiana. Early in March, 1943, he returned to his Detroit post, much strengthened.

Naturally, his body refused to obey him as readily and as tirelessly as in earlier years. At seventy-three, he carried his daily burden of human woes as patiently as always but less resiliently. Yet his ardor was undiminished. In Huntington, his thoughts were constantly with his fellow workers in Detroit. In a note to Brother Leo, beginning with his usual "God bless you and yours," he said: "I want to thank you for your practical assistance to this—I was going to say, poor old sinner—rapidly getting old, at least. Many thanks for the medicine forwarded and the personal letters. In case my friends ask—just tell them I am improving and thankful for such a restful contrast after nearly forty years—over 18 in Detroit. God willing, I hope to be well before long and possibly back 'at the old stand.' "

That he was "rapidly getting old" was a major admission. It came from one who never in all his life was known to have grumbled or complained, or willingly made known any of his physical afflictions. In another letter to Brother Leo, dated February 28, 1943, he makes a further admission. Speaking to his fellow porter of their work, he notes that it has "many advantages—if only we be of good will and cooperate with the graces never failing on God's part." To this he adds— "Sometimes, of course, it becomes monotonous and extremely boring, till one is nearly collapsing; but in such cases it helps to remember that even when Jesus was about to fall the third time He patiently consoled the women-folk and children of His persecutors, making no exceptions. How can we ever be as grateful as we ought to be for such a vocation—for such privileged positions—even in the Seraphic Order of the Poverello."

After his return from St. Felix he was at his desk daily, but there were signs that he was, indeed, "getting old." On Christmas Eve of 1943, for the first time within memory of the friars, he failed to appear at the chapel gallery opening above the crib, to play hymns to the Babe of Bethlehem.

Marvelous occurrences such as had long been associated with him continued to be reported. A mother brought him her

four-year-old daughter, whose face a birthmark seriously disfigured. Its removal, plastic surgeons said, would leave a lifetime scar. Many years later, Mrs. Dolores Kolancz of Detroit
remembered the brown-robed man with a white beard telling
her he was Santa Claus, and placing cold hands on the sides
of her face as he blessed her. From that moment the birthmark grew smaller; in about two weeks it had almost disappeared. So, incidentally, did a gland swelling she had been
suffering from at the time.

Sometimes there was no cure, but a prediction of death or
continued suffering. The Ray Garlands, visiting him one
evening, had happened to bring along their two-year-old
daughter. Father Solanus noted that she had a cold; it had
persisted, Mr. Garland informed him, for some time. Taking
her in his arms, Father Solanus talked to her. Then, drawing
the father aside, he said: "I think the chapel is still open. Take
her there, kneel down with her, and tell our dear Lord—'You
can take her.' "

Puzzled and somewhat frightened, Mr. Garland did so.
Father Solanus offered no explanation of his strange words,
but Mr. Garland, troubled, repeated them to his wife as they
drove home.

The child's cold persisted. The third doctor to whom they
took her discovered—too late—that she was suffering from
pleurisy in an area which, he said, had made detection difficult. The baby died.

All his actions, even when he predicted tragedy, were
motivated by thoughtfulness of others. His compassion might
be expressed by as ordinary a courtesy as bringing a sorrowing
visitor a cup of coffee and a cupcake, or something as startling
as the blessing of a small boy—whose toothache immediately
stopped.

At times it might be nothing more than a nonchalant response to an embarrassing situation—such as a woman lock-

ing herself out of her car. Mrs. Thomas V. Egan of Greydale Avenue, Detroit, relates the following. Driving her sister, Mrs. Vincent Kelly of Toronto, about Detroit on a sunny summer afternoon in the early 1940's, Mrs. Egan parked her car before the Monastery, and with her sister visited the public chapel. When they came out, Father Solanus was walking up and down in front of the monastery, enjoying the sunny summer afternoon. After greeting him, Mrs. Egan moved to her car. The door handle wouldn't turn—and a glance revealed the worst. Her car keys were in the ignition switch; she had locked herself out. Both sisters in turn tried the car's two doors, then miserably conceded they would have to call a locksmith.

As they discussed their plight Father Solanus, having turned at the far end of his promenade, approached. Noting their perplexity, he questioned them and was told they had locked their car keys inside the Buick.

"There's no problem," he said.

He grasped the door handle, turned it.

Mystified and dumbfounded, Mrs. Egan and her sister thanked him and drove off.

Sometimes he figured in incidents less mysterious than coincidental. One day the Soup Kitchen's bread supply was running low. Father Herman, in charge of the Kitchen, saw that it was certain to give out before all the guests were fed. As he walked from the Third Order Hall to the Monastery on some business, he was worried. Passing through the office, he said to Father Solanus, who as usual was at his desk—"We have no bread."

Whereupon, Father Solanus stood up, and made the sign of the cross towards the Soup Kitchen, saying, "Have confidence."

Father Herman returned to the Hall. He asked all the men to rise, and to take off their hats, saying, "We will say a

Hail Mary, asking God for the replenishment of our bread supply."

Then Father Herman started back again to the Monastery. As he opened the hall door, a man was starting up the stairs, carrying a large basket filled with bread from one of the city's large bakeries.

"I have a lot more in the truck," he said.

Such coincidences were common in Father Solanus' life. So common that the Friars ceased to marvel, and he himself evidently thought nothing of them. His attitude seemed to be that, if he or others were doing God's work, God's help was to be confidently expected. His faith was absolute. He was sure that God's care for his children might extend to material interventions, even to holding trains, as seemed to have happened when he was returning from the west in 1913.

Now, thirty-two years later, he was thinking of making another journey west. John McCluskey, son of the Caseys' youngest sister Genevieve, was to be ordained in Seattle in the latter part of June, 1945. For several months, the twelve Casey brothers and sisters had been looking forward to the event, and the family reunion it would occasion. It was sadly foreseen, however, that two brothers would be absent. Edward—now a Monsignor—was a prisoner of the Japanese in the Philippines. Father Maurice was still under treatment —however inadequate—in Mt. Hope Sanitarium.

Toward the last of February in 1945 a letter from Monsignor Casey reported that American troops had rescued him with hundreds of other American war prisoners. In his letter to Father Solanus he asked him to "send word to Seattle, Frisco, Los Angeles, Burkhart, Superior, etc." He also asked: "Where is Father Maurice now? What Father Maurice needs to make him contented is more work. For a year before I left the States he was practically forced to be 'idle' in the Baltimore Sanitarium."

When Monsignor Casey had visited him, during that period, Father Maurice had "been wild to teach children, or anything else."

His letter concluded: "If James Casey still lives he is nearing 80 years. God bless him living or dead. . . . I cannot expect that all are still living as in 1941; but send word of both the living and the dead that I may weave their names in the Holy Masses and the daily prayers. Pray for a just peace—whether it comes early or late."

Monsignor Casey failed to mention in his letter to Father Solanus that the day before their rescue he had acted to prevent the death of many prisoners. In the prison hospital he was surrounded by sick men, dangerously weakened by diseases and starvation. To these, any shock to their hope of survival might mean death. Despite this, the Japanese officer in charge issued a murderous directive. He ordered rations cut from a starvation 900 calories to 600 calories a day, and directed the head nurse to post a notice to that effect on the ward's bulletin board.

As she entered the ward to do so, Monsignor Casey noted her look of despair. Before she could post the order, he reached her side and took it from her hand. A swift glance, and he realized the paper's fatal significance. He crumpled it in his hand, and told her—"I'll assume full responsibility for this." Then forcing a broad smile, he said to the sick men—"I thought it might be something important—but it's hardly worth mentioning. The nurse just wants you to know that tomorrow we're going to have a big dinner of ham and eggs!"

The preposterous "announcement" brought a ripple of smiles, and prevented what might have been a fatal shock to many.

It also proved minimally correct. Next day, when American soldiers stormed into the camp, they distributed to those liberated prisoners able to eat solids, powdered eggs and proc- essed ham!

Monsignor Casey was not alone in thinking that Father Maurice's treatment in Mt. Hope Sanitarium had ceased to be beneficial. His niece, Mrs. Dean Conley, after visiting him, had concluded that for Father Maurice, Mt. Hope was a mis- nomer. She and her husband, who was professionally familiar with the most advanced techniques in sanitarium treatment for disorders such as that of Father Maurice, were positive that he could improve only if released from that institution.

Three months after receipt of Monsignor Casey's letter Father Solanus, in the casual, indirect way characteristic of him, brought about Father Maurice's discharge. Early in June, 1945, Monsignor Edward—who had come to the United States to recuperate—and brothers Owen and Patrick, des- cended on St. Bonaventure's. They had come to carry Father Solanus off with them to Seattle. To this eager proposal Father Solanus responded with an innocent question: "Would Father Maurice be going, too?"

They answered "No." They had taken it for granted that he would continue to be confined in Mt. Hope Sanitarium.

Their Capuchin brother gently replied that he wouldn't want Father Maurice to feel that he was the only one left out of the family reunion. Unless his elder brother could make the trip, neither would he.

And so, instead of going west at once, Monsignor Casey, Owen and Patrick went east to Baltimore, determined now on obtaining Father Maurice's release. They succeeded, and on Friday, June 15, accompanied by Father Maurice, they ar- rived in Chicago, where Father Solanus was to join them.

It was a memorable family reunion in Seattle, with the Casey brothers and sisters reminiscing among their children and grand-children, their nieces and nephews, their grand-nieces and grand-nephews. Those bearing the Casey name were of course the more numerous, but there were also Traynors and LeDoux and McCluskeys and Bradys, for all the four Casey sisters had married.

They were a strong, self-reliant, unfettered group. Theirs was the rich inheritance of independence and human dignity that is won only through self-control, self-respect, hard work and the desire to make best use of the talents God had given them.

At the reunion, the close-knit Caseys were plagued by one great difficulty—outsiders calling at all hours of the day and evening for Father Solanus. He seemed to be as celebrated in Seattle as in Detroit. Pastors invited him to offer Mass in their churches; Sisters in their chapels.

In Spokane, it had been much the same story. He had stopped there overnight at the home of his cousin Mrs. Euphrasia Cunningham. So many wanted his blessings, that the Cunninghams had little time for conversation with him. "Our home was packed until his departure," said Euphrasia. "I don't know where all the people came from."

Nuns at an academy, and others, were expecting him, but he couldn't get away from the crowds surrounding him at their residence. Monsignor Edward wanted him to meet Spokane's Bishop White, but he declined. His time was limited, and he said he wanted "to visit his little cousin Euphrasia."

Relatives and friends in and about Los Angeles, California, were begging him to come there, even if only for a single day. He hesitated. But when his brothers explained that it would be several days before they could obtain his transportation to Detroit—war priorities were in force—he decided to go. Moreover, he had several days leeway, and his brothers assured him that the Los Angeles trip could not possibly delay his return to St. Bonaventure's.

So he went to Los Angeles, intending to stay but a day. He was the guest of the Irish Capuchins at whose friary he greeted friends and relatives. But transportation back to Seattle had not been obtainable, and he found himself stranded. On July 9 he wrote to Father Marion, then Guardian at St. Bonaventure's—

WHETHER to my discredit or otherwise, I am still here in this part of the country. Instead of a day as I figured on, it's now coming a week since I arrived in Los Angeles—a name well-fitting such a gentle wonderland.

Last Saturday, after Fr. Stephen [O.F.M. Cap.] wired you, he informed us that the very best he could do in regard to transportation was to get reservations for next Thursday (12th) instead of yesterday (9th) for Seattle, so that I might use my "pass" to St. Paul. . . .

To get on the train as I proposed, without a reservation, he stressed would be foolhardiness. So here I am still—hoping to make the best of missing the privileges of the Chapter. [The Provincial Chapter, held every three years to elect superiors and transact other Order business was convening at St. Bonaventure's.]

*   *   *

Ending the letter, Father Solanus refers to himself in Latin as the Father Guardian's breast-beating subject. But there is no indication that he considered himself at fault. His contrition was merely for the fact that conditions beyond his control detained him. His obedience to the rule was always so complete, so exact that, as Father Marion said, any thought that he was willfully derelict never would have occurred to his superiors. His letter of explanation to Father Marion was considered ample excuse for his tardy return.

Had he been at St. Bonaventure's during the Chapter, it is probable that he would have been informed earlier of an action which would directly affect him. For among the transfers of friars decided upon, was his own.

Two things, in the superiors' opinion, made his removal from St. Bonaventure's necessary: The friars wanted to safeguard his health; they wanted also to prevent his name and prestige being further used in Mr. Garland's promotion of the Mary Agreda Society.

Father Solanus' physical welfare was of prime consideration to his brethren. They feared that his health could not stand up much longer against the public's insistent demands upon his energies. He was seventy-five years old, and suffering—severely, at times—from varicose veins and eczema. Two years before, he had been close to death. And while Capuchins prefer to wear out rather than rust out, they know how to protect their aged members in their declining years, even against themselves. The least that was called for, in the immediate instance, was the lightening of Father Solanus' burdens. And they realized that he was so outgoing, so compassionate, so unable to deny himself to anyone, that his labors would never grow less while he remained at St. Bonaventure's. Regard for his health alone, would have dictated his transfer from Detroit.

As a first step toward more complete retirement, the superiors decided to send him to St. Michael's Friary in Brooklyn, New York.

Thus Father Solanus' twenty-one continuous years at St. Bonaventure's came to an end.

Chapter 19

"A Little
More Sleep Under
the Great Archangel's Wings"

Ending his western trip, Father Solanus arrived in Detroit
on a Saturday. By Monday evening he was at St. Michael's in
Brooklyn.

His prompt departure from St. Bonaventure's was according to Capuchin custom. Like all religious, Capuchins are
expected to act on their "marching orders" without question
or delay—whether those orders take them across a city, a
continent, or the world.

Brother Leo noted that Father Solanus accepted his transfer with his characteristic, easy good humor. His departure,
though, shocked thousands who had come to consider him
their indispensable counselor.

He himself was as casual about leaving St. Bonaventure's
as if going to a suburb on a weekend "helpout."

He was probably grateful that the public was unaware of
his going. Scores would have demanded a final word with him.
Inevitably, someone or some group would have attempted to
launch a farewell party. Editors would have sent reporters to
interview him. And he was tired and aging; such demands
would have exhausted him. So Father Solanus left, and
trusted to Brother Leo to send on his few winter clothes,
stored in the community wardrobe.

A week after he had taken up his portering duties at St. Michael's, he wrote the Brother to send along a few mementos he had left behind: Old letters from Father Edward, and "a little prayer on modesty" that, he reminded Brother Leo, "we were figuring on having in the office." He had written it before going west, but had had no opportunity to bring it to the Provincial's attention for approval.

"I hope," he remarks, "to get a little more time for such things here at St. Michael's, although so far—getting acquainted, etc.—I've not had much surplus time.

"One thing, however—I've taken a little more sleep under the great Archangel's wings this past week than perhaps in three weeks before my arrival."

He was referring to a statue of St. Michael standing guard above the Brooklyn church and friary.

He had sent his best wishes "to all our friends—inside and out—who may be interested," and his friends "outside" the friary quickly made known their regret at his departure. Some refused to let distance separate them from him. Within a few days of his arrival at St. Michael's, a thin scattering of Detroiters began to show up. A great many wrote to him; so many, that his correspondence soon became heavy.

Former Detroiters living in or near Brooklyn, informed by Detroit friends of his presence there, sought him out. Within a few days after his arrival at St. Michael's a former Detroiter reached him by telephone. In his thin, patient voice, which sounded tired, Father Solanus explained that he was in Brooklyn for a rest, but that his "friends had found him there." The implication seemed clear—he was not getting all the rest he had expected. He was probably still fatigued after his long western trip. His tone of voice was not that of one positively denying permission for a visit, neither was it invitational. When assured the call was prompted only by friendly courtesy and that the telephone caller would not visit him, he seemed somewhat relieved.

His statement that he had been sent to New York for a rest was no half-truth on his part; he had been informed that this was the reason for his transfer.

His openness to a visit, had the telephone caller insisted, was characteristic. No matter how sick or exhausted he might be, he was never known to refuse anyone who asked his counsel. Knowing this, many wrote him for advice, and he would always answer them, though writing had become laborious. Some kept in touch with him by long distance telephone. One of these was Mrs. D. Edward Wolfe of Brighton, Michigan, who telephoned him when informed that her infant daughter Kathleen Ann was close to death from "early" celiac disease.

Convinced that medical science could be of no further help, Mrs. Wolfe wanted to take the baby to Brooklyn to receive Father Solanus' blessing. This he would not permit.

"Kneel down with the baby," he told her, "and I will give you my blessing over the telephone."

After he had done so, he suggested that Mrs. Wolfe use the money she would have spent in traveling to Brooklyn to "do something for a poor family."

The child recovered.

At long intervals, Father Solanus was free from both visitors and telephone calls; this was when he made a religious retreat. Shortly after arriving in Brooklyn he enjoyed a solid two weeks of contemplation at the Immaculate Conception Seminary at Garrison-on-the-Hudson. Its beautiful site on the lordly Hudson River helped to make his stay delightful.

As was his custom, he jotted down retreat notes. These included the following: "God knows as no one else knows that we need humiliations whereby to foster humility. Hence in His love He never fails to provide occasions for each one to practice penance—which means, to check self-conceit and to get somewhere in humility. Hence, for a religious the most practical penance is that which is naturally and logically consequent on the rule."

His duties were now sufficiently light to permit him to visit familiar scenes in and about New York, and to renew old acquaintances. He attended a Labor Day parish celebration at Sacred Heart Friary in Yonkers, which had been his first appointment after ordination forty-one years before, and visited the other friaries where he had once been stationed.

Letter writing became a demanding task. Many who had known him during his years in Detroit wrote to him. From various parts of the United States he received letters from people who had heard of him, and who wanted him to enroll them in the Seraphic Mass Association. Often he worked on his correspondence till after midnight, but generally he would have to stop with many letters still unanswered. At times his varicose vein condition sent him to his cell early. "Sometimes," he wrote Brother Leo, "my two faithful sentinels" —as he referred to his legs—"threaten to go on strike," and "to quiet them down" he would take to his bed, where he could lie flat.

At St. Michael's as at St. Bonaventure's, people came to him with their worries and their sicknesses. In one note he tells of a "young musical genius," Jimmy Sarchet, whom he enrolled in the "Seraphic Masses." He describes Jimmy as "only 14 years old," but the master of "piano and three other instruments. Now paralyzed, blind and deaf, he's still as cheerful as ever."

The memos he made at St. Michael's are not arranged by weeks, and are comparatively few; evidently he was not using them when talking to congregations. One memo concerns Timothy Conery, who was suffering from some disease,—

Father Solanus' word for it is undecipherable—and who came
back two weeks after first talking with Father Solanus. He
wanted to thank him for his cure and said that the doctors
were surprised.

In New York he continued to advise people to read *The
Mystical City*. Among these was the mother of a rebellious
and straying twenty-year-old girl who had disappeared from
her home ten weeks before her mother came to him. Father
Solanus suggested to the mother that she promise to read one
of the four volumes if her daughter returned within a week.

Five days later mother and daughter came to the friary,
where the daughter waited for an hour and a half to go to
confession.

This experience is recorded in the last memo he made in
his notebook relating to his several months at St. Michael's.

His correspondence with Father Maurice informed him
that the latter, in the spring of 1946, was again visiting in
and about the old Casey homesteads in Wisconsin. In one
letter, Father Solanus, recalling their boyhood, seeks to inspire confidence.

HOW WONDERFUL—he writes his brother—are the ways of
the Dear Good God!—when we think of the blessings of the
past—when we went berrying and picking hops and nuts and
digging jinsang [ginseng]. And still further back, when the
"old field" was all we had open and the prairie chickens used
to stage a picture like that of the first Paradise in the morning
sun as they shook the dew from the great oaks, up to the
East!!! You and I are all that are left now, who can go back
to our first spring in old Trimbelle. [Ellen, James and John
had died.]

I have never seen a picture—in Bible history or elsewhere
—so nearly like an earthly paradise as I remember the scenery

to be—with deer in twos, threes and more, stopping on the hill-sides or valleys to gaze at what we might be doing.

No doubt what heightened the appreciation of those days was our innocence from sin.

And how the hawks themselves, every fall, were wont to circle around and around again and again in their upward flight, right over our log-palace and plot of green. They seemed to me, as they circled to the clouds, to invite us to strive with them to get up to Heaven. They were surely an inspiration. I've often thought in later years that God in His goodness and wisdom very likely gave those simple birds a pleasure of some kind in giving us playing youngsters such an entertainment. . . . When we think of past blessings and merciful providence—notwithstanding our sins—why should we not foster confidence by thanking Him for the future, too?

All this he wrote on a three by five inch card—his customary stationery. Having covered front and back, he turned to the back again to use the slim margin unfilled there, to say —"I simply hope you get a kind of 'kick' out of this—I never intended so much. But O! what God must have ahead for us if we only leave all to His planning."

It was another effort to persuade Father Maurice toward contentment.

Seven months had now passed since Father Solanus was transferred to Brooklyn, which his superiors from the first had evidently considered a way station in his progress toward retirement. He was still doing too much work for his seventy-six years; his fellow friars felt that he needed more complete rest in a more peaceful setting.

On April 25, 1946, he was transferred to St. Felix Friary in Huntington. Here he could walk in the green Indiana. countryside and hear wild birds sing as he had heard them in his boyhood days.

Chapter 20

Retirement without Rest

St. Felix Friary rose majestically amidst rich and rolling farmlands. Here Father Solanus strolled through the friary's orchards and huge vegetable garden, which must have reminded him of the orchard and truck garden beside his home in the days of his boyhood. Here, near the banks of the Wabash, after fifty years of Capuchin labors, he could expect untroubled rest, for his brethren had prudently kept the news of his latest transfer from the public.

His days, for the most part, were uneventful. He strolled in the friary's grounds, along the borders of the huge vegetable and berry garden, under the fruit trees, and near the bee hives. He sat in the sun—lost, generally, in admiration of a bird or flower or bee.

A bee—he usually sat near the beehives—would alight on his hand, and crawl up a finger. And, fascinated by the tools with which nature had equipped it, and its instinctive efficiency, he would exclaim—"My dear God, how could You have created such a marvelous thing!" So friendly did he become with the friary bees, that Brother Bee Master enlisted him as an assistant. Once or twice the bees stung him, but this did not change his good-neighbor attitude toward them.

That his easy way with bees was not shared by all, he failed to realize. One warm day, as he was writing in his room, a bee flew in and buzzed about him. He stretched out a hand;

the bee alighted. Father Solanus started toward the window; it was screened. Hearing steps in the corridor, he stepped out, bee on hand, just as Frater Leon was passing.

"This little bee is lost," he said. "Would you take him outside so he can find his way home?"

With this, he adroitly transferred the bee to the cleric's nearest finger. Frater Leon gingerly tiptoed down the corridor—but as he reached the door, the bee stung.

Next day, nursing a swollen digit, he saw Father Solanus sitting rear a beehive. Bees crawled about his hands and arms, and he was talking to them. The cleric kept his distance, observing. When Brother Bee Master came by, he asked— "What's Father saying to those bees?"

Oh," returned the Brother, "he's praising them as God's little innocent creatures."

"They're small enough, but they're not so innocent!" exclaimed the rueful Frater Leon. "Look at what one did to me." And holding a swollen finger on high, he hurried away.

The cleric was less fortunate than Father Elmer Stoffel, who relates that in 1950, while helping Father Solanus tend the apiary, three bees stung him. He fell to the ground, writhing in pain. Father Solanus blessed him, and immediately, the pain left. He reported that he suffered no after affects whatever.

Father Solanus aided Brother Orchardist, also, but in a different way. One Saturday in May, just sixteen days after he arrived at St. Felix from New York, radio stations broadcast heavy frost warnings. Concerned with this threat to the apple crop, the friars were discussing lighting smudge fires. Father Solanus seemed not too confident that this would be effective.

He volunteered to bless the orchard. In doing so, he used the oration "ad omnia," and a special prayer invoking Blessed Ignatius, a Capuchin Brother, whose cause for canonization was then being considered.

On farms all around, the apples were lost; St. Felix' apple trees went unharmed.

Father Solanus had special reason for calling on Blessed Ignatius on that eleventh day of May; it was the saintly Brother's feastday. [Five years later, Blessed Ignatius became Saint Ignatius].

At this time, as for a considerable period before, Father Solanus was praying for the thawing of another heavy frost— a bitter coldness that had developed between his brothers Patrick and Augustine. He was praying, particularly, that they might be reconciled before Augustine's death from cancer.

As yet, few Detroiters knew he was at St. Felix. It was not until nine months later that his thousands of Michigan friends learned he was now stationed in Huntington. A story in *The Detroit News* of Saturday, January 25, 1947, carried the information that he had come to Detroit to observe the anniversary of his fifty years as a Capuchin. A multitude of Detroiters prepared to help him celebrate.

Sunday morning he offered a solemn Mass of Thanksgiving in the public chapel. Fifty years before, in the choir chapel a few steps away, he had been invested with the Capuchin habit and had taken his name in religion.

At the Mass, his brother Edward—thinking, perhaps, of Father Solanus' faculties-deprived priesthood—preached on the text—"To those who love God, all things work together for good." The jubilarian's brother Owen, and his sister Grace —Mrs. Bernard Brady—had come from Washington State, and his friends from Chicago, Joseph J. and Mrs. O'Donnell, were also present. The chapel was packed.

The Mass was followed by dinner in the Third Order Hall, which accommodated three hundred. Later, Father Solanus ascended to the auditorium on the second floor for a reception that lasted several hours. More than two thousand stood in line to congratulate him. Checks and currency—which he of course donated to his Order's activities—poured in upon him. One of the gifts was a specially designed chalice.

The printing of a memento card, customary for such an occasion, had been left to the last moment. Father Solanus was asked to write a message for it. While a friar waited, he wrote and re-wrote until he felt he had something that expressed his thoughts. It read—

PAX ET BONUM

IN MEMORY OF MY

GOLDEN JUBILEE IN RELIGION

St. Bonaventure's Monastery

Detroit, Michigan

Thanks be to God for uncountable

mercies—for every blessing!

Thanks to my neighbor for his

charitable patience.

Fifty years in the Order—almost unnoticed—have slipped away from me into eternity.—Thither I hope to follow before half another fifty; trusting in the merciful goodness of God!

Fr. Solanus, O.F.M. Cap.

DEO GRATIAS

The two Casey brothers and the O'Donnells remained with him in Detroit until his return to Huntington five days later, when the O'Donnells drove him back to St. Felix Friary.

Publicity attendant on the celebration ended his relatively untroubled rest at St. Felix. Visitors began to come, and soon demands upon him were almost continuous. Many who could not come, wrote. His correspondence became so heavy, the superiors assigned him a secretary.

The secretary lightened his load, and acted as an aid to his failing memory. For years back he had been somewhat absent-minded. One day, when stationed in Detroit, he had created, through a slip of the mind, considerable postal confusion. When posting a letter, he had dropped his morning's mail—just received—into the mail box with it. Since that episode his forgetfulness had increased. People would hand him money, and he would stash it in any odd place that was convenient. When Father Blaise, then a young priest, was appointed his secretary, he found over a hundred dollars in desk drawers, books, and unusual nooks and corners.

Women, proud of their culinary skill, brought him such offerings as pies, and these also were found in strange places—shelves behind rows of books being a favorite location. His intention was to turn the baked triumphs over to the cook, but he would forget the matter completely, and the perishable dainty might go undiscovered for days.

He welcomed Father Blaise's help. He had known the young priest since the latter, as a lad of twelve, had served Mass at St. Bonaventure's. Father Blaise remembered him, also, as the priest who celebrated Mass with such intense devotion, and who generally took longer than anyone else.

Father Blaise noticed that, while Father Solanus frequently misplaced charitable contributions, he never misplaced or failed accurately to record a Mass offering. That he considered a sacred obligation.

To letters requiring answers to moral questions, he himself responded, leaving the young priest to handle communications of a routine nature. His letters dealing with moral issues continuously awed Father Blaise by the depth of spiritual wisdom they revealed.

Father Solanus' acute discernment and theological depth

impressed many besides his Capuchin confreres. One of these was Dr. A. L. Gabriel, director of The Mediaeval Institute of the University of Notre Dame and C. Fellow of the French Academy (des Inscriptions and Belles-Lettres).

"I had the pleasure of meeting Father Solanus several times," says Dr. Gabriel. "He impressed me not only as a well-balanced, serene, cheerful man but as a religious with deep humility in his heart and in possession of abundant grace. Speaking with scholars specialized in the field of history of philosophy and theology, he was at his ease and most natural, and his conversation was that of a person inspired by the Holy Ghost. Though accustomed to a scholarly public, I found Father Solanus' companionship most inspiring. Each time I had a visit with him, I felt I left the monastery richer than before my visit."

His wisdom enabled him to help his two warring brothers to a reconciliation. Two days before seventy-year-old Augustine died—on the feast of the Sacred Heart—he and Patrick were touchingly reunited.

Father Maurice's welfare continued to concern him. In 1947, he was able to write Monsignor Edward, now working in the United States for the Philippine missions, that he had received "a very bright letter from Fr. Maurice Joachim. It was about the best in a long time. It really looks as if he is his old self once more. Thanks be to God 'a billion.' "

The next few months became the peaceful sunset of Father Maurice's troubled life. Serving as chaplain in a Catholic hospital in the little town of Graceville, Minnesota, he was useful, happy and contented.

On January 12, 1949, a wire to Father Solanus from Monsignor Edward informed him that Father Maurice had died that morning. Driven by "Father Guardian and Brother Cook"—as he relates in one of his letters—Father Solanus set out the next day by motor car for Fort Wayne, where he boarded a train for the west. To him, trains were still romantic; it thrilled him to be riding the "Golden Arrow" to Chicago, and the "Hiawatha" to St. Paul.

In Graceville's Holy Rosary Church, a bishop and fifteen priests chanted the Divine Office, and Father Solanus delivered the sermon. It centered about his favorite theme—man's debt of gratitude to God. His text was—"What shall I render to the Lord for all things He has rendered to me." It was a meditation on the meaning of death to the faithful Christian, and he spoke of death as the humiliating, purifying gateway to eternal life; "the last of the blessings God showers upon our earthly journey towards heaven." The listeners felt the deep pathos of the speaker; perhaps not all realized that its source was his intimate knowledge of his brother's twenty years of humiliation.

Father Solanus was never wholly saddened by the death of a good man or woman, for he rejoiced with them in their eternal joy. This morning, the thought of his brother's death uplifted him as he emerged from the church and saw the nearby cemetery veiled in pearly, shimmering light that sometimes results when the sun begins to pierce winter's morning mist. It was such a scene as Doré depicts in his drawings of Dante's heaven. When he returned to Huntington he said to one of his first visitors, Miss Agnes O'Neil of Detroit, that death should be considered as one of the happiest of human experiences. Miss O'Neil was one of the multitude who attributed to Father Solanus' prayers recovery from physical afflictions of long standing.

In the spring of 1953, a little more than four years after Father Maurice's death, Father Solanus' sister Grace—Mrs. Bernard Brady—died in Seattle. She was the "Gracie" he had shielded when a horse threw him as he was carrying her before him more than sixty years before. Of his fifteen brothers and sisters, only four now lived—Patrick, Monsignor Edward, Margaret and Genevieve.

He himself felt that he had years of service in him; he never seemed to realize that he had grown old. No novice was more genial and cheerful and optimistic. Even when he was very sick, he never complained. If he felt at all well, the friars knew it by the fact that he came down stairs on the run.

He wanted to keep himself physically fit, and often, late at night, he would jog around the friary garden path to—as he put it—"keep in trim." Novices would invite him to play volley ball and tennis—and he would play his heart out. Sometimes he would stumble and fall flat, but he'd struggle to his feet and continue to play. He walked barefoot in the friary grounds even when the ground was snow covered; this was one of his favorite "nature cures."

He was nearly always first in choir—generally arriving a good fifteen minutes before the day's first scheduled service at 5:15 a.m. After morning prayers, when others sought a brief rest in their rooms, or studied, or meditated, he would busy himself in the garden. He cultivated a patch of wild strawberries; he said he was "taming" them. He did tame them, too, and the friars found them delicious.

His sense of humor was unfailing, and youthful. In his easy way, he would always go along with a joke, particularly if it were at his expense. He narrated humorous anecdotes with relish, and he had a fund of them. Above all, he was what Brother Agathangelus, at one time his secretary, described as "good community man, a man of great charity."

In all Brother Agathangelus' close association with him, he never heard him utter an unkind word.

"The nearest he came to any criticism of another was to say, drolly, when one of the fathers was grouchy and showed it—'Father's a little off today.' And that," explained the Brother "was said more in excuse than in blame."

Nor did he show the slightest indication of old-age ir-
ritability, though he showed increasing signs of aging. His
eyes were failing; he had to ask others to read certain prayers
in choir which he, as senior friar, was supposed to read.
Brother Agathangelus read all letters addressed to him, and
summarized them for him. If the letter requested counsel in
an important matter, the Brother gave him the original and
remained with him until he had read and answered it.

"His eyesight had become so feeble," said the Brother, "that
he sometimes required fifteen minutes to read a single paragraph."

Yet he kept up his extensive correspondence, toiling over
his letters and sometimes using them as a shepherd's crook.
One day he learned that a fallen-from-grace Huntington
Catholic was planning to divorce his wife. He went to the
man's home, but his visits were useless; the delinquent eluded
him. Thereupon, Father Solanus began to write him, urging
him to reconsider his ways and return to the sacraments, and
stressing God's infinite love for him. He prepared the letters
painstakingly. Having written one, he would hand it to a
brother priest for criticism and correction. Then he would rewrite, and sometimes rewrite it again.

The letters were effective. The stray finally sought out
Father Solanus and returned both to his religion and to his
wife.

The writing of letters demanded patience, and not only
from Father Solanus. Frater Leon—he of the bee episode—
occupied the next cell; his bed was against the wall on the
other side of which was the little table supporting Father
Solanus' typewriter. Because the cell was small, it was impossible for Frater Leon to reposition his bed. Every key tap
fell upon his ear drums with the persistence of a Chinese
water torture. Unconscious of all this, Father Solanus would
type on, far into the night, his hunt-and-peck system further

slowed by age and failing eyesight. And Frater Leon would lie awake, suspensively awaiting the next key tap. For, so long were the pauses between taps, that the tired cleric would find himself wondering whether Father Solanus had quit for the night—when another tap would vanquish hope.

Finally he would fall off to sleep at some point between taps—aided by the fact that his day had started at 4:40.

Letter writing was, of course, the smaller part of Father Solanus' activities at St. Felix. Most of his time was taken up with people who came to him individually, in families and in groups. Many came by the bus load, particularly on weekends. On Saturdays and Sundays, it was common for two or three buses to arrive.

Many visitors were old friends; they wanted to see him, to have a few words with him, to receive his blessing. Sometimes, after visiting with a group, he would produce his violin, and soon he would have everyone singing hymns and Stephen Foster's melodies and such popular ballads as *Mother Machree,* at the top of their voices.

Some who came experienced the unexpected. Mrs. Nettie Dearbin of Milner Avenue in Detroit was an old friend and she came just to visit him. But she did have an ugly black spot on her cheek—an infection that resulted from an accidental scratch, and which medical treatment had failed to cure. She made no mention of it, but as Father Solanus reached out his hand to shake hers, she touched the back of his hand to the sore. From that time on the injury began to heal, and the black spot disappeared.

She remembered this when her daughter Eugenia, eighteen years old, was suffering agonies from headaches. She brought her down to Huntington, and Father Solanus put both hands on the girl's head and blessed her.

"Go home, my child," he said. "You won't be troubled with headaches any more."

The headaches ceased. And so when surgeons told Mrs. Dearbin's son-in-law, Jerry Shornak, that they would have to amputate his leg, she took him, also, to Father Solanus. He blessed the gangrenous, smashed ankle, and the leg wounds healed.

Mrs. Dearbin was one of many who brought the sick and the crippled to him. Mr. Alaska brought his wife, Evelyn, who had been crippled by polio. He carried her into the Monastery after driving down from Harper Woods near Detroit, and they visited with Father Solanus a while. When they were ready to go the friar blessed Mrs. Alaska.

"I'll go into the chapel and pray," he told her. "When you get home, you'll be just fine."

She immediately felt new strength in her legs, though before she had not only been unable to walk but had felt discomfort in almost every position. Now she stood up and walked out of the monastery, down the steps, and to her car, leaning on her husband's arm. When they arrived home she was the first out of the car.

"This happened to me on Tuesday, July 5, 1949," said the former Mrs. Alaska, who after her husband's death became Mrs. Martin Wachinger. "I never had any after effects, excepting a muscular feeling in my legs when I get very tired."

Father Solanus always attached utmost importance to the prayers of those who came for help.

"I can't cure you," he would say—as he said to Mrs. Alaska. —"But God can cure anyone He desires to cure. If He so wills, that is, if it is for your good, He will answer your prayers."

Frequently the cure was of the spirit rather than the body. When polio crippled Leo Brown of Mayfield Avenue, Detroit, in 1955, it left him with a useless right arm. So bitterly did he resent the handicap that he refused to cooperate with therapy treatments.

"About a month after he left the hospital," Mrs. Brown

says, "Leo's brother drove him down to St. Felix Monastery to Father Solanus. My husband and Father talked a long time, and his attitude changed completely. He accepted his affliction, trained himself to use his left arm, and was able to continue his work as a draftsman. He hunts and fishes and seems as handy as when he had two good arms."

Mrs. Brown had been a friend of Father Solanus ever since, in 1941, she had gone to him with what her doctors had diagnosed as a goitre. He blessed her, and she claimed that the growth disappeared and never returned.

Some visitors reported experiences in no way associated with physical cures. Mrs. E. J. Devlin of Dearborn, Michigan, tells of a bewildering episode which occurred when she brought two of her sisters to see him. As they were driving to Huntington, Mrs. Devlin and one of her sisters, Marion Ryan, teased the other sister, Margaret Ann Ryan, about her name. Though baptized "Margaret Ann," her given names on her birth certificate appeared as "Anna Marguerite." After she had discovered this, Margaret Ann never ceased to voice regret that she had not been baptised "Anna Marguerite," a name she greatly preferred. Father Solanus, Mrs. Devlin is sure, knew nothing about the matter; he had never met her sisters.

At the end of their visit, Father Solanus learned that the Ryan girls had never been enrolled in the Seraphic Mass Association. As a courtesy, one that he frequently extended, he offered to enroll them. Writing with the painful slowness that marked his later years, he uttered the girls' names as he wrote them on the enrollment cards. But, as he wrote out Margaret Ann Ryan's card, he did not use that name. Instead he pronounced and wrote, "Anna Marguerite."

Completely nonplussed, Mrs. Devlin and her sisters could only look at one another, mystified. Too astonished to ask him why he called Margaret Ann, "Anna Marguerite," they made their way to their car, wondering. Years later, they were still wondering.

Many, having heard about him, turned to him in desperate crises. One of these was a neighbor of Mrs. Devlin's—Mrs. William Evison. Mrs. Devlin had attributed to Father Solanus' prayers the recovery of her seven-year-old son Tom from a physician-mystifying blood infection. She related the experience to Mrs. Evison, a neighbor.

In March of 1954, Mrs. Evison's six-weeks-old daughter, suffering from a wildly erratic heart, was not expected by her physician to live through the night. Her mother remembered the story of little Tom Devlin's recovery, and she telephoned the Capuchin. Sympathetically—for Mrs. Evison was weeping—the Brother who answered the telephone said he would bring Father as quickly as he could find him.

In the meantime, another sympathizer had been listening—the long distance operator. She cut in. "I have heard wonderful things about Father Solanus," she assured Mrs. Evison. "I'm sure he will help you."

When Father Solanus came to the telephone and listened to Mrs. Evison's story, he said—"You're going to bring your baby home in a few days. I'll go down to the chapel now, and pray for her."

The next morning, when the doctor came into the infant's room, and examined her, he cried out. A nurse, thinking the baby was dead, ran to his side. But the doctor's exclamation had been one of joyful surprise. The baby's heart was beating normally. The child, Cynthia Evison, is today, in her mother's terms, "a picture of health."

Undoubtedly, Father Solanus prayed more for the cure of souls than of bodies; no effort was too great when it came to rescuing a wanderer from the fold. Even when he had become quite feeble, he seemed to gain new strength when helping others spiritually. When an alcoholic came to him in Huntington in 1955, convinced that he could not stop drinking and in despair determined to end his life, Father Solanus talked with him. He talked with him steadily for two hours. At the end of that session, the man went away, convinced that he could abstain. For the next two years—up to the time Father Solanus left St. Felix—he corresponded with Father Solanus. His correspondence, which passed through Brother Agathangelus' hands, showed that he had continued to abstain.

His effectiveness in bringing back Catholics to resumption of their religious duties was notable. One of his old friends, Mrs. Edward Clair of Detroit, encountered an example of this when she brought a little group to see him from a Catholic sanitarium in Rome City, Indiana. She did not know that Miss B, one of the group, had been out of the church thirty-two years, and Mr. L twenty-six years.

Miss B had taken a seat as far from Father Solanus as the room permitted. When he had her card made out, he walked across the room to her, and presented it. Then he talked with her several minutes.

There was a priest in the group—Monsignor Voight of Saginaw. Mr. L went to confession to him that night, and received Holy Communion the next morning.

Two weeks after Miss B had returned to her home in Cleveland she wrote Mrs. Clair, informing her that she, too, had returned to the practice of her religion.

Friars, too, talked out their problems with him. He was unfailingly serious, even in minor things, about the obligations of the religious life. To all, but especially to religious, he preached complete and joyous acceptance of God's will.

Typical of his counsel was a talk he gave to novices at St. Felix when, one Sunday morning, they were gathered on the lawn outside the chapel after Mass. Responding to the novice master's invitation to speak to them, he said in the course of his remarks: "Some fellows speculate anxiously on where they are to be sent after they receive Holy Orders. They say— 'I hope I don't have to go to this place, or to that place.' Why should we allow such thoughts and questions to bother us? What does it matter where we go? Wherever we go, won't we be serving God there? And wherever we go, won't we have Our Lord in the Blessed Sacrament with us? Isn't that enough to make us happy?"

During his Huntington years, Father Solanus was occasionally driven to various shrines in Indiana, Ohio and Michigan. He was delegated, also, to attend church dedications, anniversaries, and like events. In April of 1949, one of these journeys came close to costing him his life.

The occasion was the unveiling of a statue—that of Father Stephen Eckert—in Milwaukee. The unassuming Father Eckert had entered the Order six years before Father Solanus. He was of gigantic spiritual stature, and made the colored people of Milwaukee the special objectives of his solicitude. In a day when many white persons tended to ignore both the black man's human rights and spiritual welfare, he became their apostle and champion.

After his death in 1923, many people claimed extraordinary favors after invoking his intercession. In 1948, on the twenty-fifth anniversary of his death, his body had been reburied in Milwaukee, in a small court formed by the institutions he had helped to found: St. Benedict the Moor Mission, and St. Anthony's Hospital. The statue marked this final resting place.

To Father Solanus, the journey was a pilgrimage. Father Stephen had served in New York parishes immediately before Father Solanus. From many parishioners he had learned much about his predecessor's warm charity and friendliness.

He was completely in sympathy, also, with Father Stephen's work among Negroes, in whom he himself felt deep interest.

As was almost to be expected when Father Solanus was one of a company, this journey to Milwaukee brought pleasant surprises along the way. The Capuchin party set out from St. Felix on Monday morning, April 27. Toward noon, as they were driving through Chicago, someone remarked that a stop for lunch was about due. In his offhand way, Father Solanus responded with a direction to the driver.

"Turn here," he said. "We're near some friends who'll be sure to have something for us. . . . Stop at the house on the corner."

It was the residence of the Joseph O'Donnells, who were devoted to him. The O'Donnells served an impressive dinner. Yet Father Solanus ate little of its main dish, ham; he was allergic to it.

At the dedication dinner that evening in Milwaukee, again ham was the meat dish. And again Father Solanus ate little of it. But the ham was contaminated. Several diners later became sick, Father Solanus dangerously so.

After the dinner he visited the old Notre Dame Convent; he desired to give the Mother Superior, who was dying, his blessing. Descending the convent stairs, he collapsed.

After two days in St. Michael's Hospital, he recovered sufficiently to be taken back to Huntington. On examining him, the infirmarian discovered that his legs were raw and bleeding. His old enemies, eczema and varicose veins, had staged a violent return. The infirmarian had to bath the socks off his feet.

The next day he was taken to a hospital in Huntington. Circulation in his legs was so deficient as to make his condition critical. His physicians were on the point of amputating them to save his life. But the circulation slowly improved, and after a few days he was pronounced out of danger.

Through this painful and alarming experience he remained entirely detached. He had placed himself in God's hands.

Soon he was back at the friary, counseling visitors as before.

Through the next year and a half his health was relatively good, but in January of 1951 eczema broke out again. A skin specialist ordered him to remain off his feet, and he was confined to his room for several weeks. By April, he was again functioning as usual.

His sicknesses were becoming more frequent, but in between his seasons of disability he managed to aid a great number of people—and, at times, his own community. One day when a group of friars was setting off for Detroit in an old car that limped so badly they were doubtful about getting there, Father Solanus was standing by.

"When you get to Detroit," he suggested, "call on Jerry McCarthy, the Chevrolet dealer. He'll give you a new one."

They did call on Mr. McCarthy, and he did give them a new car.

Two months later, Father Solanus went to Detroit to comfort his friend Jerry McCarthy on his death bed.

In May of 1953 he had another bad spell when a doctor, not realizing that he was allergic to the drug, administered sulfa to combat an infection. Blisters broke out all over his body.

His physical condition in the spring of 1954 was comparatively good, and the friars began to look forward to celebration of his golden jubilee as a priest. The Father Guardian—the Very Reverend Thomas Aquinas Heidenreich—and Father Cuthbert Gumbinger [later to be an Archbishop] would observe their silver jubilees at the same time. It was decided that the great day would be Wednesday, July 28, 1954.

Several days before the event, *The Detroit Times* sent a feature writer, E. A. Batchelor, Jr., to St. Felix to do an article about Father Solanus. The story appeared on Sunday, July 18.

Mr. Batchelor mentions that the "bearded young Brother" who opened the friary door to him "expressed no surprise at the arrival of a reporter and a photographer." He attributes this to the friary's constant stream of visitors since Father Solanus' transfer there eight years before.

FATHER SOLANUS AT 83—Mr. Batchelor's story said—stands amazingly erect, although his tall frame is gaunt in its brown homespun habit from many decades of fasting and self-denial.

But his most striking characteristics are his eyes and his voice. The eyes . . . are the eyes of a man 50 years younger. At times they are shrewd and penetrating, but when he speaks of his faith they shine like the eyes of a child.

His voice is low and warm and somehow it can make his simplest remark sound like a benediction.

When the newspaperman asked why his advice was treasured by so many laymen, he answered: "One need not be a priest to be an instrument in God's hands. If a man lives as he should, he will be given the knowledge to aid people. And if we are interested in saving our own souls we must have an interest in our brothers."

This was said ten years before Vatican Council II and its Decree on the Apostolate of the Laity. His interest in his brothers had been constant through fifty years. In various ways he had taught every individual who came to him that he was "an instrument in God's hands," or should be.

Two weeks after he preached his two-sentence sermon on the layman's role to *The Detroit Times* reporter, Father Solanus was to offer public thanksgiving for his fifty years of priesthood. To provide the needed seating capacity, the jubilee Mass would be in Huntington's St. Mary's Church, and the dinner in SS. Peter & Paul's more commodious parish hall. Thus the people of both parishes would be united in the jubilation.

Early in the morning of the celebration, friends from Detroit, Chicago and other cities began arriving at the friary. From there they drove or walked to St. Mary's Church, where, mingling with Huntington people, they helped fill every seat.

Father Solanus offered the solemn Mass of thanksgiving. He was assisted by Father Thomas Aquinas as deacon, and Father Cuthbert as subdeacon. The Very Reverend Clement Neubauer, who during Father Solanus' later years at St. Bonaventure's had been Provincial, spoke the heartfelt gratitude of himself and his confreres for God's goodness.

Among the dinner guests who after the Mass gathered in SS. Peter & Paul's auditorium were more than five hundred out-of-towners. The gathering resembled a huge family party. The warm Franciscan spirit—the spirit Father Solanus generated so naturally wherever he went—suffused and animated the diners, and the speakers were eloquent and witty. Years later, the participants remembered the dinner as one of the happy, glowing experiences of their lives.

Friends showered Father Solanus with gifts, but the most substantial was presented to him ten months later. It happened that after the jubilee, Mr. and Mrs. Daniel Ryan of Detroit came across several people who regretted that they had missed honoring Father Solanus at his anniversary celebration, and desired to do something about it. The Ryans therefore suggested the raising of a purse. They expected a few hundred dollars. But as the word spread, more and more contributions poured in. Finally the purse totaled $6,000.

Mr. and Mrs. Ryan headed a delegation that presented this sum to Father Solanus on May 22, 1955, together with a list of donors of from 25 cents to $100. As the aged friar read the list, tears blinded him. Nothing like this, he managed to say, had ever happened to him before.

"The first sign of intelligence," he added, "is gratitude to God." Then with simple eloquence he thanked first the "dear Lord," and secondly, all the contributors.

He donated the money for the remodeling and redecorating of the friary chapel, and the construction of a new—and smaller—altar. This replaced one of relatively mammoth size—discarded by a Detroit church—and made for needed seating space.

There was no end to the flow of visitors. On Tuesday, June 14, three bus loads of Father Solanus' friends from Detroit surprised him by appearing for the friary's Corpus Christi procession. On July 21, the friars observed his nameday. Father Guardian extolled his faithfulness to religious exercises, despite endless demands on his time. His faithfulness included private reading of whatever spiritual passages he had missed at the mealtime reading when visitors made him late at table.

About a month after his name day, he for the first time in his career spoke to a fellow Capuchin of being unable to meet all the demands made upon him.

Nevertheless, and despite his eighty-five years, he had sufficient strength on January 2, 1956, to join with clerics and Brothers in planning the community's annual amateur entertainment. It was his last effort at St. Felix.

A day or two later he showed signs of serious physical failure. The superiors decided that he must be taken to a Detroit hospital for a complete checkup, and Brother Gabriel, the infirmarian, drove him there.

Father Clement, formerly Minister General of the worldwide Capuchin Order, who had become Father Guardian at St. Felix, also went to Detroit at this time. Returning a week later, he brought word that Father Solanus was to undergo an operation for skin cancer, but that neither the operation nor his general condition was serious.

Toward the end of the previous year his brother Owen had died in Seattle. Now, on February 15, 1956, came news of his brother Patrick's death in the same city, where for years he had lived close to a church that he might attend daily Mass. Of the ten Casey brothers, only two were left—himself, and Monsignor Ed.

A month went by, with Brother Gabriel reporting frequently from Detroit to Father Clement. The operation was performed and the patient was "doing nicely." There was, however, no word as to when he would be returning to Huntington.

More weeks passed, and reports became less favorable. Friars and clerics and Brothers at St. Felix began to wonder whether Father Solanus would ever come back to them.

Chapter 21

Father Solanus
Predicts "a Wonderful Day"

Father Bernard Burke was a friar who knew when to speak, and when to keep silent. As Father Guardian at St. Bonaventure's, he chose to keep silent about Father Solanus' presence there during the first several months of 1956. For while Detroit afforded every medical skill and facility that might aid his recovery, it was also the home of thousands of his friends and, one might say, his spiritual children. Had they known he was in the city, they would have been intent on seeing and consulting him. Some would want "just a few words"; some would be experiencing a crisis which he alone could help them solve. It would all have added up to a deadly depletion of his strength.

The thought of saving himself would never have entered his head.

To have permitted him to resume anything like his former activities would have been fatal—on this superiors and physicians were agreed. Father Bernard directed the friars, therefore, in a conspiracy of silence, while at the same time placing Father Solanus under the obedience to refuse to see any callers without the Father Guardian's specific approval. He accepted the restraint without complaint, as he always accepted his superior's directions. But it was plain that the necessity of denying his comfort and counsel to those who sought him was a greater burden to him than his own sickness. When word of his presence at St. Bonaventure's did become known to many, a few were permitted to visit him on condition that they shroud the visit in silence.

By May it had become clear that the care of his Detroit physicians would have to be virtually continuous. The superiors therefore decided that he should remain permanently at St. Bonaventure's, and on May 10 he was formally transferred.

His days now were devoted to celebrating Mass and attending choir services when he was able, and to prayer. His physical weakness was evident in his speech; one had to listen with all his ears to catch the syllables. But his presence was a continuous inspiration. On August 2, the Father Vicar being absent, he spoke, as senior Friar, to congratulate the Father Guardian on his nameday, and as the friary chronicle puts it, edified all the friars "with words flowing from his God-loving heart."

His "God-loving heart" went out to all, and he did not forget the friends of his youth. He was concerned with Chris Adam, his boyhood hunting companion of seventy-five years before, and he wrote him letters in which he sought to inspire a deeper appreciation of things spiritual. He never forgot a friend, nor willingly neglected a friendship.

On December 2, 1956, an illustrated article in *The Detroit Sunday News* rotogravure section made all Detroit and Michigan aware that Father Solanus was again stationed at St. Bonaventure's. That, of course, was not the article's objective. Its theme was the centenary of the Capuchin foundation in the United States, but its pictorial emphasis was on Father Solanus. His picture, as the friary chronicle records, "was spread all over the front cover of the rotogravure section." A small picture of him, in smiling conversation, also appeared in connection with the text.

Featuring him was simply good newspaper practice; to the public, he was "Father Capuchin." He was the only friar quoted. The quotation—part of the article's final paragraph—read: "How does a monk feel about his life of prayer, study, work? Fr. Solanus Casey, who is 86 and in his 60th year in the order, said: 'It's like starting heaven here on earth.' "

The superiors had permitted the publicity, feeling that if anyone was to be featured it should be Father Solanus. As for trying to keep his presence secret any longer, there seemed to be little point to it. It had now been eleven months since he had come from Huntington. Each succeeding month, word of his presence had become more widespread—the friars assumed that practically everyone at all interested was aware of it. Some reasoned that after his many years' absence from Detroit many who had known him had probably died, and others had lost their early interest in him.

There was much astonishment, therefore, at the tidal wave of inquiries that engulfed the monastery the day following the article's appearance. "The Brothers at the front door," recorded the friary chronicle for December 3, "were suffering a headache from answering the avalanche of phone-calls from the people who wanted to know whether Father Solanus was available for consultations and blessings."

The answer was, of course, "No," but the publicity added to Father Bernard's task of protecting the former porter of St. Bonaventure's.

On the morning of January 14, 1957, Father Solanus celebrated the anniversary of his investiture sixty years before. The Community assembled in the refectory and accompanied the celebrant in procession to the sanctuary of the public chapel. The morning was bitterly cold, yet despite the announcement that no public reception would be held, there

were a few laymen in the chapel. After Father Bernard con-
gratulated the jubilarian, Father Solanus, reading from a
mimeographed paper, began to renew his vows. He hesitated
repeatedly as he read, and finally came to a full stop. This did
not puzzle the friars; they knew his eyesight was poor. But
those near him saw that there was another reason for his
difficulty; tears blurred his vision. Father Giles came to his
rescue, and completed the reading of the vows.

As Father Solanus went through this ceremony, he was
separated by only a few feet, and a partition, from the spot
on which he had knelt when making the same vows sixty
years before in the choir chapel.

With Father Bernard holding down his activities by limit-
ing the number of his visitors, he got through the winter. His
interests were, as ever, keen and wide. They embraced the
success of the Tigers—Detroit's baseball team—and that of
the missions, including Monsignor Edward's Philippine missions. On March 17—noting that it was St. Patrick's Day—
he sent his brother $20 for the missions, mentioning that the
sum had been contributed by a friend. It was another small
addition to the total amount he had sent Monsignor Edward
for the missions during his lifetime.

In early May, skin eruptions appeared on his body. He
grew worse, and his physician diagnosed the eruptions as
severe erysipelas. On May 15, he was taken to St. John Hospital in an ambulance.

In the hospital, he became more enfeebled, and seemed
near death. Father Bernard P. Hoey, the hospital chaplain,
anointed him. An oxygen tent was placed over him, and the
hospital sisters were invited to come to his room, as their
duties might permit. They entered, one by one, and knelt to
pray for the dying man.

The oxygen invigorated him; he revived, and began to sing a hymn to the Blessed Virgin. In his sweet, thin voice he sang the first verse—then a second, a third, a fourth, a fifth.

Brother Gabriel, hovering about him, became concerned that his patient might dissipate the little energy he possessed. As one verse followed another, he became more and more anxious. Finally, unable to restrain himself longer, he burst out: "For the love of God, Father, quit for now, and finish the hymn another time when you are stronger."

Father Solanus stopped at once, and the Sisters silently filed out. They returned one by one as their duties permitted, praying the rosary for him, and with him when he was able to respond.

Always, they found him in good humor, and frequently humorous. Any remarks that were made to him, and which he deemed laudatory, he fended off with a quip. When Sister Arthur Ann first met him, she said: "Father, throughout the years I have so often heard people speak of you."

"Yes," he replied, "people often speak of Jessie James, too."

"But these people, Father, spoke of the wonderful things that occurred through your prayers for them."

"Ah," he conceded, "many wonderful things have happened—but the people had the faith."

Gradually, treatments brought relief, and he gained strength. When he could be moved in a wheel chair, Brother Gabriel or one of the Sisters began to take him to the hospital chapel for visits with his Eucharistic Lord. This quickly became known to the hospital's Catholic population. Some were alert for his wheel chair passing through the corridors, and would ask his blessing as he passed. Others would await him for the same purpose in the chapel.

When he was able to walk, he began to offer Mass in the chapel. Even on the first day he did so, a considerable congregation was present; the Sisters wondered how the word could have spread so rapidly. His Masses were not announced, and he celebrated them at irregular hours. Yet there was always a generous sprinkling of worshippers in the pews.

The chapel was the Lord's abode; he loved to be there. When Sister Arthur Ann would ask him whether he would rather have her read to him, or take him for a visit to the chapel, his reply was—"Why don't we go down to the chapel, and you read to me there?"

Such journeys were daily occurrences, Father Solanus blessing all they met as he was wheeled through the corridors.

In the chapel, after one of the Sisters had read to him for a while, and had come to a pause, he would sometimes sing the "Ave Maria" in Latin as he gazed toward the tabernacle.

Like all the Sisters, Sister Arthur Ann regarded him as a saint, and she desired to have some memento of him. One day, when he asked her to recite the rosary with him, she said: "Father, will you please use my rosary. Then I can regard it as a keepsake associated with you."

He extended his hand, and said humbly—"All right, give it to me." It seemed plain to Sister Arthur Ann that, while he flinched from the esteem her request indicated, he was too gracious to refuse.

Like Sister Arthur Ann's, the attitude of most of those who came in contact with him was one of veneration, and this he tried to offset with humor.

As Sister Arthur Ann stepped briskly into his room on one occasion, she asked—"How about a blessing, Father?"

"All right," he smiled, "I'll take one."

Then he blessed her, and talked about man's ceaseless and often futile search for happiness. "So often," he said, "people hope to find happiness in money or the things money buys. If only they would stop running around, acquiring this and that, instead of seeking happiness only where it can be found —in love of God. They are so foolish."

Some sought to speak with him about their problems. Among these was Mrs. Gladys Feighan of Utica, Michigan. She had long prayed that she might be able to bear another child—alive—for her blood carried an Rh factor. As is usual with women so afflicted, she had borne her first child successfully. Following that, however, the Rh factor had caused one miscarriage, and two of her children had been born dead.

She had long desired to consult Father Solanus. While he was still stationed in Huntington, an acquaintance had told her about him. This acquaintance was planning to go to Huntington to ask his prayers—for she, too, was an Rh factor case. She urged Mrs. Feighan to accompany her. But Mrs. Feighan was pregnant, and her physician and her pastor both advised against the journey. The acquaintance—she was only that, and later Mrs. Feighan was unable to recall her name— did go to Huntington, and afterwards successfully bore three children.

Mrs. Feighan, therefore, experienced a surge of hope when, visiting her sick mother in St. John Hospital, she learned that Father Solanus was also a patient there, and in a room directly opposite her mother's. Seeing Brother Gabriel going in and out, she asked him if she might talk with Father Solanus. Shortly thereafter, the Brother brought her word that he had spoken to his patient, and that he wanted to see her.

WHEN I ENTERED HIS ROOM—said Mrs. Feighan—Father Solanus was sitting at a little table. He welcomed me, asking me to sit down."

"What is your name?" he asked.

"Mrs. Feighan."

"No—your given name?"

"Gladys."

"What, Gladys, do you want from God?"

"I want a baby. Another baby."

"A baby! For a woman to want a baby—how blessed, to hold God's own creation in your own hands."

I told him about my Rh factor; that I was well toward my middle thirties; that I feared it wouldn't be long before I might be too old to bear children.

"I do so want another child," I told him. "Perhaps I am selfish."

"No," he answered me, "you are not selfish. For a woman to want children is normal and blessed. Motherhood entails so many responsibilities—bringing up a child as it should be brought up is doing God's work. One doesn't always meet women who want children."

I had thought with great sadness of my three children who had died unbaptized.

"Father," I said, "I sorrow over my children who died without baptism—to think that they are in limbo, not in heaven."

"That is not for you to concern yourself about," he answered. "Just have confidence in our dear Lord's infinite love."*

Father Solanus' mind seemed above earthly things. He was ecstatic—so much so that I could hardly ask him a ques-

---

*This is an example of how Father Solanus cut through theological speculation to the source of truth. He realized that all such worried concerns as that of Mrs. Feighan about limbo are blown away like mists when "we have confidence in our dear Lord's infinite love." He may, too, have been thinking of the theologians' adage —"the divine action is not tied to the sacraments.—In "Life After Death," the *Twentieth Century Encyclopedia of Catholicism* says: "The existence of limbo itself is not a matter of faith, nor even of theological certitude. It is a solution which, up to now, it has been necessary to adopt: a solution of a hypothetical nature." —Some theologians now theorize that the soul of the unbaptized is, after death, enabled to choose its eternal destiny.

tion. After answering my first few questions, he did nearly all the talking. His words to me were of God's infinite love for us, and of how we should place all our confidence in that divine, all-embracing love. As he spoke, he was trembling with emotion. Finally he said—"Kneel down, and I will bless you, and your husband and all your family."

The other Capuchin (Brother Gabriel) was there, and a Sister of St. Joseph—one of the hospital Sisters—and they knelt, too.

Then he said to me—"You will have another child, Gladys. Your Blessed Mother will give you your child. Believe me, you will—you will have another child. You must believe this with all your heart and soul. You must believe this so strongly that before your baby is born you will get down on your knees and thank the Blessed Mother. Because once you ask her, and thank her, there's nothing she can do but go to her own Son and ask Him to grant your prayer that you have a baby."

Tears were in his eyes.

When I reached home, I was shaken for a couple of days, but uplifted. I felt confident, happy.

Mrs. Feighan was not to experience proof of Father Solanus' prediction until after his death.

Two days after her talk with him, he was moved to another room, and several days later, he was taken back to St. Bonaventure's

In July, erysipelas broke out again, and on Wednesday, July 2, he was taken to St. John Hospital a second time.

He was suffering intensely. The Sisters of St. Joseph, who operate the hospital, had learned to love and venerate him. In their view, his presence blessed them and their institution.

EVEN IN HIS SUFFERING, said Sister M. Margretta, who with Sister Arthur Ann was assigned to nurse him, he showed a keen sense of humor, and interior joy. Frequently we would hear him humming a tune of some hymn to the Blessed Virgin.

He radiated Christ-like holiness.

A Sister companion and I often read to him—always from *The Mystical City of God*. Always, too, he would precede the reading by asking us to recite with him a prayer to the Holy Spirit. As we read, he would close his eyes, and seem to doze. But let a word be misread, and he would open his eyes, and we'd note a twinkle in them as he corrected us. Or some passage would strike him, and he would exclaim— "Glory to God."

He told us he had "prayed" the four volumes of *The Mystical City* through three times, kneeling.

His sickness brought excruciating suffering. He developed a skin reaction that enveloped his entire body. This alone caused intense pain. Tubes, needles, examinations—these added to his discomfort.

Yet there was never a complaint from him, and he was rational at intervals even on the morning of his death.

In his presence it was impossible not to feel his Christlikeness, his genuine simplicity and humility, his great love for mankind, his selflessness. Even in his pain, he wanted to continue working to bring more people closer to God.

"I can't die," we overheard him say, "until everyone loves Him."

Yet he realized that death was not far off.

As Sister Arthur Ann entered his room one evening, he asked—"What time is it, Sister?"

The Sister, who had learned that he relished a little bantering, replied: "Now, Father, why should you care? You're not going any place."

"Oh, yes I am. I am going to heaven."

"Well, if you're such a little prophet, when are you going to heaven?"

"I'll tell you when—when it is God's will. I don't want to go until I have learned to appreciate heaven."

He frequently spoke of God's mercy with such childlike tenderness that tears came into his eyes.

"God is so good," he would say, and then repeat, slowly and quietly, "Glory be to God, Glory be to God."

The Sisters realized that he was suffering intense pain, and sought to alleviate it.

"Where do you hurt, Father?" one compassionately asked.

"Oh, I hurt all over—thanks be to God," he responded.

Because of poor nutrition, and continuous intravenous feedings, his hands had become red and raw.

"Your poor hands," said Sister Arthur Ann, as she prepared to remove a needle, "I hate having to remove the adhesive tape."

"Well, Sister, don't feel badly about it," he comforted her. "Look at Our Lord's hands."

Sister Carmella, one of those who read to him, noted that "one could go in and out of the room, and he wouldn't know it. His mind was elsewhere; he seemed to be thinking continuously of the love of God. 'The love of God,' he would say, 'is everything.' As he said this, his face would shine with an inner light."

During his last four or five days, the erysipelas erupted and caused a red scaling over his entire body.

He seemed to be wholly unconcerned about his malady. He didn't like to be fussed over. When asked what nourishment he would prefer, he'd answer—"Whatever the good Lord wants me to have." This was his way of telling the Sisters that he desired to leave the matter entirely to them. He had no desire for food; it was almost impossible for him to take any.

Physicians and nurses tried everything to sustain his strength. But he became so feeble that he could give little help even when it became necessary to move him. For refreshment, he chewed bits of lemon peel. At times he showed a lively interest in baseball.

He prayed almost constantly, and during the long nights the nurses heard him repeating one name, that of Father Gerald Walker, over and over. He was remembering Father Gerald as a spiritual son; as the little boy who had come with his parents on visits to him back in the thirties.

To the young Provincial he seems to have confided, as to no one else excepting his brother Edward, some idea of the intensity of his sufferings. On one visit, as Father Gerald was standing over him, he began to writhe. Fearing that he might be suffering a heart attack, Father Gerald asked—"Where do you hurt?"

"My whole body hurts, thanks be to God," he answered. "I am offering my sufferings that all might be one. Oh, if I could only live to see the conversion of the whole world!"

This for years had been his constant prayer. In 1943, while talking with a Rabbi Rosenwasser, he had lamented the world-wide increase in atheism, and the disunity among believers in a Supreme Being. As the Rabbi sat beside him at his desk, he had—as if to emphasize the thought—written on a scrap of paper: "If any good is to come from atheism— itself the climax of insanity—it will be because it is going to force believers in God together."

Father Gerald, closely observing his suffering confrere, had the impression that he was very close to God, but that he was receiving no consolation from that nearness. The invalid had recourse frequently to the Blessed Mother. On one of his frequent visits, Father Gerald found him in an oxygen tent. After talking with him for a few minutes, Father Solanus suddenly interrupted himself in the midst of a sentence.

"We're talking too much," he said. "Let's sing to our Blessed Mother. How wonderful she is . . ."

Then, making up words to some tune in his mind, he sang in his thin, low voice, like a small child singing to himself his happy thoughts.

At times he spoke of suffering in general, pointing out that "suffering makes us more like our dear Lord." Frequently he was heard to say—speaking in an impersonal tone— "Thanks be to God—we are like Him in our sufferings."

It happened at this time that Monsignor Casey came to Detroit to consult with the local Propagation of the Faith Office regarding mission appeals for the Philippines. He arrived at about the time that Father Solanus became dangerously weak, and was therefore able to be with him five days before his death.

When Monsignor Edward first came to his brother's bedside, he noticed that his eyes were red and bleared, and that he didn't pay his usual close attention to him. Sunlight was flooding the room, and both the room and the day were warm. The bedsheet had been pulled down from his chest that he might get the full benefit of the sun. Despite the 90 degree temperature, he was shivering. He looked up and said, "Hello, Ed," but his mind seemed elsewhere.

His doctor came, accompanied by an assistant, and said to the Monsignor: "He hasn't eaten or drunk for the last three or four days. Try your best to get him to eat—and especially, to drink. If he doesn't, he can't last much longer."

Thereafter, Monsignor Edward urged and pleaded, but Father Solanus could not force himself to either eat or drink. He was evidently in constant anguish. Monsignor Edward questioned him about his suffering, and finally drew from him an admission. "There's not so much as a pinhead's space on my body," he said, "in which, thank God, I don't feel pain."

The Sisters told Monsignor Casey that his brother's condition was so critical, he should remain in the hospital. They provided a room. They informed him that many people desired to see Father Solanus, and that he never denied himself to any caller. They therefore asked his brother to guard against visitors. If anyone had an imperative reason for seeing him, the visit was to be restricted to five minutes or less.

Despite this injunction, and Monsignor Casey's best efforts, a caller, who had come hundreds of miles to consult Father Solanus about a personal problem which she considered all-important, violated her promise. Instead of five minutes she stayed a full thirty. Monsignor Casey was therefore relieved when Mrs. Martha Casey, widow of his brother Owen, flew in from Seattle. She was a firm, decisive lady who for some years had directed a nursing home in Seattle. When she came to Father Solanus' bedside, he opened his eyes and gazed intently at her.

"Martha, Martha," he said to his matronly sister-in-law. "Such a long trip just to see me. And on the Feast of St. Martha."

It was July 29. He hadn't forgotten the date, nor its place in the liturgical calendar.

He asked Martha about various members of the Casey families, his words coming slowly, and he thanked God for every good report.

Mrs. Casey, with a Detroit friend, Mrs. Edward Clair, remained at his bedside many hours during that day and the next. At his request Mrs. Casey recited the rosary with him and read to him from *The Mystical City*. He was obviously very sick and in pain, but no word suggested his suffering excepting his "Thanks be to God." Once he said to her: "Martha, pray for the conversion of all men, and especially my own." Another time he said to her: "I don't want to die till all men have come to know and love God."

As she read to him, he would seem to doze. But when, thinking him asleep, she stopped reading, he would open his eyes and say—"Read on, Martha." Mrs. Casey and Mrs. Clair would try to administer water and give him any possible care, but he asked for nothing, nor would he admit being in pain. His skin, however, was so red that it looked to Mrs. Clair as if it had been "baked in an oven."

When Monsignor Casey wasn't at his brother's bedside, he paced the hospital corridors. One day shortly after his arrival a cleaning woman stopped him.

"How is Father Solanus?" she asked.

"He seems to be doing pretty well."

"Oh, I am praying for him," answered the woman. "I owe him so much. I went to him after an accident with scalding water had terribly disfigured my face. My disfigurement shocked people so, that when I went outdoors I wore a heavy veil. Father Solanus told me not to worry. He blessed me, and put his hand on the wound. After that, the disfigurment almost entirely disappeared."

On Sunday morning, the day before his sister-in-law arrived, Monsignor Casey had noted that his brother was extremely weak, and this weakness continued. Mentally, he was quite himself, and insisted on talking with his brother. The latter, to prevent him using his little energy, attempted to do all the talking himself. But the sick man would break in, though every word he spoke taxed his strength.

When Father Gerald visited him Tuesday evening, July 30, Father Solanus talked to him joyfully of approaching death.

"Tomorrow," he told the Provincial, "will be a wonderful day."

To Father Gerald, his meaning was clear; he was predicting he would die on Wednesday.

Monsignor Casey knew nothing about this prediction, but Tuesday night he was particularly worried. At about 11 o'clock that night he went to his brother's room. A nurse came tiptoeing down the corridor, and he asked her whether Father Solanus had been sleeping at all.

"He does from time to time," she told him, "but he wakes easily."

While the Monsignor lingered at the door, she entered the room.

"Well, Father Solanus," she asked, "how do you feel?"

"Suffering a little, thanks be to God."

There was a pause, and he added—"I am very cold."

"Maybe you'd like another blanket?"

"Well, yes—it might help."

The nurse put another blanket over him, though it was a warm July night.

Again, between four and five o'clock, Monsignor Edward went to his room, and again the nurse met him.

"He's been pretty restless," she said.

"Does he take anything to eat or drink?"

"The only thing we can get him to take now is a little diluted whiskey."

This, Monsignor Casey knew, was a discouraging sign. Whiskey, because the system almost instantly assimilates it, is sometimes administered to patients, including infants, when vitality is dangerously low.

Wednesday morning Monsignor Casey offered an early Mass for his brother in the hospital chapel, then went directly to the sick man's room. It was 8 o'clock. To Monsignor Edward, his brother seemed more himself than at any time he had observed him.

To prevent him talking, the Monsignor tried to command the conversation. But Father Solanus wanted to talk about the subject closest to his heart—the need of the world's conversion, and his longing to do more to bring men to God. He was animated and seemed considerably stronger.

After leaving him, Monsignor Casey went to his own room and began writing notes to his relatives, informing them that Father Solanus was much improved.

Three hours later, at a little before 11 o'clock, he was still writing. At that time, in Father Solanus' room, Mother Aileen, Sister Margaretta, a nurse, a maid and an orderly were attending the patient. The orderly, a powerfully built young man, was supporting Father Solanus in his arms as the nurse and the maid straightened the bed sheets.

For several minutes Father Solanus had been whispering. His voice was too weak for anyone to catch the words, and his eyes were closed.

Gently, the orderly and the nurse laid him back upon the bed.

Suddenly, his eyes opened wide, and he who for days had lain prostrate from weakness, raised himself and said, clearly —"I give my soul to Jesus Christ."

The words were a proclamation of victory, and a testament. By them he willed his being to God, and gave final expression to his rejection of the hell of egotism and self-worship.

He fell back, and the ebbing life flowed into eternity.

Monsignor Casey, who had been summoned by telephone, rapped on the closed door.

Mother Aileen opened, and told him—"He is gone."

The Monsignor stood looking on his brother for a few seconds. Then he said—"Shall we recite the rosary?"

He led the first two decades, when his voice gave out. Mother Aileen took over and continued to the end of the five decades. After this, Monsignor talked with those present, including the orderly, asking details of his brother's last moments.

Father Solanus had died at 11 o'clock.

The date was July 31, 1957.

It had been at 11 o'clock, 53 years to the day, that he had ascended the altar steps in St. Joseph's Church in Appleton, Wisconsin, to offer his first Mass.

Chapter 22

A Friar's Legacy

At the funeral Mass, Father Gerald, the Provincial, spoke the final farewell. He spoke not so much as a superior to whom the dead friar had owed obedience, but as a spiritual son of a spiritual father. At times he was forced to pause as grief choked his voice.

"Father Solanus was a man I loved dearly," he began, and with the simplicity common to Capuchins he told why, searching for words to describe the spiritual sweetness of the man. He told how, as a small boy visiting Father Solanus with his parents, he had come under the spell of his goodness. But for the most part, he could only remind these friends of the porter of St. Bonaventure's, who filled the seats and jammed the aisles, of what they so well knew.

Father Solanus' life, he said, had been gloriously successful, because he had served God so faithfully, so earnestly, so selflessly. He had seen his Creator in every element of His creation, in every bird and flower and cloud and sunrise. Above all, he had seen Him in and served Him through men and women, and the young people who had come to him for counsel, and the children who had been brought to him. His service to them had been Christ-like, and he had been ever thankful to God for permitting him to serve Him in this way.

His hearers recognized the factuality of these statements, as they did that of Father Gerald's concluding words.

"His was a life of service and love," he said, "for people like me and you. When he was not himself sick, he nevertheless suffered with and for you that were sick. When he was not physically hungry, he hungered with people like you. He had a Divine love for people. He loved people for what he could do for them—and for God, through them."

Monsignor Edward Casey, now the last of the ten Casey brothers, celebrated the Mass. On behalf of the clergy and people of the archdiocese, Bishop Henry E. Donnelly paid a final tribute.

Then the body was carried from the chapel as Monsignor Casey raised his voice in the beautiful antiphon beginning "In paradisum deducant" . . . "May the angels lead you into paradise; may the martyrs welcome you on your arrival and bring you into the holy city of Jerusalem. May the choir of angels receive you, and may you rest eternally with the one-time poor man Lazarus."

His body would rest until the resurrection of the dead in the burial plot beside the monastery in which he had labored so long. It is a dignified and pleasant ground; a walled rectangle bordered by flowers and small shrubs. On its east side rises a large granite slab engraved with a bas relief of St. Francis greeting the setting sun, and the words—from his Canticle to the Sun—"We praise Thee, Lord, for our Sister Death." And below this, the Capuchin Order's motto—"My God and my All!"

The little door in the west wall, bordering the main street, is generally open in the warmer summer months. When it is locked, visitors obtain the key from the Brother on duty in the friary office.

Through every season, people come to Father Solanus' grave; hundreds during the year. He was a legend before his death; here the legend gains new life. Many come here to say a prayer for him or to him. Many ask his intercession as they asked it when he sat in the nearby office. Others come to thank him for some favor which, they claim, they have received through his intercession.

To this grassy patch comes Mrs. Gladys Feighan, whom Father Solanus had blessed a few weeks before his death. She comes, leading the sturdy twins she successfully bore despite her deadly Rh blood factor which, in two previous pregnancies [in which her babies were born dead] had nearly ended her life. Father Solanus had assured her she would have another baby; she had believed him. She became pregnant in 1962 and cheerfully told her husband that the child would be a girl; she was utterly confident. Her husband, promoting her confidence, voted for a boy. But her physicians were by no means assured. Despite their experience, skill, and all the safeguards medical science could provide, they were fearful of a fourth tragedy. Both parents were overjoyed—as were the doctors—when Mrs. Feighan successfully bore twins—a boy and a girl.

To offer thanksgiving at the friar's grave comes also Mrs. Gladys Redfern. On May 11, 1964, after being x-rayed and examined three times, she had entered the Highland Park General Hospital for an exploratory operation. Her physician informed her that during the operation the surgeon would remove a lump from her breast. Mrs. Redfern knew the lump was there; she could easily feel it, and she feared that it might be cancerous. Since the first suspicion of cancer weeks before, she had been praying to Father Solanus that the growth might prove benign.

At the hospital, the night of May 11, doctors made a formal examination preceding the operation scheduled for the following morning. No lump could be found.

Among several who asserted that since Father Solanus' death their prayers to him have been followed by favorable solutions of their problems was the Archbishop of Izmir, Turkey—the former Father Cuthbert Gumbinger, O.F.M., Cap. The Archbishop visited his old friend's grave when he called at St. Bonaventure's in the spring of 1966; he died a year later. Several years of almost daily observance at the Monastery, had convinced him that Father Solanus was very close to God.

While a missionary at Puerto Cabezas, Nicaragua, in 1959, Father Cuthbert received a letter from his mother in which she attributed to Father Solanus her recovery from a heart attack suffered in April of that year. About the same time, he himself experienced what he thought to be the intercessory power of Father Solanus. In a letter written May 15, 1959, to the Capuchin Provincial, he said:

FATHER SOLANUS appeared to me lately in a wonderful and beautiful dream. He looked radiant, shining and glorious, with a most heavenly expression on his face, and a gentle smile. He did not say he is in heaven, but he is [as he appeared in the dream] "happy." He seemed eager to assure me, and as though he wanted to tell me things, but hoped that I'd understand merely from seeing him. I did understand that he is in heaven . . .

I told the dream to Father Florian, who is also much impressed. We decided to prove the matter further by asking Father Solanus for some much needed material favors.

First, we needed water very much, as our tanks were practically dry after the dry season . . .

We also need money for the House for Conferences which we are building nearby, and for the new church which the town needs badly.

The two Capuchin Fathers promised Father Solanus that if they received favorable answers to these requests they would especially honor his patron; they would erect a statue of St. Francis Solanus in the new church. In addition, Father Cuthbert pledged himself to prepare, for ecclesiastical consideration, a formal statement setting forth the life of Father Solanus. His letter continues—

AN HOUR AFTER I began [to write the formal statement], Father Florian joyfully announced that a tank above our attic had suddenly filled up! After another hour, a person brought 100 Cordobas for the new church, and that evening another one brought 1,000 Cordobas! Rain came at night, and today, also, it rained heavily to fill our outside tanks.

Sometimes, a Capuchin seminarian comes to the grave to thank him for his part in paying for his education. This help is given through the Father Solanus Guild, which Mrs. Clare Ryan of Detroit established in 1960.

Knowing that his multitude of friends would welcome an opportunity to honor Father Solanus' memory, Mrs. Ryan proposed formation of the Guild shortly after his death. Father Bernard Burke, then Guardian at St. Bonaventure's, opposed the idea at the time.

When Father Cassian became Guardian, Mrs. Ryan renewed her proposal, and Father Cassian referred it to the Provincial, Father Gerald Walker. In the spring of 1960, Mrs. Ryan invited twenty-seven friends of Father Solanus to meet in her home, with Father Gerald and Father Rupert Dorn present. During the meeting, Father Gerald gave his approval to the Guild's foundation.

In 1967, the Guild's membership was 5,000 and it had contributed more than $75,000 to the support of the Capuchin seminary at Crown Point, Indiana.

One of the gifts to the Guild was $31,000 contributed by W. V. Bedolfe of Toronto. A second cousin of Father Solanus, his contribution was "in memory of Father Solanus and in thanksgiving for my own profession of faith on July 31, 1953, after being away from the Church so long." Mr. Bedolfe, though baptized in the Catholic faith, was never instructed in it. His sister had visited Father Solanus, and persuaded her brother to visit him. As a result he was instructed and became a Catholic. Soon after, his wife and son, both Protestants, followed him into the Church.

*   *   *

Several years after Father Solanus died, Capuchin superiors asked a Guild member to list his possessions, which since his death had been reposing in a trunk.

This is the list—

a small crucifix

a framed picture of the Sacred Heart

two framed pictures of the Blessed Virgin

a pair of worn sandals

a pair of shoes

two habits

three cords

an overcoat

eyeglasses

two pens

  a small alarm clock

a harmonica

undergarments and sox—threadbare, mended and tattered

an old red stole

a set of vestments (used when he offered his last Mass at St. Bonaventure's on the Feast of the Sacred Heart, June 28, 1957) a framed picture of his family (taken forty-four years before his death)

a few snapshots

a few holy cards

two volumes of *The Mystical City of God*

several pamphlets

four prayerbooks

a wooden statue of St. Anthony.

He had left a violin, also; it was being cared for by a friend.

These things, after sixty Capuchin years, he left—these, and more intense fires of love for God and fellowmen in thousands of hearts; fires to ignite other hearts through generations.

Only a man so poor could have left a legacy so rich.